Offenders or Victims?
German Jews and the Causes of Modern Catholic Antisemitism

Studies in Antisemitism

Vadim Rossman, *Russian Intellectual Antisemitism in the Post-Communist Era* (2002)

Anthony D. Kauders, *Democratization and the Jews, Munich, 1945–1965* (2004)

Cesare G. De Michelis, *The Non-existent Manuscript: A Study of the* Protocols of the Sages of Zion (2004)

Robert S. Wistrich, *Laboratory for World Destruction: Germans and Jews in the Central Europe* (2007)

Graciela Ben-Dror, *The Catholic Church and the Jews, Argentina, 1933–1945* (2008)

Andrei Oişteanu, *Inventing the Jew: Antisemitic Stereotypes in Romanian and Other Central-East European Cultures* (2009)

Offenders or Victims?
German Jews and the Causes of Modern Catholic Antisemitism

Olaf Blaschke

Published by the University of Nebraska Press, Lincoln and London, for the
Vidal Sassoon International Center for the Study of Antisemitism (SICSA)
The Hebrew University of Jerusalem

Manufactured and distributed for the Vidal Sassoon International Center for the Study of Antisemitism (SICSA), the Hebrew University of Jerusalem, by the University of Nebraska Press

∞

Library of Congress Cataloging-in-Publication Data

Blaschke, Olaf, 1963–
Offenders or victims?: German Jews and the causes of modern Catholic antisemitism / Olaf Blaschke.
p. cm.
Includes bibliographical references and index.
ISBN 978-0-8032-2522-0 (cloth: alk. paper)
1. Antisemitism—Germany—History—19th century. 2. Antisemitism—Germany—History—20th century. 3. Christianity and antisemitism—Germany—History—19th century. 4. Christianity and antisemitism—Germany—History—20th century. 5. Judaism—Relations—Catholic Church. 6. Catholic Church—Relations—Judaism. 7. Catholics—Germany—Attitudes. 8. Jews—Germany—Attitudes. 9. Antisemitism—Public opinion. 10. Public opinion—Germany. 11. Germany—Ethnic relations.
I. Title.
DS146.G4B535 2009
305.892'4043—dc22
2009019461

Editing and Typesetting: Alifa Saadya

Table of Contents

Preface and Acknowledgments

Most studies of antisemitism examine the negative attitudes of non-Jews about Jews, but do not dwell on the attitudes and acts of Jews. It's all about prejudices. This treatment of only one side has been labeled unfair. Some scholars insinuate that touching the question of Jewish responsibility means stepping on prohibited ground. They have recently set out to break what they call a "taboo" and claim that it was the Jews who provoked animosity. Can antisemitism really be explained by Jewish behavior? At least, this is what antisemites always believed. Occasionally, this "explanation" presents itself as based on a certain amount of research, though, taking a closer look, its foundations often turn out to be unquestioned traditions. Historians should consult the sources and examine the real conduct of Jews.

This book turns the tables. It studies the familiar phenomenon of antisemitism from the other side, and this in two regards. First, it takes a closer look at the Jewish material in order to check what is behind the notion that there was a real conflict between Jews and Gentiles. This might help explain the phenomenon of antisemitism. How did Jews conceive of "others"? Did they really provide reason enough to hate them? We know a lot about antisemitism, about how non-Jews perceived and hated Jews. We know much less about how Jews perceived this negative perception and its harsh effects. This is the second major issue dealt with in this study: how Jews discerned antisemitism.

This book is a case study, concentrating on German Jews and their relationship with another group, one which has often been described as being so different from Jewish culture: German Catholics. The latter seem to have had ample reason for discontent, since in comparison they were less wealthy and less successful than Protestants and even less than many Jews around the year 1900, to take an arbitrary point in time. If anything should make it easy to find "good reasons" for tensions leading to antisemitism, here it is. And if it is most difficult to challenge this notion of "good reasons" it is in this very case of Catholic–Jewish relationships.

Antisemitism was indeed widespread among Catholics, an issue I addressed in a previous book (1997). The present case study was born out of the first book. It looks less at Catholic attitudes towards Jews and more at Jewish attitudes towards Catholics and their antisemitism.

Completion of this study was enabled with the help of the Vidal Sassoon International Center for the Study of Antisemitism at the Hebrew University of Jerusalem, which granted me generous research stipends in 1996 and again in 2001. The editorial board of SICSA accepted it for publication in their *Studies in Antisemitism* series, published by the University of Nebraska Press. To both institutions I am most grateful. Till van Rahden and Leon Volovici encouraged my intention to continue my earlier work on Catholic antisemitism. Andreas Braemer, Andreas Gotzmann, and Uri Kaufmann provided me with important leads for this work. Eleanor Toal shouldered the burden of translating major parts of the (literary) German text into proper English in 2002. Any misunderstandings remaining are due to my own clumsy attempts to write in a foreign language and to update the text ever since, integrating new ideas and important literature which appeared since then. With painstaking and sensitive editing Yohai Goell in 2004 managed to allow the text to be presented to the English-reading public. Alifa Saadya took over the technical part, competently transforming the manuscript into a book. Lizzie Collingham undertook a last critical review of the proof copy. Lotte Nawothnig prepared the index. Many thanks to them all.

Olaf Blaschke
Trier
Spring 2007

Introduction

Could it be that Jews and their behavior were partly responsible for antisemitism? Is it true that "the rise of the Jews in modern times," as a recent academic study published by Cambridge University Press maintains, has been "the most fundamental cause of modern racial and political anti-Semitism"?[1] The idea is an old one: antisemites, of course, were convinced that Jews were the cause of their animosity. They were the offenders. Even several scholars have pointed to the Jews in order to find an explanation for antisemitism. In 1983, Dennis Prager and Joseph Telushkin proclaimed: "The ultimate cause of antisemitism is that which has made Jews Jewish—JUDAISM." Modern attempts, they claim,

> to dejudaize antisemitism, to attribute it to economic, social, and political reasons, and universalize it into merely another instance of bigotry are as opposed to the facts of Jewish history as they are to the historical Jewish understanding of antisemitism. . . . Antisemites have hated Jews because Jews are Jewish.[2]

Another very recent example is provided by Konrad Löw, emeritus professor of political science in Bayreuth. In 2002 he published a book about "Christians and Jews as Judged by National Socialists and Contemporaries" which polarized the reading public: Radio Vatican, some official diocesan journals (Munich, Trier), and right-wing newspapers (*Nationalzeitung*) have praised it; for others it was the object of criticism. Löw identifies Jews as the "perpetrators of world history" and turns "perpetrators into victims."[3]

Did Jews incur the hatred of Christians through their behavior? Seen from a moral perspective, particularly after the atrocity of Auschwitz, as well as from an analytical point of view, this question seems simply undue and irrelevant. For a long time now, antisemitism has been regarded by most researchers as a kind of delusion. Yet, despite every study of antisemitism, despite every effort to find a rational explanation for the phenomenon since its beginnings, instances of anti-Jewish comments and actions by right-wing extremists have recently been on the increase. These extremists are supported by a surprisingly high number of approving onlookers. At times they are even supported by indiscreet third-rate politicians—not to mention the overt antisemitism in Arab countries. And what is more, even scholars who are supposed to have a command of the literature fuel the notion that antisemitism is due to Jewish behavior.

A wide range of authors have assumed the task of standing up both to those who deny the Holocaust and to right-wing legends by exposing and pulling apart their respective arguments. Unfortunately, such efforts will continue to be of importance as long as such misleading and hostile texts remain an influential genre. It has recently been argued that there is a tendency towards re-nationalization in German historiography since 1990.[4] I would not apply this generalization to all German historians. Revisionist views could be observed before 1990 and in other scholarly communities as well. However, antisemitism seems to be experiencing a resurgence. In the summer of 2000 the problem of right-wing radicalism finally came to the fore as a permanent theme of discussion in the German media, followed by a government campaign which placed its messages in locations such as cinemas with the objective of stimulating civil courage.[5] At the beginning of the twenty-first century a wave of riots against synagogues and Jewish cemeteries occurred in France. In 2003, German neo-Nazis planned bomb attacks against synagogues in Bavaria. However, the incidents in Western societies around 2000 were not “the highest wave of antisemitism since 1945.” In fact, antisemitic activities are a cyclical phenomenon, having occurred around 1959/1960, 1980, and 1990.[6]

The suggestion that the cause of anti-Jewish attitudes lies in the behavior of the Jewish people themselves seems dubious, but has recently been circulating again, even among respected academics. Some circles seem to have unshakeable faith in the proverbs, “There’s no smoke without fire” and “There is a grain of truth.” Such claims remain extremely topical. Therefore, the old question of whether the Jews really were to blame for antisemitism must be examined anew. One should be careful in weighing the arguments. Alarmingly, it is quite evident that the best contemporary refutations of antisemitism have an all too limited half-life, and that the clearest explanation for anti-Jewish attitudes seems to have been completely forgotten. However, our purpose here is not to once again prove antisemitic accusations to be incorrect, for this could turn out to be awkward. Explaining stereotypes as being mistaken and portraying the victims as angels has driven intellectuals to sarcasm in former times: Jewish historian Heinrich Graetz, for example, scornfully accused his contemporary Isaak Marcus Jost (1793–1860) of trying to prove, in his *Geschichte des Judenthums und seiner Secten* (A history of Judaism and its sects), written between 1857 and 1859, "that the Jews [have] always been peaceful citizens and loyal subjects." In 1888 Graetz wrote that the book was biased, despite Jost's many merits.

> The Jews on the whole, he [i.e., Jost] says, have always been honest, upright people, who never slaughtered Christians and do not deserve the accusations which are piled upon them. It was only the Pharisees and their descendants, the Rabbis, who have earned these reproaches; they were absolutely disgusting people, filled with superstition and darkness. This is the prevailing tone of Jost's depiction of Jewish history. He wanted to prove wrong both the admirers of Jewish history and its critics.[7]

A number of academics have long since endeavored to thoroughly refute antisemitism, recognizing that there is a long history of conflict related to the issue.[8]

Ever since modern antisemitism first came to light in the nineteenth century, non-Jews supporting emancipation and Jews have been able to contradict it with good arguments. Right from the beginning, quiet resistance has always accompanied a more strident antisemitism. However, explanation alone has not been enough to halt its triumphant progress. Almost every argument which countered antisemitism with an explanation can be found, for example, in the *Antisemitenspiegel,* written in reaction to the much-discussed smear pamphlet, *Judenspiegel.* The latter had been published in Paderborn in 1883 and in turn had taken up the argument of a paper from 1819.[9] The *Antisemitenspiegel* first appeared in 1890 and was put together by the Verein zur Abwehr des Antisemitismus (Association for combating antisemitism), a society supported by liberal non-Jews and concerned *Kulturprotestanten.* The *Antisemitenspiegel* contains the most important counter-arguments, which are still as relevant today as when they were first published. The second edition appeared in 1900. Throughout more than 500 pages, every stereotype is meticulously examined and then disproved or put into its correct sociological and historical contexts. There is no need to repeat this, particularly as more recent works have also attempted a comprehensive explanation of antisemitic impressions and prejudices.[10] The 1995 volume about antisemitic myths edited by Julius H. Schoeps and Johannes Schlör examines the origins of twenty-four anti-Jewish stereotypes, including "Murderer of God," "Profiteer," "Shirker," and "Communist."[11]

Instead of refuting these once again, it is essential to tackle the most recent claims, which are expressed by revisionists and apologists. Revisionists want to rewrite the history of antisemitism, whether from radical right-wing motives or as a result of other factors. A book that claims to be breaking a "taboo" is always more likely to become a bestseller. The aim of apologists, on the other hand, is to make excuses for the history of their own group or to present it in a good light. Their motive is not radically right-wing, nor do they need to rewrite history, but they feel obligated to the traditional discourse of their national or religious heritage.

The subterranean movement that disseminates Jewish stereotypes surfaces again and again in society and in research; therefore it must be taken very seriously. Simply sweeping aside the claims of revisionists and apologists with one outraged moral gesture is not sufficient. Morally superior motives are no substitute for analytically superior arguments. It is empirical plausibility, rather than superior moral validity, that will carry weight in the final tally.[12]

A very striking example of a book that relies more on the pose of breaking a taboo than on valid evidence is the work of Albert S. Lindemann, a history professor at the University of California in Santa Barbara. *Esau's Tears: Modern Anti-Semitism and the Rise of the Jews* first appeared in 1997 with a second edition in 2000. For Lindemann, antisemitism is not a projection but an "understandable development" caused by the conduct of Jews. Despite the fact that his work has attracted a certain degree of praise, it has also been severely contested. William Rubenstein went as far as to suggest that "the author deserves a medal for bravery in writing the book."[13] Others voice dissappointment, such as Robert S. Wistrich, who calls it a "deeply pernicious book."[14] "The antisemitic stands are always taken as credible," writes Leon Volovici in his review. This work is a "paradigmatic case in which an experienced historian has fallen victim to a premise transformed into a kind of priori 'truth.'"[15]

What exactly has Lindemann done to attract such praise and criticism? He rejects the notion that "Jew hatred is one-sided" and "functions independently of its object," calling this the "comfortable approach." For him, "the opposite position" means accepting "that Jewish conduct is the main cause for hatred of Jews." However vague and slippery the manner in which Lindemann expresses his opinions (for example, by failing to distance himself from outrageous quotations and by using negating sentences), he does reveal his aims clearly:

> My position is that, whatever the power of myth, not all hostility to Jews, individually or collectively, has been based on fantastic,

> chimerical visions of them, or on projections unrelated to any palpable reality. As human beings, Jews have been as capable as any other group of provoking hostility in the everyday secular world.[16]

Lindemann knows that antisemites might misuse his "observations" and that his approach could be accused of committing "the cardinal sin of blaming the victim."[17] Yet this makes him all the more inclined to adhere to his unorthodox perspective. Critics are "impressed by the way in which he tackles taboo after taboo in the litany of anti-Semitic historiography."[18]

He sets out to analyze and compare "some ten different countries"[19] over the course of more than two centuries. He pays special attention to Germany and France, but also examines antisemitism in Romania, Russia, Britain, the United States of America, Italy, Austria, and Hungary and also touches briefly on antisemitism in Poland. Unfortunately I am not an expert on Romanian, Russian, Italian, or Hungarian history, so I have concentrated on Germany in this work, notwithstanding a small amount of comparative information about Austria and France. Since I am not conversant with the Romanian, Russian, Polish, Hungarian, or Italian languages, which would be necessary for any academic study with new findings, I cannot inspect the original sources and scholarly literature; I have, however, been able to examine Lindemann's claims about German history. Given that a large-scale historical work like this should be based on historical texts, it is striking that Lindemann relies almost exclusively (quite typical of many Anglo-Saxon historians, but most annoying to others) on secondary literature (in English), instead of consulting primary sources, as far as Germany and other countries are concerned.[20] Rather than analyzing ten countries over two centuries, I think it is enough of a challenge to conduct a case study that looks closely at one example, Germany and its Catholics, and to study it carefully, using and referring to original sources, including several Catholic newspapers and Jewish journals in addition to other Jewish documents. I have chosen to concentrate on the nineteenth century, the age of Jewish emancipation. If the "ultimate cause" of antisemitism, as Prager and Telushkin maintain, is the distinctiveness of Jews, antisemitism should have decreased in the wake of assimilation and acculturation. But, in fact, the very opposite happened. Prager and Telushkin fail to answer the pertinent question that arises: why did antisemitism increase the more Jewish distinctiveness disappeared? How can it be that, in the course of emancipation and acculturation, Jew-hatred did not fade away but increased dramatically?[21]

Why is the case study of Catholicism a proper test for our question? The social and economic gap between Catholics and Jews was considerably wide regarding rural and urban lifestyles, attitudes toward modernity and emancipation, different levels of education, etc. There could be many reasons why growing alienation turned into antisemitic resentments just because Jews and Catholics, as groups, were so different from each other. At the same time, both German Catholics and Jews shared a minority position. Both were looked down upon by the dominant Protestant elite and society. This is one reason why, for too long, the issue of Catholic antisemitism has been virtually ignored in the field of antisemitism research. Historians in Germany, as well as in the United States, tended to focus on the dominant groups, on White Anglo-Saxon Protestants or on White Prussian-German Protestants. Catholic antisemitism is a topic about which few studies have as yet been carried out—though many more than Daniel J. Goldhagen claims in his recent, superficial book about the Catholic Church and the Holocaust.[22] With regard to our question, the topic appears to be particularly provocative. If Catholic attitudes towards Jews have attracted little interest, what has attracted even less scholarly attention is the inverse set of issues: how did Jews behave towards Catholics and how did they regard Catholic antisemitism? This line of questioning seems especially inflammatory because Catholics succeeded in drawing a great deal of negative attention, if not enmity, to themselves during the nineteenth century. Therefore the prospect of finding Jews who were anti-Catholic and anticlerical is especially high, so high, in fact, that some scholars firmly discern Jewish anti-Catholicism like a *fata morgana* before their very eyes. In any case, it is higher than the prospect of coming across anti-Protestant Jews, since German society was dominated to an increasing degree by Protestant, bourgeois, and national value patterns and ideals. Many Jews leaned on this hegemonic culture, which was frequently anti-Catholic. If Jews actually played a part in the omnipresent anti-Catholicism, was Catholic antisemitism therefore just a reaction to it? I will attempt to prove that this was not the case; Catholic antisemitism should not be mistaken for a simple reaction to a perceived Jewish provocation.

All three questions—Catholics' attitude to the Jews, Jews' attitude to Catholics, and, finally, the Jewish perception of Catholic antisemitism—are tightly interwoven. A sober analysis of the role and opinion of the Jews makes it possible to dispel some misjudgments about Catholic antisemitism. Yet the function of this study, to put it explicitly, is not to explore Catholic–

Jewish relationships but primarily to analyze Jewish attitudes towards Catholics in order to get a balanced picture of both sides of the coin. I have therefore offered only a rough thematic outline of the profile of Catholic antisemitism itself; the information which is briefly reviewed in the first chapter has already been the subject of a separate analysis.[23]

In addition to moral and analytical components, another factor plays a crucial role in contributing to the forming of various academic attitudes, namely a particular interest. Academics closely connected to the Church—often called apologists—are, of course, frequently interested in exonerating Catholicism from the charge of antisemitism. Their first strategy is to deny the fact that modern antisemitism is also taking root in Catholicism, either by playing down anti-Jewish resentment as primarily religious "anti-Judaism" or by claiming that the remarks of Catholic antisemites are mere exceptions. In order to present examples of resistance against Jew-hatred, some apologists employ an interesting argument: They rely on Jewish witnesses, who allegedly certified that Catholics were rather philosemitic, or at least not anti-Jewish.

Yet when historians who set out to defend Catholicism are faced with the overwhelming burden of proof, they have to admit to a latent antisemitism among Catholics. How do they react? They change their strategy and finally resort to looking to the Jews themselves as its cause. These scholars of Catholicism claim that there was a real conflict between Jews and Catholics, which led to anti-Catholicism on the one side and to antisemitism on the other side. If there were tensions on both sides, are antisemitism and anti-Catholicism essentially, then, the same? Are they equivalent, but referring to different objects? This was certainly the argument Rome put forward in 1998. The papal Commission for Religious Relations with Judaism published its long-awaited and sensational millennium document worldwide in March 1998, with an accompanying text by John Paul II entitled "We Remember: A Reflection on the Shoa." It was intended to represent an apology. Yet it surreptitiously compared the persecution of Jews with the persecution of Catholics. National Socialist ideology rejected Christianity and the idea of the divine. This extreme ideology became

> the basis of the measures taken, first to drive the Jews from their homes and then to exterminate them. The Shoah was the work of a thoroughly modern neo-pagan regime. Its anti-Semitism had its roots outside of Christianity and, in pursuing its aims, it did not hesitate to oppose the Church and persecute her members also.

What is more, the document also parallels the hatred of Jews with hatred of Christians by maintaining:

> We wish to turn awareness of past sins into a firm resolve to build a new future in which there will be no more anti-Judaism among Christians or anti-Christian resentment among Jews, but rather a shared mutual respect."[24]

This formulation can no longer be found in the official statement of Pope John Paul II's sensational plea for forgiveness which was broadcast on television on 12 March 2000. It emphasized much more that the "hostility or the mistrust of many Christians towards the Jews over the course of time is a depressing fact." Thus the document encourages historians to make constant re-analyses.[25]

The present study is structured so that it can be neatly divided into three parts. First, Catholic antisemitism is introduced and studied in the context of its time, one of severe confessionalism. Second, Catholic antisemitism is examined in relation to the attitudes and behavior of Jews. Finally, the question whether Jews perceived some Catholic antisemitism is raised.

The first and second parts are closely interrelated. Both examine the question of whether the causes of antisemitism among Catholics (chapter 1) can be traced back primarily, or at least partly, to the Jews (chapter 2). Certain historians claim this to be possible. However, this is not the only basis of explanation and must therefore be compared with other models which assume that the causes of anti-Jewish attitudes lie not with the victims, but with the culprits, and which look not to antisemites for witnesses of Jewish "misdeeds" but examine Jewish sources. Ever since the issue of antisemitism came to light, it has concerned both supporters and critics. One thing was always clear to the antisemites: that "there is a Jewish question, which was not brought into being by the Christian side, but by the Jewish side," as the Catholic dean Albert Wiesinger emphasized in 1894. He claimed to have dedicated his full attention to the "Jewish question" for thirty years, as both orator and author. By that time the activists in the Verein zur Abwehr des Antisemitismus and the Centralverein deutscher Staatsbürger jüdischen Glaubens (the central association of German citizens of Jewish faith) were already forming completely different opinions with regard to the motives and reasons behind antisemitism. For them, the so-called "*Judenfrage*" was a problem which belonged to the terrified Gentiles. It was seen as a construction and group-projection. In 1926 Fritz Bernstein published a study entitled "Antisemitism as a Collective Phenomenon," and even today his sharp observations can still compete with modern sociological and psychological studies.[26]

Meanwhile, it is astounding how frequently some of today's historians still rely on hypotheses which are of antisemitic origin. Although they dutifully pay lip-service to the notion of a "Christian–Jewish dialogue," some "Christian" researchers still refer to antisemitic stereotypes, such as the Jewish profiteer, or the explanation that antisemitism is the fault of the Jews. What really lies behind the opinion that Jews were anti-Catholic and that there was a genuine Jewish–Catholic conflict? Sometimes it seems that research into antisemitism has simply been plagued by a degree of intellectual naïveté. But in the work of some historians it is often obvious that they have a determined interest in portraying their own group, the group to which they feel they belong (Catholicism in this case) in a good light. It is possible to adopt a number of alternative approaches towards the analysis of Catholic antisemitism in relation to a "Jewish reality" which are much better suited to finding the causes of Catholic antisemitism than the reasons behind the *Realkonfliktthese,* the belief in a real conflict between Jews and non-Jews in economic, political, and everyday life. These alternative approaches conclude chapter 2.

The third part of this study deals with the way in which the Jewish side perceived Catholic antisemitism. We have to ask whether Jews blamed Catholics for antisemitism or whether, on the contrary, they themselves proved that the Catholic side was actually relatively free from such prejudice. This would be very good evidence for apologetic historians defending the Church's interest. Indeed, it is possible to find that there were those on the Jewish side who treated Catholicism with courtesy and praised it for being free of antisemitism. This would entirely confirm the opinion of the philo-Catholic historians who maintained that Catholicism was not antisemitic. However, their theory that the Catholics were unreasonably provoked by the Jews would then appear dubious.

It could also well be that Jews perceived antisemitism on the Catholic side and uttered this in public, consequently provoking verbal attacks from Catholics. If this were the case, the apologist historians would be correct in suggesting that the Jews criticized, angered, and provoked the Catholics. That, however, would make their claim that the Jews had not perceived any animosity from Catholics incorrect.

This study is based on Jewish material from the nineteenth and early twentieth centuries. Whereas a former book of mine was based on Catholic journals, pamphlets etc., showing Catholic antisemitism, the present volume changes the perspective. It looks at Jewish books, letters, and—above all—newspapers in order to find out what this minority thought about those who defamed them. My research included the study of some newspapers which were always suspect of being "Jewish," especially the *Frankfurter Zeitung,* and also an examination of the following truly Jewish papers, both Liberal and Orthodox:

Allgemeine Zeitung des Judenthums: Ein unparteiisches Organ für alles jüdische Interesse, published in Leipzig from 1837 onwards and edited by Rabbi Ludwig Philippson (Bonn) until the 1880s;

Im Deutschen Reich, the monthly leading organ of the Centralverein deutscher Staatsbürger jüdischen Glaubens, which was called *CV-Zeitung* as of 1922;

Israelitische Wochenblatt: Zentralorgan für die gesamten Interessen des Judentums, which was also liberal and edited by Felix Fabian Schach;

Der Israelit, which contrasted sharply to the papers above. It called itself the "Central Organ of Orthodox Judaism" and was edited by Rabbi Marcus Lehmann (Mainz);

Israelitische Wochenschrift für die religiösen und sozialen Belange des Judentums, and *Jüdisches Literaturblatt,* both published in Magdeburg and edited by Rabbi Moritz Rahmer.

I also consulted the *Jüdische Volksblatt: Unabhängiges Organ für die Interessen von Gemeinde, Schule und Haus,* as well as the *Israelitische Familienblatt,* published by L. Neustadt (Breslau).[27]

What will become apparent from this study is that Jews neither provoked Catholics nor ignored Catholic antisemitism. There was no typical Jewish position but rather, as will be shown, three strategies stand out which are all related to the issue of Catholic antisemitism.

NOTES

1. Albert S. Lindemann, *Esau's Tears: Modern Anti-Semitism and the Rise of the Jews,* 2d ed. (Cambridge 2000), 532.

2. Dennis Prager and Joseph Telushkin, *Why the Jews? The Reason for Antisemitism* (New York 1983), 21–22.

3. Antonia Leugers, "Review of Konrad Löw, *Die Schuld: Christen und Juden im Urteil der Nationalsozialisten und der Gegenwart* (Gräfelfing 2002)," *Gegen Vergessen: Für Demokratie* 41 (2004): 56–57; see idem, "Salonfähiger Antisemi-

tismus?," *Newsletter zur Geschichte und Wirkung des Holocaust, Fritz Bauer Institut,* no. 26 (Autumn 2004). He is no longer prepared to respect the "taboos" which were "dictated by political correctness" and reaches out to look for Jewish complicity before and after 1933; Konrad Löw, *Die Schuld: Christen und Juden im Urteil der Nationalsozialisten und der Gegenwart* (Gräfelfing 2002), 221, 280–81.

4. Stefan Berger, *The Search for Normality: National Identity and Historical Consciousness in Germany since 1800* (Oxford 1997).

5. See Deborah Lipstadt, *Denying the Holocaust: The Growing Assault on Truth and Memory* (New York 1993); Brigitte Bailer-Galanda, Wolfgang Benz, and Wolfgang Neugebauer, eds., *Die Auschwitzleugner: "Revisionistische" Geschichtslüge und historische Wahrheit* (Berlin 1996). Worth recommending for its didactic approach is Markus Tiedmann, *"In Auschwitz wurde niemand vergast": 60 rechtsradikale Lügen und wie man sie wiederlegt* (Mühlheim an der Ruhr 1996).

6. Simcha Epstein, "The 'Highest Wave of Antisemitism since 1945'—Is It So?" *Vidal Sassoon International Center for the Study of Antisemitism Annual Report 2001* (2001): 7–8; Werner Bergmann, "Antisemitismus in öffentlichen Konflikten 1949–1994," in *Antisemitismus in Deutschland: Zur Aktualität eines Vorurteils,* ed. Wolfgang Benz (Munich 1995), 64–88.

7. Heinrich Graetz, *Volkstümliche Geschichte der Juden* (Vienna 1888; rprt. Cologne 2000), 2:1001.

8. The following are a few classic and important titles in the field of antisemitism research: Werner Jochmann, "Struktur und Funktion des deutschen Antisemitismus 1878–1914," in *Antisemitismus: Von der Judenfindschaft zum Holocaust,* eds. Herbert A. Strauss and Norbert Kampe (Bonn 1985), 95–142; Peter Pulzer, *Die Entstehung des politischen Antisemitismus in Deutschland und Oesterreich* (Gütersloh 1966); Helen Fein, ed., *The Persisting Question: Sociological Perspectives and Social Contexts of Modern Antisemitism* (Berlin 1987); and the following works by Shulamit Volkov: *The Rise of Popular Antisemitism in Germany: The Urban Master Artisans, 1873–1896* (Princeton 1978); "Antisemitismus als kulturelle Code," in *Jüdisches Leben und Antisemitismus im 19. und 20. Jahrhundert* (Munich 1990), 13–36, first published in *Leo Baeck Institute Year Book* 23 (1978): 24–45; "Das geschriebene und das gesprochene Wort: Über Kontinuität und Diskontinuität im deutschen Antisemitismus," in ibid., 54–75, first published in *Vierteljahrshefte für Zeitgeschichte* 33 (1985): 221–43. For some good overviews see Helmut Berding, *Moderner Antisemitismus in Deutschland* (Frankfurt 1988); Wolfgang Benz and Werner Bergmann, eds., *Vorurteil und Voelkermord: Entwicklungslinien des Antisemitismus* (Freiburg 1997); taking the opposite view, but poorly argued: John Weiss, *Der Lange Weg zum Holocaust: Die Geschichte der Judenfeindschaft in*

Deutschland und Österreich (Hamburg 1997). See also Susan Sarah Cohen, ed., *Antisemitism: An Annotated Bibliography*, vols. 4–6 (1988–1990) (Munich 1997); and the current bibliography in *Leo Baeck Institute Year Book*. A good summary of recent research is provided by Massimo Ferrari Zumbini, *Die Wurzeln des Bösen: Gründerjahre des Antisemitismus: Von der Bismarckzeit zu Hitler* (Frankfurt 2003).

9. See Dr. Justus [=Aron Briman], *Judenspiegel, oder 100 neuenthüllte, heutzutage noch geltende, den Verkehr der Juden mit den Christen betreffende Gesetze der Juden. Bonifacius Broschuren: Populaere Eroerterungen über den Katholizismus und die Einsprüche seiner Gegner,* nos. 3–5 (Paderborn 1883, rprt Paderborn 1921); Hartmut von Hunt-Radowsky, *Judenspiegel: Ein Schand- und Sittengemaelde alter und neuer Zeit* (Würzburg 1819).

10. C. Burger, *Antisemitenspiegel: Die Antisemiten im Lichte des Christentums, des Rechts und der Wissenschaft,* 2d ed. (Danzig: Verein zur Abwehr des Antisemitismus, 1900); compare the 3rd ed., with same title, Berlin 1911. This is a study of the development and character of antisemitism that examines its "lies" and prejudices about the Alliance Israélite Universelle, "Jewification," white-slave trafficking, Jews in the armed forces, Jews as tradesmen and farmers, *Güterschlächterei* and profiteering, the Jewish contribution to crime, the Shulhan Arukh and the Talmud, Jews in the administration of justice and education, as well as the economic power of the Jews. Burger then goes on to deal with the ritual murder legend in great detail. For the Verein, see the following: W. Fritsch, "Verein zur Abwehr des Antisemitismus (Abwehrverein) 1890–1933," in *Die bürgerlichen Parteien in Deutschland: Handbuch der Geschichte der bürgerlichen Parteien und anderer bürgerlicher Interessenorganisationen vom Vormärz bis zum Jahre 1945,* ed. Dieter Fricke (Leipzig 1974), 4:375–78; Barbara Suchy, "The Verein zur Abwehr des Antisemitismus, Part 1: From its Beginnings to the First World War," *Leo Baeck Institute Year Book* 28 (1983): 205–39.

11. See Julius H. Schoeps and Johannes Schlör, eds., *Antisemitismus: Vorurteile und Mythen* (Munich 1995).

12. See Jörn Rüsen, *Historische Vernunft: Grundzüge einer Historik,* vol. 1: *Die Grundlagen der Geschichtswissenschaft* (Göttingen 1983), 76–136.

13. See the quotations on the back cover and first page of Lindemann's book (Zuccotti in *The Nation*; Rubinstein in *History*). Susan Zuccotti proclaimed it a "superior sourcebook for students of anti-Semitism and a brilliant analytical work."

14. See Robert S. Wistrich's review, "Blaming the Victim," *Commentary* (Feb. 1998): 60–63.

15. Leon Volovici, "Discussion: A Broken Balance," *Vidal Sassoon International Center for the Study of Antisemitism. Annual Report 1998* (1998):15–17; see also the

review by Andrea Hopp, *Historische Zeitschrift* 269 (1999): 126–38. Some historians still use "classic antisemitic phrases" now and again, as confirmed by Stefan Rohrbacher, "Über das Fortwuchern von Stereotypvorstellungen in der Geschichtswissenschaft," in *Shylock? Zinsverbot und Geldverleih in jüdischer und christlicher Tradition,* eds. Johannes Heil and Bernd Wacker (Munich 1997), 235–52, quote on p. 251.

16. Lindemann, *Esau's Tears,* xvii.

17. Ibid., xix, 9. In fact, looking for Lindemann on the Internet, I came across the infamous American neo-nazi Zundel page.

18. Steven Beller, in the *Times Literary Supplement,* quoted from the back cover of Lindemann's book.

19. Lindemann, *Esau's Tears,* xv (actually, he examines nine countries).

20. See Wistrich, "Blaming the Victim."

21. Prager and Telushkin, *Why the Jews?,* 22.

22. Daniel J. Goldhagen, *Die katholische Kirche und der Holocaust: Eine Untersuchung über Schuld und Sühne* (Berlin 2002), first published as *A Moral Reckoning: The Role of the Catholic Church in the Holocaust and its Unfulfilled Duty of Repair* (New York 2002). See Olaf Blaschke, "Hitlers willige Katholiken? Goldhagens Moralpredigt gegen die katholische Kirche aus der Sicht eines anderen Kritikers ihres Antisemitismus," *Zeitschrift für Geschichtswissenschaft* 50 (2002): 1099–1115; idem, "Goldhagen und Hitlers willige Katholiken zwischen Sensationshascherei und Wirklichkeit: Ein ernstes Themenfeld droht zu verbrennen," *Menora: Jahrbuch für deutsch-jüdische Geschichte* 14 (2003) [=*Goldhagen, der Vatikan und die Judenfeindschaft,* eds. Julius H. Schoeps et al (Berlin and Vienna 2003): 163–93]; Christopher Clark, "Doctrine or Death?" *Times Literary Supplement,* 1 Nov. 2002: 14.

23. Olaf Blaschke, *Katholizismus und Antisemitismus im Deutschen Kaiserreich,* 2d ed. (Göttingen 1999); idem, "Einleitung: Die Anatomie des katholischen Antisemitismus: Eine Einladung zum internationalen Vergleich," in *Katholischer Antisemitismus im 19. Jahrhundert: Ursachen und Traditionen im internationalen Vergleich,* eds. Olaf Blaschke and Aram Mattioli (Zürich 2000), 3–56.

24. For the complete text see "Wir erinnern: Eine Reflexion über die Shoa: Erklärung der päpstlichen Kommission für die religiösen Beziehungen zu den Juden vom 12. März 1998," *Blätter für deutsche und internationale Politik* 43 (1998): 755–61, quote on 761. See also Olaf Blaschke, "Nicht die Kirche als solche? Anfragen eines Historikers an die vatikanische 'Reflexion über die Shoa,'" ibid., 862–74. For the text in English see Commission for Religious Relations with the Jews, "We Remember: A Reflection on the Shoa," *Menora: Jahrbuch für deutsch-jüdische*

Geschichte 14 (2003): 101–12 (quotes on 107, 110); also in http://www.vatican.va/roman_curia/pontifical_councils/chrstuni/documents/rc_pc_chrstuni_doc_16031998_shoah_en.html For Catholic antisemitism see also Michael Langer, *Zwischen Vorurteil und Aggression: Zum Judenbild in der deutschsprachigen katholischen Volksbildung des 19. Jahrhunderts* (Freiburg 1994) (very descriptive); Uwe Mazura, *Zentrumspartei und Judenfrage 1870/71–1933: Verfassungsstaat und Minderheitenschutz,* Veröffentlichungen der Kommission für Zeitgeschichte Reihe B: Forschungen, vol. 62 (Mainz 1994) (apologetic); a critical analysis of both monographs: Olaf Blaschke, "Kontraste in der Katholizismusforschung: Das antisemitischen Erbe des 19. Jahrhunderts und die Verantwortung der Katholiken," *Neue politische Literatur* 40 (1995): 411–20. See also Walter Zwi Bacharach, *Anti-Jewish Prejudices in German-Catholic Sermons* (Lewiston, N.Y. 1993). Various essays already examined the problem earlier: David Blackbourn, "Roman Catholics, the Centre Party and Anti-Semitism in Imperial Germany," in *Nationalist and Racialist Movements in Britain and Germany before 1914*, eds. Paul Kennedy and Anthony Nicholls (London 1981), 106–29; Ernst Heinen, "Antisemitische Strömungen im politischen Katholizismus während des Kulturkampfes," in *Geschichte in der Gegenwart: Festschrift Kurt Kluxen*, eds. Ernst Heinen. and Hans J. Schoeps (Paderborn 1972), 286–301; two works by Helmut W. Smith: "Religion and Conflict: Protestants, Catholics, and Anti-Semitism in the State of Baden in the Era of Wilhelm II," *Central European History* 27 (1994): 283–314, and "The Learned and the Popular Discourse of Anti-Semitism in the Catholic Milieu of the Kaiserreich," ibid.: 315–28. See also Uriel Tal, *Christians and Jews in Germany: Religions, Politics and Ideology in the Second Reich, 1870–1914* (London 1974); Wilhelm Damberg, "Katholizismus und Antisemitismus in Westfalen: Ein Desiderat," in *Verdrängung und Vernichtung der Juden in Westfalen,* eds. Arno Herzig et al (Münster 1995), 44–61; specifically concerning the post-1918 era, see three works by Hermann Greive: *Theologie und Ideologie: Katholizismus und Judentum in Deutschland und Österreich 1918–1933* (Heidelberg 1969); "Between Christian Anti-Judaism and National-Socialist Antisemitism: The Case of German Catholicism," in *Judaism and Christianity under the Impact of National Socialism,* eds. Otto Dov Kulka and Paul R. Mendes-Flohr (Jerusalem 1987), 169–79; *Geschichte des modernen Antisemitismus in Deutschland* (Darmstadt 1988); for apologist views see Walter Hannot, *Die Judenfrage in der katholischen Tagespresse Deutschlands und Österreichs 1923–1933* (Mainz 1990); Amine Haase, *Katholische Presse und die Judenfrage: Inhaltsanalyse katholischer Periodika am Ende des 19. Jahrhunderts* (Munich 1975); for works concentrating more on anti-racism see Clemens Thoma, "Die katholische Weltkirche und der Rassenantisemitismus 1900–1939," in *Antisemitismus in der*

Schweiz 1848–1960, ed. Aram Mattioli (Zürich 1998), 445–64; see also Urs Altermatt, "Das Koordinatensystem des katholischen Antisemitismus in der Schweiz 1918–1945," in ibid., 465–500.

25. Gerhard Ludwig Müller, ed., *Erinnern und Versöhnen: Die Kirche und die Verfehlungen in ihrer Vergangenheit* (Freiburg 2000), 92 (the quote), 69–70, 97.

26. Albert Wiesinger, *Literarische Bildergalerie von "Antisemitischen Dummköpfen, Narren und Verbrechern": Erstes Christenwort zur Judenfrage* (Münster 1894), 3–4; Fritz Bernstein, *Der Antisemitismus als Gruppenerscheinung: Versuch einer Soziologie des Judenhasses* (Berlin 1926).

27. It was not possible to consult and analyze the publications from every year on a similar scale. The volumes actually focused on were as follows: *Allgemeine Zeitung des Judenthums* 29–57 (1865–1893); *Im deutschen Reich* 1–5 (1895–1899); *Der Israelit: Ein Zentralorgan für das orthodoxe Judentum* 12–22 (1871–1881); *Israelitische Wochenschrift für die religiösen und sozialen Belange des Judentums* 1–13 (1870–1883); *Israelitisches Wochenblatt: Zentralorgan für die gesamten Interessen des Judentums* 11 (1912): *Jüdisches Literatur-Blatt* 8–19 (1879–1890); *Jüdisches Volksblatt: Unabhängiges Organ für die Interessen von Gemeinde, Schule und Haus* 8–17 (1902–1911); and *Israelitisches Familienblatt* for 1908.

CHAPTER 1

Catholic Attitudes toward Jews

It is a common phenomenon that people maintain attitudes towards other people. To understand these attitudes, we can either interpret them as a reaction against "the other," or we can look for indigenous reasons that underlie such attitudes. What problems, world-views, and traditions lead some people to nurse stereotypes against others? The same questions can be asked about Catholic attitudes towards Jews. Some would interpret them against the backdrop of specifically Catholic constellations, but there seem to be many who would prefer to understand Catholic attitudes towards Jews as a response to an outer challenge. There are even those who deny that Catholic antisemitism ever existed. This chapter examines Catholic antisemitism and its different interpretations in the literature.

CHALLENGING EXPLANATIONS OF CATHOLIC ANTISEMITISM

Albert S. Lindemann is only one outstanding example of a significant number of historians who maintain that the Jews were at least partly responsible for antisemitism, nowadays a minority view. Ever since the beginnings of antisemitism, opinions about the phenomenon have been divided in two. While one side, including all antisemites of course, maintained that the Jews were themselves guilty of certain misdemeanors which justified attacks against them, others, Jews first and foremost, saw and still see antisemitism as a system of prejudices. However, Lindemann suggests that "Jews, perhaps more than non-Jews, were firmly convinced that the new, racial anti-Semitism of the 1870s and 1880s was entirely justified, given the arrogance and immorality of large numbers of newly-successful, highly placed, and all-too-visible Jews."[1]

These claims are highly questionable and not supported by any evidence. There might certainly have been some Jews who tried to make the best out of the situation, using Gentile antisemitism as an instrument to address their Jewish comrades in order to improve something, but many more Jews were afraid of the increasing antisemitic attitudes and suffered because of them. Who among them thought that "racial anti-Semitism . . . was entirely justified"? Lindemann only quotes a few Zionists and some Reform Jews. Moreover, who, except antisemites, have ever proven the "arrogance of large numbers" of successful Jews? On what does Lindemann actually base his statements?

The position of the antisemites was clear in any case. They implied that there was Jewish aggression, or at least unreasonableness, or an actual conflict between Jews and non-Jews. In fact, people tend to compete, for instance, for scant resources or the hegemony of different world-views. If we consider equal rights and the opportunity to participate in a system to be resources in which one can share or from which one can be excluded, then the *Realkonfliktthese* would be convincing, since Jews were excluded before they achieved equality and were often still socially ostracized afterwards. Yet the *Realkonfliktthese* is only seldom understood this way; on the contrary, it usually takes the view that the Jews behaved improperly.

Since the near-extermination of European Jewry, the dominant position has obviously been that which sees antisemitism not as a result of a real conflict, but as a result of a construct of the antisemites. When one considers the monstrous catastrophe which murdered millions of Jews, it is sacrilegious, immoral, and politically incorrect to maintain that the Jews paved the way for this catastrophe.[2] Yet insofar as this Western consensus is based on morals instead of on well-based arguments, in the end it is not always convincing. Moral appropriateness and political correctness don't serve the rational case. They might actually help those who like to break taboos, since in rebelling they can stylize themselves as martyrs, defiantly opposing the powerful opinion of the general public. They boast of revealing unpleasant truths despite the overwhelming power of the "Auschwitz-hammer" *(Auschwitz-Keule*), the fact that one needs only to mention the Auschwitz atrocity in order to contest any anti-Jewish argument.

Lindemann is right in assessing that the analysis of Jewish–Gentile relationships should pose no moral obstacle. To convince his critics to look at the Jews, and not just at the antisemites, he writes that it is dangerous to offer representations which merely present a one-sided treatment of the issue, "for that provides ammunition to those who maintain that Jews and their supporters twist history to their advantage, that they are critical of all except Jews, and that they exaggerate the flaws of their critics while covering up Jewish misdeeds."[3] Lindemann believes that he himself has overcome moral restrictions and that he offers a "non-polemical analysis." Revealing that the Jews were largely responsible for their own persecution might be dangerous, he concedes, since antisemites could feel exonerated, but the danger of not exploring the topic properly seems much more significant.

Making it a taboo to question the role of the Jews is, admittedly, not very helpful, but I do not agree with Lindemann's claim that Jewish history has been "twisted" and do not consider most studies to be polemical. Nor do I agree with his suggestion that a closer examination of the relationship between Jewish history and antisemitism must necessarily lead to the result he presents. A precise interpretation should rather come to the conclusion that it is by no means satisfying to explain antisemitism by looking at Jewish behavior.

Being politically correct and overly sensitive towards antisemitism goes hand in hand. Accordingly, breaking the rules of political correctness and re-negotiating the scope of antisemitism are promising strategies to attract attention. It is helpful to insinuate that one is nowadays forced to be absolutely silent about alleged Jewish misdeeds. The other way of attacking the taboo is to de-dramatize antisemitism, a tactic that claims that the alarm often sounds too early. What we today understand as antisemitism was not seen, revisionists maintain, as a serious problem at all at the time. It was, they claim, much more harmless and not meant as it is represented today. It has been suggested that Auschwitz has over-sensitized us. "The fact that people today tend to use the phrase [antisemitism] in a sloppy way," wrote a historian in 1994, "has inevitably been influenced by the Shoa; this is why it is doubtful whether one can do justice to the phenomenon at the end of the nineteenth century with such a perspective. What is more, antisemitism is, particularly today, still a political catchword used to defame and silence opponents." This quote is from a historian whose study of political Catholicism and the "Jewish question" was published by the Kommission für Zeitgeschichte (Commission for Contemporary History), a body founded with the support of the German episcopacy. The core of his work consists of his theory that Catholicism has never been anti-Jewish in any way and that its party, namely the Zentrumspartei (Center Party), "never participated in any antisemitic actions."[4] It is alleged that antisemitism at the time was only understood to be racial antisemitism and consisted of depriving the Jews of their rights. This is too narrow a definition. To legitimate his narrow definition, Uwe Mazura suggests that today we have a wide-ranging and moralizing concept of antisemitism. Here he refers to Michael Wolffsohn to support his case: "Auschwitz signifies a kind of knockout. When somebody says 'Auschwitz' every conversation suddenly comes to an end, every argument becomes pointless." He called this the *Auschwitz-Keule*, i.e., "Auschwitz hammer."[5] It may not be easy to simply dismiss this observation, especially with regard to Germany, Israel, and the United States, where in 2000 the debate about the "holocaust-industry," initiated by Peter Novick and Norman Finkelstein, raised similar questions about the special gravity of this issue.[6] But the question whether the genocide is abused for moral or economic purposes distracts from the antisemites. With this image of a fictitious opponent, we make it too easy to exculpate Catholicism, since this stance assumes that whoever calls Catholicism antisemitic today or denies that the Jews were partly to blame is employing ahistorical categories and at the same time just taking the comfortable path on high moral ground. It is therefore all the more important to deal with such strategies of argument on an analytical level. We must use empirical data and analytical precision to check whether the Jews represented a cause for Catholic antisemitism and whether they actually judged it to be harmless.

Let us remain with Mazura's book, which was the first to examine the relationship between political Catholicism and antisemitism from 1890 to 1933. The fact that Mazura persistently uses the term "*Judenfrage*" without quotation marks, as though it were an objective problem in need of a solution (like the social question), is disturbing in itself. Until legal emancipation was finally achieved in Germany in 1870, the "Jewish question" consisted of whether and how Jews could be emancipated. Afterwards, the "new Jewish question" was a fiction created by antisemitic non-Jews who thought that Germany, or Christendom, must now emancipate itself from the Jews. The unthinking use of the term "Jewish question" for the post-emancipation era encompasses the antisemitic usage. In fact, there is a further consensus among researchers that "antisemitism was not brought into being by a Jewish question—contrary to its self-conception—but, much more on the contrary, it was antisemitism which created the modern 'Jewish question.'"[7]

It is not only the use of the term "Jewish question" which suggests that there was a real problem at the time, and Mazura is much more frank concerning this point. Though his general conclusion does show Catholicism as not being anti-Jewish, he however has to admit after all that among "certain deputies of political Catholicism" there were indeed "demonstrable anti-Jewish and antisemitic tendencies." What is now decisive here is how such "tendencies" are to be interpreted and explained. According to Mazura, they "obviously" had "their cause in the proximity of a large part of the non-Orthodox Jewry to the Kulturkampf. Here surely lies an explanation as to why anti-Jewish comments came about." As an example of these anti-Jewish tendencies following 1870 he refers to the *Historisch-politische Blätter für das katholische Deutschland* (Historical-political Papers for Catholic Fermany). However, the findings there, he says in an attempt to ease his conscience, "are not to be generalized."[8] These papers were related to the papally-loyal Catholic publications which set the tone at the time. If Mazura had really leafed through them a little, not just after 1870, he would have noticed that antisemitic elements had been present in them since they were first published in 1838, which is something for which the Jews cannot be held responsible. Yet the author continually gives the impression that the Jews initiated the conflict. Church propaganda at that time maintained the same thing, claiming that everything was simply a "reaction" to Jewish provocation. "Large sections of Jews and their press supported the *Kulturkampfgesetzgebung* [the Kulturkampf legislation], this in turn strengthened anti-Jewish resentment among the Catholics."[9] From the beginning of the Kulturkampf onwards, in this fundamental conflict between Bismarck and the Catholic Church, between liberalism and ultramontanism, "some Jews as well as Jewish newspapers and publications displayed open support for Bismarck's measures." And "as a reaction to the defense of the Kulturkampf by means of papers such as the *Allgemeine Zeitung des Judentums* and the *Israelitische Wochenschrift,* the *Germania,* which was connected to the Center Party, began a series of articles in 1874–1875 in which it launched into a polemic against the Jews and Judaism." Mazura even states that actually, at the time, "the overwhelming majority of Jewish literary figures adopted a very hostile attitude towards Catholics."[10]

The excuse that Jewish writers adopted anti-Catholic attitudes was the standard cry of antisemitic contemporaries. It was based on prejudice. One would expect those academics who still share this fatal premise today to have reached their conclusion after careful, empirical research, yet Mazura only quotes one piece of evidence to support his case. It is antisemitic in origin, which is perhaps why he conceals its source in the footnotes: Ludwig Windthorst, the leader of the Center Party.[11] Obviously, Mazura is so convinced that his hero was a supporter of the Jewish side that the fact that Windthorst, a Catholic, makes an antisemitic remark here completely passes him by. Like most of his contemporaries, this Catholic politician, still relatively liberal, was not completely free of antisemitism, even though he was aware that the radical antisemitism within the Center Party must be diminished. Mazura has daringly transplanted Catholic prejudices into his analytical argument, so an antisemitic remark is therefore cited here as evidence that its contents (i.e., antisemitism) are correct.

Discussing the possibility of the Catholics' distancing themselves from antisemitism, Mazura suggests that had the Jews only remained peaceful, there would have been no further reason to defend oneself against them: "From the end of the 1870s onwards the behavior of the Jewish press changed; gradually it began to make peace with the Center and accept its political viewpoints, subsequently, in the media which was linked to the Center, the tone became more moderate."[12] This sounds like an original Catholic voice prior to 1900, but it is Mazura who unquestioningly takes over the *topoi* of the time. Applying a rough generalization, Catholics were targeted by "the Jewish press" in the 1870s. The author does not realize that Catholics were basing their ideas on an antisemitic pattern of interpretation. Historians should always be careful not to give too much credit to the convictions of the people they study. Where is the evidence to support Mazura's insinuations, or the claim that Catholicism was just reacting to Jewish provocation? Where is the proof that, when these Jewish "provocations" were curbed, "subsequently" Catholics acted more moderately?

Are those claims and scholarly explanations, so dubious and unproven, a mere exception? Unfortunately, they are rather typical of the argumentation of numerous authors writing from the point of view of the Catholic Church. In 1992, in the same series, Wolfgang Altgeld maintained that national liberalism and Jewish emancipation appeared to the Catholics to be a joint de-Christianizing offensive—"no wonder, considering the liberal 'Jewish' *Kulturkämpfer*." Altgeld complains that this aspect of liberal-Jewish *Kulturkämpfer* is barely noted in German research on Catholic anti-Jewish attitudes.[13] Should we therefore seek out Jewish *Kulturkämpfer* in order to summon up understanding for Catholic antisemitism? Heinz Hürten expressed an even clearer view on this in 1998. The emeritus professor at the Catholic University of Eichstätt admitted that he believed there could be some truth hidden behind antisemitic rhetoric. If Catholics attacked the "Jewified" press, then, logically, they would not have meant the few papers which really considered themselves "Jewish." Hürten, however, is quick to concede the following:

> The expression "Jewified" deserves our complete abhorrence; that does not, however, mean that it is not philologically exact. "Jewified" could just describe that which was not originally Jewish, but, despite its claim to a denominationally indifferent identity, was controlled, i.e., dominated, by Jews. Therefore the reasons behind the defamation of the weekly journal *Simplizissimus* and the newspaper *Frankfurter Zeitung* were actually based on reality, since Th. Th. Heine and Leopold Sonnemann, who founded them, were Jews, just as were the founders of the press empires of Mosse and Ullstein.

Anyone who claims that these were not "Jewish" phenomena, says Hürten, either knows nothing about it or is trying to play "a cheap gag."[14]

Konrad Löw went furthest with his book and his article about antisemitism and the Church in the conservative *Deutschen Tagespost.* Since antisemitism is nowadays (1998) seen as an evil, he complains, "every criticism of the Jews [by the Catholics at the time] is antisemitism. The possibility that the criticism could have somehow been justified is ignored."[15]

We should not ignore this issue. What is the purpose of such comments? It is to explain of Catholic hostility towards the Jews as a "justified" reaction to Jewish aggressions. In this way do all the authors cited play down Catholic antisemitism. It would be easy to dismiss this transparent strategy as intended purely to serve their own interests. One could well bring up counter-arguments here, but we should not make it too easy. Any study of this issue must be carefully argued and provide convincing evidence. Otherwise its author would be too easily accused of applying different sets of standards. The defenders of Catholic integrity could argue that the study is too sensitive, that "every criticism" of Jews is labeled antisemitism, even if it was justified. The question might arise: Why then can we not term Jewish criticism of Catholicism "anti-Catholicism," all the more if it was not justified?

This issue is also worth debating because conservative Catholics and supporters of the Catholics are not the only ones who circulate such convictions. They have been propagated by scholars of Protestantism, in the right-wing conservative spectrum, of course, and by antisemites of all periods. In 1969 the well-known historian of Protestantism, Erich Beyreuther, exposed the anti-Jewish tendencies of Protestants before and after 1933, but at the same time emphasized: "One must also recognize that Judaism and Jewry represented a genuine problem. Neither the Jewish part of the radical left-wing leadership nor the strong and growing economic power of the Jews could be overlooked."[16] Kurt Nowak, another renowned expert on

Protestantism, presented a similar argument in 1991. In his book he throws light upon *Kulturprotestantismus,* describing it, quite rightly, as a protector of Judaism, but at the same time he asserts that the "Jewish problem" was not an antisemitic invention and claims that the Jews were the cause of "some tribulations." Nowak understands the "Jewish press" to be the liberal daily press.[17] Lindemann, too, maintains that "the liberal press was overwhelmingly in the hands of the Jews."[18]

Berlin-based historian Ernst Nolte provoked a fierce argument among historians when he suggested in 1986 that Auschwitz could be considered to have been derived from the Bolshevik model and the Jewish "declaration of war" in 1939. Despite the fact that his suggestion met with large-scale opposition in the so-called "*Historikerstreit,*" he continued to contribute to the trivialization of antisemitism by assuming that its variants were normal conflicts. "It is inappropriate," he wrote in 1990, "to condemn these antisemitisms as evil. They were components of important debates in world history and can only be condemned as morally corrupt if all other historical conflicts are corrupt."[19]

Can antisemitism therefore be classified with other "anti-isms" such as anti-socialism, anti-Catholicism, or anti-capitalism? Was there a hidden truth in antisemitism, which means that we must bid farewell to the accepted idea that it was a conglomeration of prejudices? Were the accusations against the Jews, therefore, based on reality, on a real conflict between Jews and non-Jews? As long as certain circles, including revisionists, pious Catholics and Protestants, right wing extremists, antisemites, and apologists of every shade of opinion put forward such claims, it is tempting to counter them with the usual standard argument. Yet how are we to do this when serious scholars of antisemitism—even Jews—support these claims? In 1956 sociologist Eva Reichmann warned against employing an apologia to defend anti-Jewish actions. She differentiated between a "genuine" and a "false" Jewish question, suggesting that the "genuine Jewish question" had an "objective crux," whereas the "false Jewish question" inflicted foreign, manipulative, elements onto the real tension of the group.[20] Progressing from Reichmann's hypothesis, Herbert A. Strauss, head of the Center for Antisemitism Research in Berlin, and Norbert Kampe wrote in 1985 that "group tensions between Jews and Christians could arise due to economic competition, political hostility and a different philosophy of life, as a result of complex friction from social advancement and declining social status," or due to envy. This model of explanation they called the *objektive Spannungstheorie,* or "objective theory of tension." A precondition for its validity, the authors emphasized, is the relative unity of the group which is to be assessed. Since the structure of Jewish employment varied widely in the nineteenth century, the "objective theory of tension" could not be taken any further. In the final tally, Strauss and Kampe decided on a socially contextualized *Wahrnehmungstheorie,* or "perception theory," in which prejudice is based completely upon "existing characteristics or semi-characteristics of the minority (the Jews) being assessed."[21]

"The Jews reached an outstanding position which was unique in German society," wrote Fritz Stern with regard to the nineteenth century. "They were relatively richer and better educated than their fellow citizens and they held—at least in their own areas—better positions than their Christian colleagues and competitors. In a few sectors, such as banking and journalism, the Jews were so outstanding that they almost dominated them completely." This was fertile breeding-ground for Christian resentment. In the 1870s the Protestant newspapers and those of the Center Party accused the Jews of having begun taking over Germany and corrupting its traditions, citing their economic success as proof. Stern therefore speaks of the "burden of success," which at least produces a connection between the Jewish condition and anti-Jewish resentment.[22]

Jacob Katz, the doyen of modern Jewish research into antisemitism, critically examined the role of Jews in several studies. In one of them he wrote: "Irrespective of the issue of responsibility, I regard the very presence of the unique Jewish community among the other nations as the stimulus to the animosity directed at them. The responses to this stimulus, however, have varied from time to time and from place to place, and insofar as these variations relate to each other chronologically, one can speak of a history of anti-Semitism."[23] Taking up Katz's conclusion, Steven E. Aschheim of the Hebrew University of Jerusalem recently established that the antisemites treated the Jewish dimension with "deadly seriousness": "Anti-Semitic observations about Jews could at times be as revealing and insightful as their evaluation and interpretations were repugnant." Historians should neither be apologist nor antisemitic, Aschheim affirms, but this factor requires serious consideration. He suggests that the Weimar Republic, for example, was often described as "Jewish" or "Jewified," as was modernism, and this interpretation can be classified on the one hand as pure antisemitism, on the other hand as pure philosemitism. This is true, and Aschheim therefore immediately offers a solution to the problem: these phenomena, described as

"Jewish," were constructed by both Jews and non-Jews. In this way he offers the conceived idea of "co-constitutionality," that Jewish-German and non-Jewish-German culture are deeply interwoven.[24] Nonetheless, part of the problem remains: some Israeli and Jewish historians, as well as researchers of antisemitism, maintain the same thing as do philo-Catholic or right-wing conservative authors, namely that there could be some truth hidden behind at least some antisemitic accusations.

This attitude can even be found in the case of the pro-Jewish Verein zur Abwehr des Antisemitismus. Its aim was to observe antisemitism carefully and minutely and to counter it progressivly and vigorously in an informed manner. It attempted to do this not only in the *Antisemitenspiegel,* but also in the Sunday *Mitteilungen aus dem Verein* (News from the Verein), which was edited by the pastor of Kolberg's Protestant cathedral. In 1893 the *Mitteilungen* published a statement by a Protestant layperson without commenting on it. He protested strongly against antisemitism, which was beginning to take root in his Church, because he thought that it was contradicting Christianity and that antisemitic tirades about "Jewification" were "unworthy of the German folk." Nevertheless, he stressed that "there's no smoke without fire," since "fundamentally, the Jews themselves also carry blame for the hatred which is shown towards them, which is blazing up with such bright flames and having such large repercussions, even if their share of guilt is mainly due to the fact that the pressure of the centuries has led them to develop the characteristics in question. Yet they do also have faults which generally make them unpopular." The conclusion here was that the Jews should therefore make a great effort to gain the trust of non-Jews. Even some of the strongest supporters of the Jewish cause refused to completely relinquish the idea of a "kernel of truth."[25]

The Abwehrverein, however, lent more weight to the opposite opinion, simply by repeatedly pointing out that the stereotypes of the antisemites were untenable. Today this stance is without doubt considered to be the dominant view. After 1945 it was well received or, at least corroborated by Jean-Paul Sartre's revolutionary text. "It has become evident that no external factor can induce anti-Semitism in the anti-Semite," he wrote. It is induced neither by historical nor social facts, but is much more a passion and way of viewing the world. "It precedes the facts that are supposed to call it forth; it seeks them out to nourish itself upon them." The Jew serves the antisemite as a pretext. Elsewhere his counterpart "will make use of the Negro or the man of yellow skin." According to the French philosopher, the Jews are not the cause of

Jew-hatred. The antisemite "is a man who is afraid. Not of the Jews to be sure, but of himself, of his own consciousness, of his liberty." Sartre even went as far as to claim that a Jew was a person "whom other people considered to be a Jew . . . anti-semitism creates the Jews."[26] This statement naturally met with substantial opposition from the Jewish side. In their polemics against Sartre, Dennis Prager and Joseph Telushkin complain about his "dejudaization of Jew-hatred" and even his "dejudaization of the Jew." In their eyes, the "incredible conclusion" of Sartre's approach and of modern interpretations is: "Jews do not cause antisemitism, Jews are not hated by antisemites, Jews do not actually have their own existence; Jew-haters have invented them. For well over two thousand years people have hated a group which does not really exist outside of the haters' minds."[27]

Sartre's thesis, however, causes fewer problems if it is seen in the light of perception theory. In postmodern times, people are familiar with the notion of constructivism. What we think we see is not always what is really out there. Antisemites construct their own image of the perceived out-group. However, Prager and Telushkin try to make Jews responsible for being hated. They do not do this from an antisemitic perspective, both authors being Jews: Prager is a prominent preacher, and Telushkin a rabbi. Their intention is to offer a "universal explanation of Jew-hatred": antisemites have hated Jews "because Jews are Jewish." They also found the ultimate remedy for antisemitism: to convince the world of "Jewish and ethical monotheist values."

Prager and Telushkin are correct in observing that the standard argument of most researchers today is that antisemitism is the problem of antisemites, but don't accept this interpretation. However, to see antisemitism as a prejudice sounds more convincing than to take it as an objective reflection of a Jewish reality. Most scholars see antisemitism exclusively as the product of individuals or cultures tainted by prejudice. Eleonore Sterling described the *Hep-Hep Krawalle,* the anti-Jewish pogroms which broke out throughout Germany in 1819, as a "displacement of social protest," which corresponds to Sartre's fundamental thoughts. The issue here was not really the Jews, Sterling asserted, as they only served as scapegoats for economic crisis and political oppression. In 1973 Jacob Katz convincingly pointed out the conflicting character of these excesses, maintaining that the violence was caused by tension between Jews seeking emancipation and non-Jews who opposed Jewish emancipation, a factor which should be taken into account alongside the socio-economic conditions. Since Katz wrote this in Hebrew, it was seldom taken into consideration for two decades, until the publication of the German edition. Katz claimed that Sterling's interpretation, on the other hand, represents an "archetype of antisemitism research."[28] However, there are two different stages: When Jews tried to attain emancipation, Jews and conservative Christians experienced a massive conflict of interest over this issue. In the subsequent stage equal rights were achieved and Jews no longer needed to struggle against Christian privileges to obtain their share of civil rights, even if they still had to fight for a long time to be recognized as part of society.

Yet, today the *Ersatzkonflikt* theory and the scapegoat theory still prevail over the theory of tension, the only point of contention being the question of *which* factors can explain why this strategy of aggression and distraction from other problems is employed. Were economic trade cycles the crucial factor which gave rise to anti-Jewish demonstrations, as Hans Rosenberg notoriously claimed in 1967, or were social, cultural, regional, or religious factors just as significant?[29]

This is not the point at which the argument should be settled between the two sides—let us call them realists and nominalists. Nowadays, certain historians are often tempted to deviate from "mainstream" perspectives and embrace moral taboos, such as suggesting that the Jews too are to blame for antisemitism. Yet if one takes a mindful and cautious approach and asks whether some reasons for anti-Jewish attitudes could not have had some basis in reality after all, this should not be regarded as taboo, for such a control is necessary in order to be able to present the opposite view. There is a basic assumption that antisemitism is a prejudice which has its roots in the particular world-view of the person who bears it. Antisemitism says more about its bearers than about the object of its hostility, a viewpoint which I consider to be plausible. A separate examination of each case, listing the hundreds of stereotypes[30] which were circulating, then disproving them individually, is not generally pursued here, since attentive contemporaries have already engaged in this, although the importance of good arguments cannot be stressed enough. Some stereotypes, insofar as they relate to Catholics talking about Jews, should be examined carefully. But the purpose of the present study lies above all in challenging revisionist approaches and apologetic views in Catholic scholarship. One such influential apologetic view is that Catholics were more or less free of antisemitism. In spite of hundreds of representative examples, some historians maintain rigorous resistance, refusing to accept the historical evidence. Shock about antisemitic traditions in the midst of the group with which they identify lies deep. Wolfgang Altgeld, an eminent scholar of Catholicism, even in 2004 confessed openly that he always viewed antisemitism "as an problem external to Catholicism." To preserve this idea, his research attempts to prove that antisemitism is not "established as an internal phenomenon of Catholicism." For those who find they cannot ignore the evidence of Catholic antisemitism, another apologetic approach is to claim it was not really the Catholics' fault: they would not have opposed the Jews if the Jews had not first attacked Catholicism.[31]

THE NATURE OF CATHOLIC ANTISEMITISM

In order to be able to reach an objective conclusion about the relationship between antisemitism and those who are its victims, the profile of antisemitism in general and of Catholic antisemitism in particular must first be defined. Antisemitism is a general term for negative stereotypes about Jews. It comprises resentments and behavior which are directed against Jews as Jews, or against Judaism or Jewry, or against other phenomena because they are seen as Jewish.

Some would consider this too broad a definition, preferring to reduce antisemitism to racism. This, however, would exclude most prejudices from any study, which seems to be the purpose of some authors who make this claim. Others criticize every definition of antisemitism, which originally was a political battle cry, finding exceptions everywhere that do not fit into any scheme. Berger Waldenegg and Georg Christoph have recently (2003) discarded every term—antisemitism, Judeophobia, Jew-hatred, anti-Judaism—without leaving much to work with.[32]

But we need to operate with a definition. Ours is based on the motives of the speaker, not on any given utterance as such. A semantic approach, focusing on language and stereotypes, might miss the point. To say that Marx was Jewish can be construed as being antisemitic or not, depending on the standpoint of the speaker and his ideological background. No stereotype is ever freely hovering in the air. This is why an approach which takes seriously the speaker-ideology dependency of the stereotype is preferred to one which concentrates on language dependency. To say that all French Jews should leave that country and settle in Israel is neither negative nor positive as such. It depends on who is speaking: If demanded by a French conservative Catholic or Le Pen, it is supporting antisemitism; if, by contrast, former

Israeli Prime Minister Ariel Sharon suggests it, as he did in summer 2004, it is aimed against antisemitism. If a German in 1935 would have said: "A Jew is a Jew is a Jew. . . . A faithful Christian can turn into an atheist, and vice versa;... Yet you can never cease to be a Jew, even if you cease to believe in Judaism," that would serve as proof of a racist ideology. But when a New York rabbi makes a similar statement in an article against antisemitism—as indeed was the case in 2004—it was meant to construct a Jewish identity for the American community.[33]

Over the past few years much has been written about both Catholicism and Catholic antisemitism. Although we have a much clearer picture now, we can still distinguish several different positions. Some say that antisemitism was a predominantly Protestant problem. Catholics were less affected by Jew-hatred; in fact, Catholicism is even depicted as being philosemitic. And indeed, the most famous antisemites were of Protestant descent, Adolf Stoecker being the most prominent example. This is why most books about antisemitism devote much more space to Protestants who defamed Jews than to the Catholic contribution.[34] Catholic historians are not unhappy with this situation, which implies that Catholics seem to have been less responsible for antisemitism. Most historians would not argue that there was no resentment at all among Catholics, but they claim the existence of an ambivalent attitude—partly hostile, partly friendly—towards the Jews.

The radical contrary opinion emphasizes the deep involvement of the Catholic Church. Daniel J. Goldhagen recently published a book on this subject. Whereas in 1996 he held the Germans responsible for "eliminatory antisemitism," in 2002 he put the blame for it on international Catholicism.[35]

A third position takes no interest in either Protestants or Catholics. It does not look at the attitudes and interests of antisemites but rather at the number and behavior of the Jews. Thus, we have three totally different traditions. Who is responsible for antisemitism in Germany: Protestants, Catholics, or Jews? It is my opinion that Catholicism was not to any great degree less antisemitic than Protestantism, if compared on the same level of attitudes and prejudices, rather than that of politics. The argument of an ambivalent position towards Jews is misleading: negative attitudes were much more virulent than positive attitudes. There was an ambivalent position toward modern antisemitism, however, because some elements of it were supported while others, such as racism, were regarded with caution.

When discussing Catholicism, it is just as important to avoid a sweeping generalization as it is when taking Judaism as one's theme. Any discussion of

Catholics or Catholicism, a milieu which survived the Kulturkampf in the nineteenth century and later on allegedly withstood National Socialism, tends to refer to Church-affiliated Catholics. Critics as well as pro-Catholic academics always have an "average Catholic" in mind who, of course, does not necessarily represent all Catholics. Some Catholics did not attend church regularly, read liberal newspapers, were suspicious of their priest, or did not vote for the Catholic party, which in Germany was the Zentrum (the Catholic Center) Party. Those who were not loyal supporters of the Center risked becoming targets for accusations. In the evening in the pub they were met by shouts of: "You really seem to have lost your faith."[36] These Catholics are barely significant for our study, as is the minority movement of *Kulturkatholizismus,* a term which refers to the Old Catholics from 1870 onwards and the reform Catholics around 1900. It is the average Catholics who are much more relevant to our investigation, those who were affected by ultramontanism from the middle of the nineteenth century onwards. They viewed themselves as a relatively homogenous group until the middle of the twentieth century and are seen as a "subculture" or "milieu" by many historians.

Critics of Catholicism, as well as its defenders, refer to this Church-affiliated majority when they speak of "Catholicism," which encompassed about 60 to 80 percent of all Catholics, depending on the time and specific conditions.[37] At the same time, the milieu also depends on the perspective of its observers. Those who dislike the idea that Catholics were antisemitic and prefer to see them as heroic members of the resistance against racism and National Socialism change their opinion about the milieu depending on the argument they try to defend: if they find Catholics opposing the Nazi regime, they generalize it as typical for Catholicism and proudly explain this conduct as "rooted in an enclosed Catholic milieu." If, on the other hand, someone finds Catholics opposing Jews, they declare this should not be generalized since there was no homeogenous milieu. Sometimes these contradictions can be found in one and the same text. The milieu is instrumentalized to prove Catholic resistance; it is denied as soon as it comes to antisemitism.

What is sure is that the Catholic milieu does not include Old Catholics, since their attitudes differed significantly from ultramontane ideals, as did their behavior towards the Jews. In comparison, Catholic antisemitism turned out to be as homogenous as the "Catholic subculture" or "milieu" (a term introduced by M. Rainer Lepsius), even though the homogeneity of a Catholic mentality should not be overstated. The recent study by Christopher

Dowe and Stephan Fuchs has shown, for example, that antisemitism was hardly circulating in the journals of Catholic student fraternities between 1888 and 1918 (though they assume that it did previously), in contrast to Austrian Catholic fraternities and to other social groups within Catholicism.[38]

The "good" Catholics, however, in general stood firmly behind their "good" antisemitism. The *Kirchliche Handlexikon* (an ecclesiastical dictionary) of 1907, for example, contains information about the nature of "good," "better," and "legitimate" antisemitism. It was published by the prominent theologian Michael Buchberger and received the imprimatur of the Generalvikariat des Erzbistums München (General Curatory of the Munich Archdiocese). The following appears under the heading "Antisemitism": "It is possible to differentiate between two types of antisemitism. The first opposes Jewry as a race, together with everything which is related to it (including, therefore, the revelations of the Old Testament); this racial antisemitism is un-Christian."[39]

Thus did the encyclopedia—like many other Catholic lexicons—openly state its disapproval of a type of antisemitism which could be harmful to the Church, as well as the Jews. Such invectives have led modern historians and supporters of the Church to conclude that antisemitism was condemned by Catholics, since true Christianity and the hatred of Jews seem incompatible. Catholics, they believe, could only have succumbed to antisemitism by forsaking their Christian beliefs. Due to their "observance of the Christian commandments and the moral laws [*Sittengesetze*] which derive from them," they supposedly rejected antisemitism. Antisemitism and Christianity seemingly contradict each other.[40]

Historians who make such a claim—one that looks like a very sound argument—dismiss the fact that Catholics in those days held quite a different opinion. Many were hostile towards Jews precisely as a result of the duties and moral obligations of Catholics. They even had no problem in constructing a "Christian antisemitism." This was in fact a plausible consequence of the character of contemporary Catholic Christianity, which viewed opposition to Jews as more important than resistance to antisemitism. We only have to read the full version of the entry in the *Kirchliche Handlexikon* quoted above to see that this is true. After having demarcated un-Christian antisemitism, it goes on to speak of acceptable antisemitism:

> The other variation [of antisemitism] simply calls for special laws to protect the Christian population from the harmful advance of the Jews. Catholic social politicians share this point of view. In fact, the Jewish

> people since their full emancipation in most European countries. . .have shown the extent to which they have become unfamiliar with the original purpose of Judaism. . .; the rapacious hunt for material goods, in particular, is part of their typical character. . . . Jewry [*das Judentum*] wields a pernicious influence on religion and customs, the social institutions, literature, and art of Christian society through its powerful daily newspapers; this stands the radical movements (nowadays Social Democracy) in good stead. This is the purpose of *Christian* antisemitism: to achieve a change [emphasis in original].[41]

The author openly called this concept of distinguishing between good and bad antisemitism "double" or "dual" antisemitism (doppelter Antisemitismus). At the time, contemporaries were already aware of the difference between a baseless type of antisemitism and one which, it was claimed, was merely a reaction to a "reality" they believed to exist. This reality was the "harmful advance of the Jews." It seemed fair to do something to meet this challenge. On the other hand, there was the latest variant of racist antisemitism which targeted supposed "races" and was unappealing to Catholics, to whom it appeared to be "un-Christian" because of its anti-ecclesiastic impetus.

Most prejudices about Jews were interpreted as judgments, which were related to "existing facts." Such anti-Jewish patterns of interpretation were woven deeply into the modern Christian faith. Antisemitism contaminated Catholic conscience not because Catholics neglected their Catholicism but, on the contrary, because they obeyed its rules strictly and exactly. This can be proven not only on a lexical level; it can also be verified historically by the mentality of Catholics at the time.[42] The question, "Can a Catholic be an antisemite?" was answered positively in a reader's letter of 1894 to the Catholic paper *Gladbacher Merkur*. "We, the decisively Catholic, are as convinced of the legitimacy of antisemitism as we are of the truth of the Catholic religion!" In 1880, in exactly the same way, the pious, papally-loyal paper *St. Paulinusblatt* of Trier declared its belief in antisemitism in the face of the "power of today's Jews in many countries, where, like vampires, they suck out the marrow and the blood of the people and brag about their dominance of the financial world and the press, and have war and peace at their disposal." It proclaimed that "the fight against the Jews has got going again. It is wrongly called an anti- Jewish smear campaign; it is an effort to protect the Christian people from Jewish haggling." Every man should make his contribution towards the protection of Christianity. Protecting the Christians became a magic formula with which Catholics immunized themselves so that their hatred of the Jews would not be perceived as intolerance and antisemitism. As has been shown in a recent study, this is the reason why even among Catholic students and academics there was no sign of any critical opposition to even the most blatant injustice and the most stupid prejudices, among them the belief in ritual murder. Who should have had a greater vocation to react against superstition with enlightenment, humanism, and a tolerant, pro-emancipation attitude if not academics? Instead, they widely ignored antisemitism.[43]

The cornerstones of ultramontane *Wagenburgideologie* (defense ideology), which had become increasingly established during the pontificate of Pius IX (1846–1878), proved to be immovable, and the concept of dual antisemitism remained just as stable. In 1925, Paderborn theologian Friedrich Murawski simply copied out what Würzburg pastoral theologian Franz Adam Göpfert had already formulated in his *Moraltheologie* (moral theology) three decades earlier. Both in 1897 and 1925 we find the same message: When it "consists of hatred against Jews because of their religion or nationality," "antisemitism" is "a sin." But, Murawski wrote, like Göpfert before him, "it is allowed, provided that . . . its purpose is . . . to defend the Christian religion." However, the scope of what could be seen as an attack on true Christianity was wide. Criticism of the papacy or of civil marriage already counted as aggression toward Christianity. Thus, there were plenty of opportunities to "defend" Catholicism and to defend it against Jews by means of a "good antisemitism." In 1927, Center Party MP Karl Bachem was still convinced that there was legitimate antisemitism, and that if one took matters into one's own hands to defend oneself against the "harmfulness" of Jewry, one could "achieve a better and more lasting effect in the long run" than with the blatant *Ausnahmegesetz* or "stirring up agitation," which could easily lead to injustice. The "entire" press of the Center, boasted Bachem, "naturally does not allow itself to be prevented from continually expressing its opinions against the harmful growth of Jewry." The Center, its press, and the Bauernvereine (peasant associations) had, so they thought, already "solved part of the Jewish question."[44]

It would be wide of the mark to downplay all of this as "anti-Judaism," as many historians still do. First of all, Catholics definitely referred to their antisemitism as "antisemitism." Secondly, anti-Judaism was, after all, not simply a theological issue. It served as a basis for a dichotomous world-view.

The Crucifixion, for example, was not just a historical event but bore a profound meaning and carried a timeless message of eternal salvation, which—as is evident from any Passion play—differentiated between Christians and Jews: "The crucifying Jew as the personification of evil and the crucified Jesus as the embodiment of good."[45]

Most devout Catholics read little. Instead of pursuing an extensive consumption of a wide range of publications, they devoted themselves to the intensive reading of a handful of life-accompanying works.[46] They would be familiar with at least parts of the Bible, a prayer book and hymnal, and the catechism or a religious school textbook. True, Catholic newspapers were circulating, confirming their readers' world-view, but some texts had a special status. It was normal to become attached to a single devotional book, passing it on down the generations, and to commit oneself to daily silent devotions for atonement, worship, comfort, or encouragement. In its presentation and its dreariness, the sacred *Blumensträußlein* by Josef Freudl, which dates from the 1860s, is a typical example of such a book. Catholics were to adopt its sacrificial prayers intended to be recited at certain times of the year. They dramatized the innocence of Christ as well as "the raging fury . . . with which the Jews attacked You" or dealt him "slaps in the face," as well as "the despicable treatment, as the Jews spat their impure, stinking saliva into Your holy face." These were by no means texts which provided information about biblical events; rather they offered a pious contemplation of reconstructed experiences, which were indelibly recorded in the consciousness of the compassionate Catholics. "The great cry, which rose up from the Jewish people, as they shouted 'Crucify him!' through which they gave You to recognize their great envy and fury towards You, which...saddened You beyond expression," was just as liable to upset people as "the great shame which You suffered as the faithless Jews . . . led you away . . . with a cross . . . ridiculed in front of all the people . . . between two murderers."[47]

William Wilmers' religious textbook, *Lehrbuch der Religion,* demonstrates the unproblematic transfer of such "experiences" into the present and is exemplary of many Catholic works. Its eight editions enjoyed huge popularity from the 1850s right up to the Weimar Republic. Wilmers graphically explains the function of Jews for the Christian faith: "Everyday the Jews living among us remind us" of the "truth of Christianity" and of "the Old Testament," which was passed down to us by them ("in the hands of our enemies!" [!]). This is what can happen if texts which are hundreds or thousands of years old like the Bible are construed as if they contain timeless messages. Many religions, not only the fundamentalists, practice such devotion to certain holy texts. However, the danger of regarding historical texts as authoritative is evident. Wilmers accuses the Jews of having murdered God and stigmatizes them as being depraved. The ahistorical logic is that the Jews were haters of Christ and Christians and thus are eternal haters of Christ and Christians. Wilmers asks in astonishment: "How has it happened that the Christian population has never reached the common decision to rid itself of the unpleasant visitor by violent means?" In the 1885 edition he glossed over the true situation, claiming that the Christians had only seldom "made use of self-defense," in spite of Jewish profiteering. Although it was a religious textbook, it bound together theological, historical, and economic motives. They were frequently underpinned by references to the antisemitic compilation of Johann Andreas Eisenmenger (1654–1704, professor of oriental languages in Heidelberg), and also commented on the present, which was rife with antisemitism. "If we just look at how the Jew gives up his home…, depending on whether hope of bigger profit attracts him or not."[48]

The belief that the Jews crucified Christ, bore a collective guilt, were rejected by God, and served, until very recently, as the antithesis of brightly shining Christianity, caused conflict even in everyday encounters between Christians and Jews. In 1882, a priest asked in his sermon: "Friends, have you any desire to be associated with this people who were rejected by the creator?"[49]

Because of this consensus on antisemitism Catholics should, on the one hand, defend themselves against the Jews, but on the other hand, not be too racist and unjust. What is more, it was not a good idea to vote for the antisemitic parties, as, for example, the chairman of the Catholic Bürgerverein Liegnitz in Silesia emphasized in 1893. In that year the Catholics of that constituency were unable to put forward their own candidate. However the chairman warned them against supporting antisemitism. It was "un-Christian," he stressed, "to give the antisemites the impression of being aggressive. Aversion to the Jews, which frequently exists in the German people," had, he proclaimed, partly developed into "passion and into hatred," not towards the Jews as a religious group, but as a race. He judged the smear campaign against the Jews to be as unjust and un-Christian as the hate campaign against the Catholics, the latter having "suffered enough under the *Ausnahmegesetz*" against the Jesuits, for example. Then, however, the speaker once again traveled the well-trodden paths of Catholic antisemitism by referring back to the enemies in the Kulturkampf. He stated that it was, in fact, "primarily Jews and the Jewish press . . . who instigated the introduction of the *Ausnahmegesetz* against the Catholics and greeted it with joy." Indeed, he continued, Christians were "obliged to stand by those under pressure, but not obliged to fortify the enemy, so that he can then raise his fist anew and inflict a crushing defeat." In any case, this approach allowed Catholics to feel fair and to call their antisemitism "just," because it only served as a defense against Jewish provocation.[50]

The concept of dual antisemitism in Catholicism was widespread in Germany, whether in Freiburg or in Liegnitz, in Ratibor, in Munich or in Berlin. In the Upper Rhine Valley a reader of the *Kölnischen Volkszeitung* held exactly the same view. His article, "Seven Theses Regarding the Jewish Question" was printed in this paper in March 1892. The ostentatious Catholic *Kölnische Volkszeitung* had already made a name for itself in the 1870s with antisemitic articles without, however, coming close to the fierce agitation of papers such as *Germania* or the *Schlesischen Volkzeitung*. Now a reader, who was obviously very familiar with the ultramontane pattern of thinking, had his say.

Thesis one reads:

> As the Jews are notorious for taking part in exploitation of economic weaknesses and poverty, the fight against the interests of the Catholic Church, the weakening of the religious and moral foundations of our public life, and the socialist-revolutionary movement, Jewry must be considered aggressive.

The Jews were therefore left looking like the aggressor, not only against Catholicism, but also against the nation, tradition, common decency, and order, in particular. Considering the tiny number of Jews, thesis two claims, this "Jewish aggression" appeared to be "greatly injurious to and provocative for the Christian population." In his third argument, the reader bases his opinion of Judaism as a whole on his supposed observation of Reform Judaism. In this way he legitimizes an attack on all Jews. "Since it is not yet known for certain that the rest of the Jews have prevented the Reform Jews from following the abovementioned course of action, held them back, or even just shaken them off, there is no compelling reason for the defensive Catholic press to only expressly oppose Reform Judaism."

What, then, was to be done? The fourth thesis reveals: "The primary activities of the resistance are as follows: referring explicitly and critically to the actions described in number 1 at every opportunity; searching for, organizing, and constantly recommending all means which are not morally and legally improper to be used to protect the Christian population from Jewish exploitation; ruthlessly and thoroughly rejecting the philosophical-religious misconceptions which are the cause of the Jewish actions."

With this, a rejection of the *Ausnahmegesetz* was indeed implied, but anti-Jewish polemic was in no way rejected. On the contrary, the reader demanded that this should be expanded:

> 5. The defensive activities of the Catholic press must not, for example, be regarded as trivial and only carried out occasionally; they must constantly remain apparent as an essential, methodically organized element, with the same rate of output as any other editorial department.
>
> 6. Resistance of this kind cannot be described as an un-Christian racial conflict, it is as compatible with the theologically fixed demands of Christian love, as harmonized with that love, as all other types of resistance among humans can and should be.

The author was aware that radical antisemitism, as an unseemly hatred, contradicted the Christian ethos of loving one's neighbor and could also be interpreted as racism. Therefore his attacks bordered on perfect agreement with the phenomenon of "dual antisemitism": there was a legitimate and an illegitimate way of fighting the Jews in the Catholic press and politics.

He highlighted the same point in his seventh theses, as though his conscience was telling him that there could be something wrong about anti-Jewish resentment: "This means of defense has, at most, something material in common with that which we call 'antisemitism'; but due to philosophical-religious insight we reject a formal participation in antisemitism." If one were to quote this sentence alone, according to which partaking in antisemitism is rejected, one could then classify Catholicism as not being anti-Jewish. But the whole context reveals in intention and characteristic style that this judgment would be totally out of place. The *Kölnische Volkszeitung* did not express reservations about this letter. On the contrary, it even commented positively on it. The letter was being published, wrote the editors, because it without doubt expressed an opinion that was also widely held in the Catholic Church and was spreading significantly. They claimed that its formulation of an antisemitic program was by far the best that they had encountered. It differed advantageously from the antisemitic press, particularly as it did not recommend an *Ausnahmegesetz* and, the paper concluded, one could agree to theses four to seven without second thought, while points one to three were the most far-reaching.

This text did not escape the notice of the vigilant Verein zur Abwehr des Antisemitismus. The "News from the Verein" complained about the behavior of the *Kölnische Volkszeitung*: "The Center and the Center's press are mistaken if they think they can regain lost influence among Catholic people by indirectly encouraging antisemitic efforts. For the time being we are holding on to the expectation that the calm and prudent elements of the Center Party make up the majority, that they still remember their terrible experiences from the time of the Kulturkampf and will have reservations about embarking on the dangerous path which this newspaper has just trodden." Clearly, the Verein, against its better judgment, is trying to stylize this text as "new" ("just trodden") and as an exception. This indicates that the Verein was taking great pains to appeal to the few anti-Jewish powers in Catholicism who had learned a lesson from the Kulturkampf, which had only recently been settled. All in all, however, the letter from the Upper Rhine testifies that despite certain modifications by the *Volkszeitung,* there was a fine line between accepted Catholic opinion and that which was unacceptable. Above all "dual antisemitism" was not restricted to lexicon entries or clerical campaign pamphlets but was the expression of the views held by wider circles of the Catholic population, where it in turn found resonance.[51]

This antisemitism was an integrated element of dualist thought, which condemned liberalism, rejected the modern arts, distrusted capitalism and the modern press, and connected all of these with the Jews. This was not just the case in Germany, but applied similarly to Austria and France.[52] Manfred Böcker, for example, convincingly pointed out the international similarities visible in the antisemitism of Catholics in Spain during the 1930s. Thus it can be confirmed that the analytical concept of "dual antisemitism" is universally applicable to other types of Catholicism, like that in Spain, Poland, or Austria.[53] In 1999, a case study of Catholic Switzerland confirmed the capacity of the model of "dual antisemitism" as it had earlier been examined for Germany. In Switzerland, just as in Germany, there was also a predominantly negative Catholic attitude towards the Jews, not an ambivalent one, as apologist historians maintained, such as Rudolf Lill in 1970. Clear lines of continuity prevail between about 1850 and 1950 in Germany and in Switzerland and, as was the case in Germany, Swiss Catholics refrained from racial antisemitism, but did not reject racial antisemitism on account of the Jews. At the same time they held onto an "acceptable" antisemitism, whose purpose was to protect Christendom from the Jews. In Switzerland this standardized resentment, like in other countries, also had an anti-modernist direction, and the Catholics' hostile stance can be explained by their special social status since the nineteenth century.[54]

Probably encouraged by the fact that in recent years even a few loyal members of the Catholic scholarly community started to corroborate the phenomenon of Catholic antisemitism between 1850 and 1950, which made it more and more difficult to evade the evidence, some of the most dedicated Catholic historians and apologists finally seem to have corrected their perspective. Their former consensus was that Catholics were ambivalent towards Jews, if not even philosemitic. Now, in his recent study (2004), even Hubert Wolf, a historian in the Theology Department in Münster, admits that "the Catholics," though distancing themselves from racist antisemitism, promoted the "better," "Christian antisemitism." If Catholics were not equally antisemitic and philosemitic but rather antisemitic instead of being philosemitic, the conventional thesis of ambivalence, as it originated in the works of Rudolf Lill, is obsolete. Catholics did not maintain a "middle position" towards Jews, as Lill asserted. In the nineteenth century they did not hold ambivalent—that is, positive and negative—attitudes towards them, but rather negative, antisemitic ones. However, at the same time that they were not ambivalent towards Jews, it remains evident that Catholics were ambivalent towards modern *antisemitism*: wary of political racism and open towards most modern aspects of antisemitism.[55]

In the 1920s the homogeneity of Catholicism, if it ever existed, eroded. The voices on either side became louder—of those who defended the Jews, which hardly ever happened before, and of those who promulgated antisemitism or even racism.[56] Thus, Wolf rightly points to the Amici Israel (Friends of Israel), founded in 1926, which was a movement of more than 3,000 priests from various countries. They wanted to reform the anti-Jewish parts of the ecclesiastical liturgy in order to bring the Jews "back" to Christianity. For Wolf, the program of the Amici Israel is evidence of "philosemitism" and "anti-antisemitism" within the Church. Certainly, in the interwar period we can observe a growing number of Catholics who stand out as exceptions to a former consensus in the Catholic antisemitic mentality. But this was not the mainstream, not even in the 1920s. In fact, Wolf openly concedes that the Catholic "group which set the tone" was anti-modern and antisemitic. It was but one party among others. However, this tradition of "intransigent, radical-ultramontane anti-modernistic Catholicism" had "gained the lead in the Church in the nineteenth century and would only be overcome in the Second Vatican Council."[57]

In 1928, the "Friends of Israel" organization was suppressed by the Curia. In the same document of suppression, and in order to avoid any misunderstanding, the Catholic Church officially condemned antisemitism for the first time! They did not want to be accused of supporting antisemitism if they forbade a pro-Jewish movement in times of ever-growing hostility toward Jews. Thus, the famous rejection of antisemitism in 1928 was less a campaign for the Jews than an image campaign on behalf of the Church. Wolf interprets this situation as the decline of any antisemitic consensus and of ultramontane dominance. Different voices could be heard in 1928, pro- and anti-Jewish. Thus it can also be interpreted as evidence that antisemitic traditions survived until then because the ultramontane group, rejecting any anti-antisemitic reform, proved its authority once again and stabilized it.[58]

Around 1930, and in the face of fascism in Italy and Germany, things became more complex for Catholics than a few decades earlier, though some traditions proved to be quite stable. Thanks to Catholicism, their own all-embracing, cure-all ideology which they had at their disposal, Catholics had no need to turn to racial ideology. They saw the present problems not as racial degeneration, but as increasing "de-Catholization." They believed that the world had been Christian and pious in the past, until Martin Luther and, later, the French Revolution came along and paved the way for the Antichrist. Many Catholics hoped, however, that the world would one day become Catholic again and that every problem would then be solved, be it the social question or the "Jewish question." The ultramontane paper *Neue Mosel-Zeitung,* edited by Wilhelm Koch, announced in 1875: "Turning back to Christianity and a resolute fear of God in marriage, family, and upbringing, that is firstly the motto, that is the essence of the solution to all modern questions. Without that, all holy affectation is just quackery."[59] Only a Catholic Church which was free to act independently and unrestrictedly in its sphere of influence, with family men appointed as agents, could steer the pathological de-Catholization back to a salutary, utopian re-Catholization, which also served as a model for the "solution of the Jewish question." The important issue for the Catholics was not so much the influence of the Jews, as it was for the radical antisemites, but to reestablish true Christianity.

ANTISEMITISM IN AN AGE OF CONFESSIONALISM

Jews were by no means in the front line of the enemies of Christ. Good Catholics blamed bad Catholics, Protestants, or non-believers for shattering the Divine order. Protestants were more preoccupied with feuding with each other and with Catholics than with Jews. Orthodox Lutherans and Pietists accused liberal "Kulturprotestanten" of being immoral, whereas liberal Protestants looked on the latter as holy Joes. All of them looked down on Catholics.[60]

In the face of antisemitism, this factor of neo-denominationalism has often been overlooked. There are many more studies about antisemitism than about anti-Catholicism and anti-Protestantism, although both affected far more people. When in 1989 I began my search for antisemitic articles in Catholic journals and publications I found several, but ran across many more texts against Protestants or non-Catholic Christians. German society was dominated by severe confessionalism, not by antisemitism. Even Christian antisemitism was often just part of the inter-confessional conflict. In comparison with Gentile anti-Catholicism, anti-clericalism, and anti-ultramontanism, which is narrower and more political than anti-Catholicism, anything said by Jews against Catholics appears rather harmless.[61] While Jews positively tried to defend "humanity," fierce Gentile anti-Catholics labeled the Church "Vaticanaille" or accused priests of chasing young women or boys. In order to understand Jewish attitudes towards Catholics in the light of the general anti-Catholic libel and how antisemitism and denominationalism are related to each other, it is helpful to employ the concept of the second confessional age. What is to be understood by this approach?[62]

In the past, prejudices against "stupid Catholics," "disbelieving Protestants," and "anti-Christian Jews" determined the scope of interpretation and behavior. Catholics did not marry Protestants and Protestants did not vote for Catholic parties. Pious people did not read the daily newspapers of a religion other than their own and even their bookcases housed different works and lexicons—the *Herder* in a Catholic house, the *Brockhaus* in a Protestant living room. Even school children were brought up strictly segregated according to denomination and they happily visited extra-curricular clubs with others of the same faith.

For a long time historians have collectively ignored, almost tabooed, this context. Among historians, the belief in a progressive loss of Christianity and the triumphant progress of secularization since the late eighteenth century has predominated. For this reason the nineteenth century has been referred to as "the age of secularization" or the "century of emancipation." We may term the nineteenth century the "age of nationalism"[63] or materialism, and that allows us to see how these forces were emerging to power. It is a legitimate point of view. But it is the winners' view. Who, in 1850, would have foreseen the disastrous consequences of nationalism in 1914 or 1939? Other influences were as strong as nationalism in the nineteenth century but their impact seems less obvious on the surface. The renaissance of Christianity was overlooked in the face of the modern driving forces of history—enlightenment, industrial capitalism, the civil society, and nationalism. Instead of viewing the nineteenth century as an "age of secularization,"[64] the period between 1830 and 1970 can be seen as a second confessional age, because faith and the religious divide in European societies played an important role, perhaps at least as important as the "secular" elements which are so often emphasized. The master narrative of secularization seems to still be very strong.[65] But secularization and sacralization are not mutually exclusive. Both are dialectically related to each other.[66]

To take religion in the nineteenth century seriously does not necessarily mean to see it as an all-encompassing force, but it played the same major role as other forces which were permanently confronted by it. Religion shaped modern *Weltanschauungen* in the age of ideologies. Even nationalism, bound to be an integrative ideology, was divided along confessional lines. Confessional convictions divided nations, very obviously in Germany, but also in France and the Netherlands.

Of course, some thought should be given to the question whether the terms confession or confessionalism are too broad, too narrow, or appropriate at all. In mono-confessional countries like France or Belgium, Catholicism was not fighting another confession, like in Germany, but laicism. Thus, Anthony Steinhoff rejects the notion of confessionalism in uni-confessional societies. On the other hand, laicism has been labeled as a sort of confession or religion by some contemporaries. In 1912 Protestant republican politician Ferdinand Buisson spoke of "la foi laïque," and historians today are still undecided on how to view it. In any case, French Catholicism was permanently building its identity against laicism and Judaism, especially in the Dreyfus Affair, just as laicism was stabilizing its character in fighting the Catholic Church.[67]

The full dimension of this topic has as yet not been adequately addressed. The events that took place between 1800 and 1970 are strikingly reminiscent of the periods of the Reformation and the Counter Reformation. The parallels are remarkable. The nineteenth century has been called the "age of the neo-styles," referring to the tendency to eclectically adopt historical styles for castles and churches, public buildings, and even factories.[68] In fact, the same century can just as well be called the age of neo-confessionalism, since it reinstalled elements of former religious ages in an eclectic manner: neo-scholasticism, neo-Thomism, neo-Lutherism, and the confessionally poisoned climate of the sixteenth-seventeenth century.

The denominations emerged and developed gradually between Martin Luther's *Thesenanschlag* of 1517 and the Thirty Years' War. This "denominalization" or confession-building divided the population into followers of various strands of belief and trained them to master the required appropriate norms and behavior of their respective Churches. However, distinctiveness soon gave way to enmity. Fierce propaganda led to bloody clashes. Due to denominalization and the extreme growth of denominationalism, this period of approximately 150 years has been called "The Age of the Religious Wars," "The Denominational Age," or "The Confessional Age." The Westphalia peace settlement of 1648 can be regarded as a turning point —in the century-and-a-half which followed, the various denominations were supposed to live strictly separate from one another.

Influenced by the Enlightenment and increasing tolerance, denominalization was seemingly overcome and the French Revolution seemed to have finally conclusively broken the power of the Church. What could still stand in the way of secularization and a pluralist, civil society? It was then that something unexpected happened: the various faiths pulled themselves together and slowly began to defend themselves anew against the threat of secularization. Protestants celebrated the three-hundredth anniversary of Luther's *Thesenanschlag* in 1817. Mixed marriages were condemned in the 1830s. Organizations were split along denominational lines. Graveyards and churches held in common lost popularity as distinctiveness gained power. A second wave of denominalization swept through society, and with it the "demon of denominalization" returned, much to the horror of tolerant contemporaries. Only now were different denominations forbidden to merge with each other and their religious practices effectively standardized. It was only now that the differences between the denominations became completely clear and recognizable to everyone; only now did priests succeed in having their position recognized as a full-fledged profession. Christianity is certainly not a nineteenth-century invention, but during this period it experienced an unexpected upswing and let society disintegrate into denominational groups that were easily distinguishable.

Soon the boundaries between the confessions grew increasingly impenetrable and with them came those resentments that would culminate in open enmity in the Kulturkampf of the Bismarck era. People held separate values and moved in separate circles. There were different levels of training and career possibilities for different denominations, as well as differing utopian dreams and susceptibilities. This played a crucial role in relation to National Socialism, and even prevailed in the Adenauer period. The second wave of denominalization in the nineteenth century and the newly awakened denominationalism are reminiscent of the dramatic events in "The Denominational Age," therefore giving rise to talk of a "second confessional age." The conflict between confessions did not decrease after the 1830s; on the contrary, it increased, culminating in the Kulturkampf in Germany, Belgium, France, and other countries, and evaporating into thin air since the 1960s. This is why I prefer to speak of a *second* confessional age rather than a process of re-Christianization. The emergence of different spheres of living, even of *subcultures,* is a major characteristic of both ages. In the sixteenth and seventeenth centuries this separation was manifest in exclusively mono-confessional territories, whereas in the nineteenth century it was represented in more or less exclusive milieus.[69]

It was only the social and cultural upheaval in the 1960s that finally signaled the end of the "Second Denominational Age." Since then people's attachment to the Church and its principles of belief has been dwindling from one generation to the next. In politics and everyday life the regime of denominational apartheid has long since been abandoned. It has almost been forgotten how influential and, at times, devastating it was for politics and society, in commerce, industry, and culture over a period of about 150 years.

This era spans a period from about 1820–1830 to 1960–1970. Seen from the religious perspective, this period appears to me to constitute a unity. There is broad consent among historians that the original Confessional Age began in the early sixteenth century and ended in 1648. Those nearly 150 years were followed by a fifteen-decade period of confessional appeasement and growing enlightenment (1648 until about 1800) when finally, in my view, another century-and-a-half of confessionalization were launched. Of course these figures are presented only to simplify understanding. The terminology makes it possible to compare the "first" and "second" confessional age or, in a slightly more moderate definition, a second age of confessionalism.[70] Contemporaries already compared events of the seventeenth century with those of the nineteenth century. No wonder that Ernst Troeltsch coined the term "confessional age" in the middle of the second confessional age, in 1906.[71]

The eminent German historian Franz Schnabel observed as early as 1937 that there had been a religious aspect to the battle between opposing world-views since the 1830s. Protestants, liberals, and free thinkers "argued in the name of Luther, who was reinterpreted as the hero of intellectual freedom, as the earliest pioneer of the secularized state. The methods of the modern democratic age were developed and introduced everywhere. The tone of the Church's communication, of writers and of newspapers was, as it had only ever been in the era of the *Glaubenskämpfe*. Once again a 'denominational age' was approaching."[72]

Many contemporaries were aware that this was a new phenomenon. They were also familiar with the term "confessionalism" [*Konfessionalismus*] by the second half of the nineteenth century at the latest. At this time denominational differences were dramatized as demarcation emphasized the individual denomination, leading to orthodoxy.[73] By the 1960s, the term could still be found in the lexicons, but later it faded into oblivion. "The cultural and political differences were increasingly exaggerated, one no longer shrank away from petty and coarse forms of dispute," we read in one entry from 1959. "The extensive denominalization of public life in Germany, which . . . was not overcome . . . in spite of weak attempts . . . constituted one of the most decisive foundations for the National Socialist seizure of power. However, the common battle in the so-called 'Third Reich' then provided an opportunity for overcoming political D[enominationalism] to a large extent."[74]

The resurgence of Christianity in the early nineteenth century at first remained interdenominational. Very soon, however, the denominalization engineered by the Church led Catholics and Protestants to grow apart. Though pregnant with conflict, it did not inevitably lead to practical conflict. Both Christians and Jews often preferred to avoid associating with each other in business-related or political affairs. The denominational sub-societies inside society provided adequate scope for autonomy, enough to prevent conflict in everyday matters. When the situation could no longer be concealed, when denominalization appeared too vociferously, "denominationalism" made itself felt.

The omnipresence of confessionalism in the nineteenth century can be discerned in nearly every sector of society. Ten areas of confessionalism might serve to illustrate this argument:

1. *Religion*. This is too obvious to call for any elaboration. In the area of religion there are different dogmas and rites, different practices and festivals, different hymns and texts. All that widely unfolded and consolidated during the nineteenth century, but today ecumenical efforts have reduced many of the differences.

2. *Mentality*. Religious dispositions exerted a fundamental influence on different world-views, ethics, stereotypes, and even on sexuality. Max Weber's ideas about the spirit of capitalism born out of Calvinist asceticism were written against the background of experienced confessionalism. Confessionalism shaped the matrix in which the world was interpreted.

3. *Ideology*. Confessional differences were also manifest in antagonistic political ideologies. Some tended more to liberalism, others, like Catholics, condemned it. The same is true for nationalism, antisemitism, and racism: different religious beliefs encouraged variant opinions about deviant political and social approaches.[75]

4. *Politics*. Different denominations tended to support different political parties. Priests played an enormous role in fostering Catholic parties. Even beyond this influence it is obvious in several societies that the decisive impact on voter behavior was less social or economic than confessional. The decision to support the Nazi movement depended more on confessional than on social or regional factors.

5. *Everyday life*. With whom to live and where to drink a beer in the evening depended much on confessional affiliation. Mixed marriages were rare, mixed drinking could be avoided by going to a confessionally correct pub, and godless salesmen could be boycotted. Confessionalism was omnipresent. In the period between 1800 and 1970, when entering someone's home people could easily recognize whether it was a friendly environment or the territory of the confessionally significant "other." The Catharijneconvent museum in Utrecht has reconstructed a living room from the 1930s, showing a Catholic and a Reformed type: with the Catholics we find the crucifix above the door, diverse devotionalia, and a holy corner; in a Reform home there are a house-organ and plenty of books and journals. This indicates how deeply rooted confessionalism was in everyday life, not just in politics: it even invaded private homes.

6. *Organizations and societies*. Around 1900 we encounter separate clubs and societies, and segregated leisure-time activities (around 1910, Konrad Adenauer played tennis in a Catholic club, called the Black Custodis Club), separate trade unions, and more.

7. *Media and communication*. There was a growing market for Catholic newspapers and eventually, for radio stations, but in the early twentieth century, there was also a boom of Protestant institutions, Protestant libraries, and the like. This market collapsed in the 1960s, along with the end of the second confessional age.

8. *Business and economy*. Differences in education, economic success, and the uneven distribution of high-ranking positions in society between Jews, Protestants, and Catholics were remarkable. In Prussia, for example, Jews were liable to pay the highest taxes, followed by the Protestants, while Catholics—even in parts of the Rhineland, where they were clustered—were outnumbered by Protestants when it came to filling leading, high-ranking positions. On the average, being wealthy was not a Catholic trait. Discrepancies were already clearly visible in high schools and universities, where 10 percent of the students were Jews (who accounted for only one percent of the population), about 20 percent were Catholics (36 percent of the population), and the majority Protestant. Literature informs us about the topos of *Catholic inferiority* and backwardness.

9. *Education*. In the second confessional age it was important for parents to send their children to confessional schools. They did not like them to be in contact with people of different creeds at the risk of being "contaminated" with wrong beliefs. The struggle to preserve confessional schools was at its height in Germany around 1927 and again in the early Bundesrepublik. The issue of Catholic inferiority in education is well known. Even in universities there was a borderline between different camps: students associated either in national, Catholic, or Jewish fraternities.

10. *History*. Finally the topic also touches upon professional historians. In nineteenth-century Germany more than 80 percent of historians were Protestant, such as Ranke, Treitschke, Sybel, etc. After 1945, Catholic historians were still discriminated against, so it is no wonder that Catholicism and religion played a minor role in historical writing. There are still too many studies which ignore the deep impact of religious factors on politics, culture, and society. The bias against church history and the history of confessions is deeply rooted in the unquestioned assumption of an ongoing secularization. Religion is held to be an old-fashioned relict from pre-modern times.

Certainly this assumption itself is a result of confessionalism, of Whig history about modernization; perhaps it reveals some optimistic vision of secular historians.

In the last few years, studies of religious phenomena have proliferated. They often concentrate on purely religious topics, isolating themselves from wider issues. The results of these studies are hardly integrated into the textbooks and volumes of general history. Since many historians still tend to neglect the religious dimension, we should not forget: confessionalism proved to be at least as strong as other ideologies—as socialism or liberalism, and perhaps even more influential than nationalism, racism, or antisemitism.

Even if we prefer to stick to the notion of a "century of liberalism," we should not forget how important anti-Catholicism proved to be for the liberal identity. The recent study of anti-Catholicism among liberals by Michael B. Gross has demonstrated how important confessionalism really was in the post-1848 period. The Catholic revival, the people's missions after 1848, and the enormous growth of Catholic monasteries posed a threat to liberalism. In the liberal mind they were also closely linked with each other through misogyny: the Catholic revival and Catholicism in general were viewed as irrational and feminine; the missions were followed by an uncontrollable, emotional mob, primarily women; the monasteries, which in fact were predominantly female, were accused of being effeminate even if they were male, because monks, Jesuits, and priests represented unmanliness. Thus, the Kulturkampf was the culminating point of tendencies that began decades before, and the Kulturkampf was not simply an attack on the Catholic Church but the attempt of liberals to preserve an entire moral, political, social, and sexual identity and order.

Anti-Catholic intolerance was a central and inherent feature of liberalism. Above all the Jesuits served as negative foil for liberals who wanted to emphasize their vision of individual and social freedom. Jesuits stood for hostility to freedom, science, and humanity; they strangled individuality. Gross's central argument is that liberals placed anti-Catholicism at the "core of their identity," yet the core's core was biology. The Kulturkampf "ultimately emerges as a *Geschlechterkampf,* a contest between men and women for the public sphere." A complete universe of dichotomies, a vision of illegitimate and legitimate social and cultural order, opened up when monasteries and Catholicism were seen as an antithesis of liberalism and the nation: medieval versus modern, darkness versus light, obsolescence versus progress, sloth versus industry, fanaticism versus reason, subservience versus freedom, stupidity versus *Bildung*. All this, according to the gendering approach of Gross, was overshadowed by binary gender oppositions: female versus masculine, prurience versus propriety, celibacy versus family. His point of the "biologization" of the Kulturkampf certainly overshoots the mark. The Kulturkampf was neither only a gender struggle nor only a class struggle, as other historians claim. But Gross rightly shows how important confessionalism was for one of the most important forces in the nineteenth century—liberalism. What he demonstrates is the co-constitutionality of liberalism, gender, confessionalism, and nationalism. Nothing was primordial; every factor was co-constructed by the dynamics of challenge and response.

Even the revival of Protestantism was directly linked to the Jesuit missions. They promoted a reawakening of popular Protestant religiosity, but they also led to severe responses by jealous Protestant pastors. Protestant anti-Jesuitism and anti-Catholicism grew, and with it liberal anti-Catholic hysteria. Gross emphasizes that "without recognizing the revival of Protestantism," which contradicts the notion of an ongoing secularization, "we cannot fully appreciate in general the social and cultural history of Germany and in particular the rise of confessional conflict" between 1848 and 1870.[76]

Confessional affiliation was strong in the nineteenth century, maybe even more than ever before and in some ways to a greater degree than in the sixteenth and seventeenth centuries, as its penetration into all segments of society in modern times was more extensive than in earlier periods. Margaret L. Anderson recently wrote: "For a century or more, nothing could be said or done in Germany that was not said or done by a Protestant, a Catholic, or a Jew."[77]

The framework—the second confessional age—may help us take a further look at the nature of Catholic antisemitism and the position of the Jews. The Romantic-Christian rebirth of Christianity in the early nineteenth century had already awakened fears among Jews, even before neo-denominalization did so. Rahel von Varnhagen, a Jewess who converted to Christianity, wrote her brother after the "Hep-Hep" pogrom of 1819 expressing her dismay at the Christian revival and her endless sympathy for the Jews:

> They want to keep them—but in order to torment them, to hold them in contempt, to denounce them as 'Jewish wheeler-dealers' . . . to kick them and throw them down the stairs . . . the hypocritical new love for the Christian faith (God forgive me my sins), for the Middle Ages

> with its art, poetry, and cruelty provokes the people to carry out the only act of cruelty to which, reminded of old experiences, they can still be incited.[78]

At this early stage Varnhagen was referring to the "new love for the Christian faith." Yet, in the final tally, for the Jews it was denominationalism, whose language, replete with stereotypes and polemic attack, became ever more threatening.

It is true that the rays of denominationalism equally hit ultramontanes and Lutherans, yet soon the Jews also became its victims. In May 1870, when the leading article of the *Israelitische Wochenschrift* pondered the retrograde religious steps, the paper recalled the following process:

> For once let the reader look back a few centuries and answer a few questions himself. Could anyone have predicted forty years ago what the situation would be like today? Forty years ago, when Protestant rationalism was in full bloom and enjoying success, when Catholicism, especially in Germany, appeared to be so peaceable, good-natured, tolerant, when its bishops were, for the most part, broad-minded, enlightened men, when one hardly needed to ask whether a citizen or official was Catholic or Protestant in countries of mixed population and people of different faiths could marry and live peacefully without any trouble—who would have thought, when Pius IX steered the course of the reforms . . . or even earlier, when the spirits of Friedrich II and Joseph II ruled the world, when the monasteries were closed and the bishoprics were secularized . . . who would have believed after Lessing, Schiller, indeed, after Herder, after Kant, Hegel, and Strauß . . . who could have foreseen or guessed at the things which we now read, see and hear every day?[79]

In 1872 that paper described the relationship between denominationalism, the Kulturkampf, and antisemitism even more clearly:

> We can shout at our old tormentors and new allies: "You deserve it because of us!" namely in the sense that they have nurtured and strengthened their enemies through the wrongs they did to us. We could say: "With your petit bourgeois small-mindedness, you encouraged denominationalism [*Confessionalismus*] before 1840 in Prussia. After 1848, with Romantic fallacy and cunning spitefulness, you further rejected the Jews by making your Church even more exclusive. Then, with uncompromising malicious zeal, you adopted

dishonest, backward-looking policies and as of 1866 you fought the Jewish people for everything they had. If you hadn't done all this, then you wouldn't have to face up to these difficulties now. But we cannot gloat."[80]

The denominational conflict between Catholicism and Protestantism is frequently forgotten in the face of the catastrophe to which antisemitism led. But it was one of the conditions which created a mutual enemy: the Jews.

Therefore confessional hate promulgated antisemitism, for Catholics and Protestants could try to overcome the tension between them by turning against a third enemy. The Jewish minority paid a high price for confessionalism among Christians. At the same time, confessionalism was just as fierce and more widespread than racism and antisemitism. "That is why antisemitic Catholics persecute Protestantism just as much as they do Judaism," recognized the Verein zur Abwehr des Antisemitismus in 1900, "that is why antisemitic Protestantism often equates Judaism with ultramontane Catholicism."[81]

In fact, the return to denominalization, with its potential for conflict in Germany, is certainly one of the most prominent causes of the escalation of antisemitism. A mutual enemy could be found in the "Jew" and, what is more, it was quite easy to link "the Jew" to the current opponent. Some Catholics considered Protestants to be friends of the Jews, while radical National Protestants regarded Roman Catholicism as a victory of Jewry over the Germanic people. In their official slogan the "Pan-German League" (Alldeutschen), a prominent nationalist group, declared that they would build the Germanic cathedral without the help of Judea or Rome ("Ohne Juda, ohne Rom, bauen wir Alldeutschlands Dom"). Yet racism and antisemitism were also supposed to offer a way out of denominational discord. This is one reason why it became so popular in this country of strict denominational division.

In 1924, Hitler proclaimed that he was furious that "nowadays religious feelings still go deeper than all national and political loyalties." He warned that this could have serious repercussions: "Catholics and Protestants are engaged in a merry war with one another, while the deadly enemy of Aryan mankind and of all Christendom is laughing up its sleeve." He wanted to replace the "war of mutual destruction between the two denominations" with a joint battle against the Jews. This shows the dangerous implications of Christian denominationalism.

The idea of using the confessional conflict to turn it against Jews did not originate with Hitler. It had already been suggested by the popular notion that there were no important motives or state interests at the root of the Kulturkampf, but rather disguised interests that were foreign to Christianity, namely financial gain and the rise of the Jews. Catholics believed that the Kulturkampf was a kind of screen behind which the Jews could carry out their financial transactions without being discovered. In 1880 the *St. Paulinusblatt* of Trier proclaimed that "the Jewish press and Jewish profiteering have instigated the Kulturkampf." This belief had already been part of the ultramontanes' standard repertoire for some time. Nationalism, racism, and antisemitism cannot be understood without the denominational parallelogram of power and its pattern of socialization, but there were efforts to make the new ideologies of integration seem an attractive alternative.[82]

Observant contemporaries also saw the disastrous effect wrought on Germany by the "demon of denominalization," as it was described in 1902 by Franz Overbeck, a Protestant theologian from Basel.[83] In 1881, Joseph Edmund Jörg, editor-in-chief of the leading intellectual Catholic journal, the *Historisch-politischen Blätter,* made it clear that he did indeed believe in the misdemeanors of the Jews. Firstly however, he believed that it was not only the Jews but also the Christians who were to blame for the so-called Jewish question. Second, and more importantly, he claimed that there was still a great, superordinate conflict, namely that being waged among the Christians themselves. He wrote that other countries could hardly accuse Germany of antisemitism for, after all, there were more Jews living in Berlin alone than in the whole of France or England.

> Yet if the Jews in Germany have erected their own stronghold and expanded their power more hastily than in any other country, then there are even deeper reasons for this. They are based on the dreadful inner turmoil of German Christendom. The tree of Jewish power, striving to reach the sky, has sunk its roots into this crack in the rock of the German nation and has succeeded in breaking through, right down to the foundations. This has been the foremost task of its [the Jewish] press, to enlarge the crevice and act like dynamite on the broken-up elements of the nation. The Prussian policy of supreme authority has been the Jews' most valuable ally. While this policy caused the denominational discord to culminate in a bloodless war against German Catholicism, a long line of new laws exclusively promoted Jewish interests. The Jews only needed to beckon, and the

> entire National Liberal movement was at their service, just as eagerly as it had been in the Kulturkampf.

After thus analyzing the consequences of inner turmoil among the denominations, Jörg went on to deal directly with antisemitism, to which he dedicated his article. "It goes without saying that the antisemitic movement has its repulsive aspects." Yet thousands were ardent followers of it, he claimed, because they had been victims of profiteers. He then returned to the subject of denominationalism and the lack of genuine Christian community spirit, since

> it is certain that there is an even greater number of people who do not believe that the Jewish plague is nothing but a well-deserved punishment for German Christendom, because of the things it has done and the things it has allowed to happen. What image, then, does this Christendom offer in the German nation? Can we really hold it against the Jews if they consider us a people already de-Christianized, the overwhelming majority of whose so-called cultured individuals have lapsed into cold indifference to or even hatred of Christ? And why should the Jew have any respect for a nation which, due to denominational loathing, is at war with itself, as though it were two completely separate peoples, and whose majority has been forearmed for this war against the minority by the State with its violent methods? Is it too much to say that the average German Protestant feels more closely related to the Jews, in spite of ethnic differences, than to the Catholic, who belongs to his own race?

We can see how the appeal to Protestants and Catholics, who ultimately shared a mutual belief in Christ, was no longer regarded as sufficient and how this Catholic tried to strengthen it by referring to the common "race."

"As long as the situation remains like this," continued Jörg, "antisemitism has its purpose. We would only be able to solve the Jewish question if the still-Christian and conservative elements of society, regardless of denomination, joined together against the throngs of all who are opposed to Christianity and against the legislation which these allies want to see put into effect in the empire." In spite of the real conflict between Jews and Christians, in which Jörg firmly believed, he held the Christians themselves responsible for the "Jewish question." He regarded the return to Christianity as a central function of antisemitism. "After such a unification the entire social issue will become evident. The Jewish question and capitalism are only the most basic and, let us not be mistaken, the most difficult part of it." His closing sentence read: "Yet let nobody use the word 'the Jewish question' without first asking himself what he has achieved for the Christian world order, without striking his own breast and saying, 'Mea culpa!' "[84] Catholics regarded the "Jewish question" as an ultimately Catholic affair. Their aim was to initiate re-Catholization, or at least re-Christianization, and not to eliminate the Jews, as Daniel J. Goldhagen declared in two books, absolutely removed from any evidence to substantiate his claim and completely blind towards the wider context.[85]

It cannot be stressed enough that the "Christian society" for which Catholics longed would have been almost the worst thing that could have happened to people of other faiths, i.e., the Jews. Such a society, not being pluralistic, would have largely excluded Jews, denying them all official positions. It would have based itself on Christian upbringing and the denominational school, condemning all non-Christian thought and, therefore, the so-called "liberal-Jewish" ideas and principles as well. Consequently, Jews would not have been allowed to become teachers, civil servants, judges, or politicians. The Papal States were regarded as an exemplary ideal for the society which many Catholics wished to establish. Only Catholic principles were valid there until 1870 and Jews, indeed, were forbidden from becoming civil servants, doctors, teachers, etc. What is worse, they were forced to live in ghettos in conditions unfit for human habitation. Considering the almost hysterical veneration which Pius IX and the Vatican enjoyed among the ultramontane believers, it is improbable that the conceived "Christian society" would have pushed for the emancipation of Jews. Yet what does all of this have to do with the Jews as offenders?[86]

Even if Christians were in severe conflict with each other, a condition which stimulated their antisemitism, it could still be true that Jews played their own active role. Maybe they were part of a "Jewish–Christian conflict" or perhaps they really did what they were reproached for: challenging the traditions of the "Christian society" and, in particular, provoking Catholicism? These questions will be the subject of the next chapter.

NOTES

1. Albert S. Lindemann, *Esau's Tears: Modern Anti-Semitism and the Rise of the Jews,* 2d ed. (Cambridge 2000), 23.

2. For the discussion see Thomas Kröter, "Political Correctness: Vom linken Wahn zur rechten Wirklichkeit," *Blätter für deutsche und internationale Politik* 40 (1995): 1367–74; Uwe Mazura, *Zentrumspartei und Judenfrage 1870/71–1933: Verfassungsstaat und Minderheitenschutz,* Veröffentlichungen der Kommission für Zeitgeschichte, Reihe B: Forschungen, vol. 62 (Mainz 1994), 23–24.

3. Lindemann, *Esau's Tears,* xix.

4. Mazura, *Zentrumspartei,* 23, 187, here basing his decision on a quote by Georg Kareski from the *Jüdischen Echo,* 12 Nov. 1930. Kareshi was a Zionist who stood as a candidate for the Berliner Zentrumspartei in 1930.

5. Michael Wolffsohn, *Keine Angst vor Deutschland* (Erlangen 1990), 118–19; Mazura, *Zentrumspartei,* 23–24.

6. See Peter Novick, *The Holocaust in American Life* (Boston 1999); Norman Finkelstein, *The Holocaust Industry* (London 2000); Hilene Flanzbaum, "The Americanization of the Holocaust," *Journal of Genocide Research* 1 (1999): 91–104; Ernst Piper, ed., *Gibt es wirklich eine Holocaust-Industrie? Zur Auseinandersetzung um Norman Finkelstein* (Zürich 2001).

7. Reinhard Rürup, "Die 'Judenfrage' der bürgerlichen Gesellschaft und die Entstehung des modernen Antisemitismus, in *Emanzipation und Antisemitismus,* 2d ed. (1975; Frankfurt 1987), 93–119, quote on 94; see also Jacob Toury, "'The Jewish Question': A Semantic Approach," *Leo Baeck Institute Year Book* 9 (1966): 85–106.

8. Mazura, *Zentrumspartei,* 219.

9. Ibid., 187. For information about the Kulturkampf see Donald J. Ross, *The Failure of Bismarck's Kulturkampf: Catholicism and State Power in Imperial Germany, 1871–1887* (Washington 1998). For a collection of sources from a Catholic perspective see Rudolf Lill, ed., *Der Kulturkampf* (Paderborn 1997).

10. Mazura, *Zentrumspartei,* 80–81. Mazura's evidence shows that he has not done any original research of his own in this matter and relies on a small number of other authors, including Jacob Toury, *Die politische Orientierung der Juden in Deutschland: Von Jena bis Weimar* (Tübingen 1966), 171. Toury wrote about the *Allgemeine Zeitung des Judentums* (1875, p. 643) and the *Israelitische Wochenschrift* (1875, p. 316) simply claiming, however, that Jewish criticism of ultramontane antisemitism had surpassed perception of conservative and racist antisemitism. A piece of evidence which is not quoted, from the *Israelitische Wochenschrift,* no. 25 (16 June 1886) and no. 26 (24 June 1886), can hardly be responsible for the anti-Jewish hate campaign led by *Germania,* which had begun ten years previously.

11. Mazura, *Zentrumspartei,* 81.

12. Ibid., 188.

13. Wolfgang Altgeld, *Katholizismus, Protestantismus, Judentum: Über religiös begründete Gegensätze und nationalreligiöse Ideen in der Geschichte des deutschen Nationalismus,* Veröffentlichungen der Kommission für Zeitgeschichte, Reihe B: Forschungen, vol. 59 (Mainz 1992), 210.

14. Heinz Hürten, "Antisemit, weil Katholik?" *Stimmen der Zeit* 216 (1998): 497–500, quote on 499. His fierce (and partly untenable) criticism is aimed at the first edition of my book, *Katholizismus und Antisemitismus im Deutschen Kaiserreich* (Göttingen 1997).

15. Konrad Löw, "Kirche und Antisemitismus im Kaiserreich und im Dritten Reich," *Deutsche Tagespost,* 1 Oct. 1998; idem, *Die Schuld: Christen und Juden im Urteil der Nationalsozialisten und der Gegenwart* (Gräfelfing 2002), 277.

16. Erich Beyreuther, "Die Vorgeschichte des Kirchenkampfes zwischen 1918 und 1933," in *Frömmigkeit und Theologie: Gesammelte Aufsätze zu Pietismus und zur Erweckungsbewegung* (Hildesheim 1980), 327–48, quote on 328 (first published in *Tutzinger Hefte,* Munich 1969).

17. Kurt Nowak, *Kulturprotestantismus und Judentum in der Weimarer Republik* (Göttingen 1991), 7–8. See also Till van Rahden, "Ideologie und Gewalt: Neuerscheinungen über den Antisemitismus in der deutschen Geschichte des 19. und frühen 20. Jahrhunderts," *Neue politische Literatur* 41 (1996): 11–29.

18. Lindemann, *Esau's Tears,* 115.

19. In this be the case, then antisemitism, with its terrible consequences, would be equivalent to the *Tarifkonflikte* or the struggle for women's right to vote; see Ernst Nolte, *Nietzsche und der Nietzscheanismus* (Frankfurt 1990), 100–102. See also *"Historikerstreit": Die Dokumentation der Kontroverse um die Einzigartigkeit der nationalsozialistischen Judenvernichtung* (Munich 1987); Walter Grab, "Kritische Bemerkungen zur nationalen Apologetik Joachim Fests, Ernst Noltes und Andreas Hillgrubers," *1999* [*Sozialgeschichte des 20. und 21. Jahrhunderts*] 2 (1987): 151–57.

20. Eva G. Reichmann, *Flucht in den Haß: Die Ursachen der deutschen Judenkatastrophe,* 6th ed. (Frankfurt 1969), 99–107.

21. Herbert A. Strauss and Norbert Kampe, "Einleitung," in *Antisemitismus: Von der Judenfeindschaft zum Holocaust,* eds. Herbert A. Strauss and Norbert Kampe (Bonn 1985), 9–28, esp. 17–18.

22. Fritz Stern, "Die Last des Erfolgs: Gedanken zum deutschen Judentum," in *Demokratie und Diktatur,* eds. Manfred Funke et al. (Bonn 1987), 95–108, quotes on 96, 100.

23. Jacob Katz, "Anti-Semitism through the Ages," in *The Persisting Question: Sociological Perspectives and Social Contexts of Modern Antisemitism,* ed. Helen

Fein (Berlin 1987), 45–57, quote on 51 (also in idem, *From Prejudice to Destruction: Anti-Semitism 1700–1933* [Cambridge 1980]).

24. Steven E. Aschheim, "German History and German Jewry: Boundaries, Junctions and Interdependence," *Leo Baeck Institute Year Book* 43 (1998): 315–22, esp. 317–18.

25. "Der Antisemitismus in der evangelischen Kirche," *Mitteilungen aus dem Verein* 3 (31 Dec. 1893): 471–73.

26. Jean-Paul Sartre, *Anti-Semite and Jew,* tr. George J. Becker (New York 1948), 17, 53–54 (First published as *Réflexion sur la question juive* [Paris 1954]).

27. Dennis Prager and Joseph Telushkin, *Why the Jews? The Reason for Antisemitism* (New York 1983), 11, 21–22, 79, 193: "Our concern has been only to show that Jewish religious and moral values are both the ultimate cause of and solution to antisemitism."

28. Eleonore O. Sterling, "Anti-Jewish Riots in Germany in 1819: A Displacement of Social Protest," *Historia Judaica* 12 (1950): 105–42; idem, *Er ist wie du: Aus der Frühgeschichte des Antisemitismus in Deutschland (1815–1850)* (Munich 1956); Jacob Katz, *Die Hep-Hep-Verfolgungen des Jahres 1819* (Berlin 1994), 13 (Hebrew version: *Zion* 38 [1973]: 62–115).

29. Hans Rosenberg, *Große Depression und Bismarckzeit* (Berlin 1967); Helmut Berding, *Moderner Antisemitismus in Deutschland* (Frankfurt 1988); compare: Stefan Rohrbacher and Michael Schmidt, *Judenbilder: Kulturgeschichte antijüdischer Mythen und antisemitischer Vorurteile* (Hamburg 1991).

30. Christoph Cobet, *Der Wortschatz des Antisemitismus in der Bismarckzeit* (Munich 1973), catalogues several hundred stereotypes; see also Wolfgang Benz, *Bilder vom Juden: Studien zum alltäglichen Antisemitismus* (Munich 2001).

31. Wolfgang Altgeld, "Katholizismus und Antisemitismus. Kommentar," in *Zeitgeschichtliche Katholizismusforschung: Tatsachen—Deutungen—Fragen: Eine Zwischenbilanz,* Veröffentlichungen der Kommission für Zeitgeschichte, Reihe B, ed. Karl-Josef Hummel (Paderborn 2003), 100: 49–56, 51. A classic apologetical, though very useful, text is Rudolf Lill, "Die deutschen Katholiken und die Juden in der Zeit von 1850 bis zur Machtübernahme Hitlers," in *Kirche und Synagoge: Handbuch zur Geschichte von Christen und Juden,* eds. Karl Heinrich Rengstorf and Siegfried von Kortzfleisch (Stuttgart 1970), 2:370–420; Lill holds that Catholics were ambivalent towards Jews. Mazura, *Zentrumspartei,* asserts that Catholics were not antisemitic but rather philosemitic. The "scientific" strategy of apologetic scholars affiliated to the Catholic "Kommission für Zeitgeschichte" is quite revealing: In May 2003 they organized a big conference in the Catholic Academy in Bavaria (Munich), summing up decades of research into Catholicism and Catholic antisemitism but

without inviting those who dealt with this problem in a way that is not to their liking. The poor results of this "discussion" among the like-minded have now been published: *Zeitgeschichtliche Katholizismusforschung: Tatsachen—Deutungen—Fragen: Eine Zwischenbilanz,* Veröffentlichungen der Kommission für Zeitgeschichte, Reihe B, vol. 100, ed. Karl-Josef Hummel (Paderborn 2003). For a critical review of this book (he writes of "Anti-Blaschke" and "Anti-Goldhagen") see Benjamin Ziemann, *Neue Politische Literatur* 50 (2005; forthcomng). In May 2004, also in the Catholic Academy, the same influential circle of Catholic historians held a three-day conference, even directly dealing with Catholicism and Judaism, but inviting speakers who favor their opinion and excluding experts who revealed antisemitism within Catholicism. This did not keep them from happily engaging in target shooting at those not present. The poor results of this "debate" have been published: Florian Schuller, Giuseppe Veltri, and Hubert Wolf, eds., *Katholizismus und Judentum. Gemeinsamkeiten und Verwerfungen vom 16. bis zum 20. Jahrhundert* (Regensburg 2005).

32. See Berger Waldenegg and Georg Christoph, *Antisemitismus: "Eine gefährliche Vokabel"? Diagnose eines Wortes* (Wien 2003); the alternative proposed by Wolfram Meyer zu Uptrup in his review of Waldenegg and Christoph (H-Soz-u-Kult, H-Net Reviews, May, 2004. URL: http://www.h-net.org/reviews/showrev.cgi?path=175011089995351) is in my opinion much too narrow, despite its positive aspect, that it does not define antisemitism as a world-view or system that explains the world: "Antisemitism is an intensified form of opposition against Jews [*Judengegnerschaft*] with paranoid thinking that has basic racist assumptions and a mixture of unrealistic and realistic attributions about Jews, which devaluates them and grants them minor rights to exist, deducing from this the struggle against Jews in the context of competition about social, economic, and political power." Antisemitism is not always paranoid or racist, but it is certainly helpful to keep reflecting about this term, which is long established, and will probably remain so.

33. Ben Tzion Krasnianski, "The Untold Truth about the Passion," in IsraelNationalNews.com, 18 Mar. 2004 (http://www.israelnationalnews.com/article.php3?id=3464).

34. See the latest work on Protestantism: Wolfgang E. Heinrichs, *Das Judenbild im Protestantismus des Deutschen Kaiserreichs: Ein Beitrag zur Mentalitätsgeschichte des deutschen Bürgertums in der Krise der Moderne* (Cologne 2000); Massimo Ferrari Zumbini, *Die Wurzeln des Bösen: Gründerjahre des Antisemitismus: Von der Bismarckzeit zu Hitler* (Frankfurt 2003), 151–94. Still important is Günter Brakelmann et al., eds., *Protestantismus und Politik: Werk und Wirkung Adolf Stoeckers* (Hamburg 1982).

35. Daniel J. Goldhagen, *Hitler's Willing Executioners* (New York 1996); see idem, *Die katholische Kirche und der Holocaust: Eine Untersuchung über Schuld und Sühne* (Berlin 2002), first published as *A Moral Reckoning: The Role of the Catholic Church in the Holocaust and its Unfulfilled Duty of Repair* (New York 2002). For an opposing view see Olaf Blaschke, "Die Elimination wissenschaftlicher Unterscheidungsfähigkeit: Goldhagens Begriff des 'Eliminatorischen Antisemitismus'—eine Überprüfung," in *Geschichtswissenschaft und Öffentlichkeit: Der Streit um Daniel J. Goldhagen,* eds. Rainer Erb and Johannes Heil (Frankfurt 1998), 63–91.

36. *Nachrichten der deutschen Vereinigung,* nos. 5–6 (1908), quoted in Hartmann Bodewig, *Geistliche Wahlbeeinflussungen in ihrer Theorie und Praxis dargestellt* (Munich 1909), 143–44. For "*Durchschnittskatholizismus*" see Urs Altermatt, *Katholizismus und Moderne: Zur Sozial- und Mentalitätsgeschichte der Schweizer Katholiken im 19. und 20. Jahrhundert* (Zürich 1989), 73–74.

37. Ulrich von Hehl and Christoph Kösters, eds., *Priester unter Hitlers Terror. Eine biographische und statistische Erhebung* (Paderborn 1996), 1:114–15; Christoph Kösters, "Katholische Kirche im nationalsozialistischen Deutschland. Aktuelle Forschungsergebnisse, Kontroversen und Fragen," in *Die katholische Schuld? Katholizismus im Dritten Reich,* ed. Rainer Bendel (Münster 2002), 21–42, n. 39; Margaret L. Anderson, "Piety and Politics: Recent Work on German Catholicism," *Journal of Modern History* 63 (1991): 681–716; Olaf Blaschke and Frank-Michael Kuhlemann, "Religion in Geschichte und Gesellschaft: Sozialhistorische Perspektiven für die vergleichende Erforschung religiöser Mentalitäten und Milieus," in *Religion im Kaiserreich: Milieus, Mentalitäten, Krisen,* eds. Olaf Blaschke and Frank-Michael Kuhlemann (Gütersloh 1995), 7–58; Martin Baumeister, *Parität und katholische Inferiorität: Untersuchungen zur Stellung des Katholizismus im Deutschen Kaiserreich* (Paderborn 1987).

38. M. Rainer Lepsius, "Parteiensystem und Sozialstruktur: Zum Problem der Demokratisierung der deutschen Gesellschaft," in *Demokratie in Deutschland: Soziologisch-historische Konstellationsanalysen* (Göttingen 1993), 25–50; see also Altermatt, *Katholizismus und Moderne* for the terms "subculture" and "substructure." For a critical assessment of antisemitism among Catholic students see Christoph Dowe and Stephan Fuchs, "Katholische Studenten und Antisemitismus im Wilhelminischen Deutschland," *Geschichte und Gesellschaft* 30 (2004): 571–93.

39. Karl Hilgenreiner, "Antisemitismus," in *Kirchliches Handlexikon: Ein Nachschlagebuch über das Gesamtgebiet der Theologie und ihrer Hilfswissenschaften,* ed. Michael Buchberger, 2 vols. (Freiburg 1907–1912), 1: 257–58.

40. Walter Hannot, *Die Judenfrage in der katholischen Tagespresse Deutschlands und Österreichs 1923–1933* (Mainz 1990), 287.

41. Hilgenreiner, "Antisemitismus," 257–58. Compare: "Antisemitismus," in *Der Große Herder* (Freiburg 1931), 725–26.

42. Numerous pieces of evidence are to be found in Olaf Blaschke, *Katholizismus und Antisemitismus im Deutschen Kaiserreich,* 2d ed. (Göttingen 1999); Michael Langer, *Zwischen Vorurteil und Aggression: Zum Judenbild in der deutschsprachigen katholischen Volksbildung des 19. Jahrhunderts* (Freiburg 1994).

43. *Gladbacher Merkur: Organ für die christlichen Handwerker, Arbeiter und Landleute,* 20 Mar. 1894; *St. Paulinusblatt,* 14 Mar. 1880. In their publications, Catholic students and academics neither criticized antisemitism nor did they instrumentalize radical antisemitism, though there were exceptions on either side; see Dowe and Fuchs, "Katholische Studenten," 579, 585.

44. Friedrich Murawski, *Die Juden bei den Kirchenvätern und Scholastikern: Eine kirchengeschichtliche Skizze als Beitrag zum Kampf gegen den Antisemitismus* (Berlin 1925), 2, 66; see also Friedrich Adam Göpfert, *Moraltheologie* (Paderborn 1897), 1:309; Karl Bachem, *Vorgeschichte, Geschichte und Politik der Deutschen Zentrumspartei* (Cologne 1927), 3:417, 422–23.

45. Walter Zwi Bacharach, *Anti-Jewish Prejudices in German-Catholic Sermons* (Lewiston, N.Y. 1993), 59.

46. See Jeffrey T. Zalar, "The Process of Confessional Inculturation: Catholic Reading in the 'Long Nineteenth Century,'" in *Protestants, Catholics and Jews in Germany 1800–1914,* ed. Helmut Walser Smith (Oxford 2001), 121–52.

47. Joseph Freudl, *Geistliche Blumensträußlein gepflücket aus dem großen Baum- und Myrrhengarticleen des ehrw. P. Marticlein von Hochheim und aus anderen schönen Büchern,* 3d ed. (Hilbetten 1865), 348, 353–54.; see 36: "Sei gegrüßt, o süßester Jesu! Ich bete dich an . . . der du unbegreifliche Peinen . . . gelitten, da dich die Juden bei allen diesen Leiden noch muthwillig verspotteten, und gegen dich allerlei Lästerungen aus ihrem gottlosen Munde ausstießen." Langer, who examined the image of the Jews in catechisms and sermons, describes these topoi as mere prejudices, which were internalized but not "laden with hatred." See further examples in Langer, *Zwischen Vorurteil und Aggression.*

48. Wilhelm Wilmers, S.J., *Lehrbuch der Religio: Ein Handbuch zu Deharbe's katholischem Katechismus,* 4th ed., 4 vols. (Münster 1884–86), 2:49–50, 52, 56–57 (1st ed. 1851–56). Wilmers (b. 1817 in Boke, d. 1889 in Exaeten) was a Jesuit and advisor of the first Vatican Council. See K. Martin, *Lehrbuch der katholischen Religion für höhere Lehranstalten,* 13th ed., 2 vols. (Mainz 1869), 1: 80–81.

49. Pfarrer Gretsch, quoted in Bacharach, *Anti-Jewish Prejudices*, 52, unfortunately without complete proof. Further documentary evidence can be found in Langer, *Zwischen Vorurteil und Aggression* (n. 41 above).

50. Quoted in "Die Juden im Kulturkampf," *Mitteilungen aus dem Verein zur Abwehr des Antisemitismus* 3 (1893): 58. The leaders of antisemitic groups hardly circulated any propaganda in Catholic regions because ties with the Center were too strong there. Nevertheless the Center supported antisemites in run-offs in some places. See Stefan Scheil, *Die Entwicklung des politischen Antisemitismus in Deutschland zwischen 1881 und 1912: Eine wahlgeschichtliche Untersuchung* (Berlin 1999).

51. *Mitteilungen aus dem Verein zur Abwehr des Antisemitismus* 2 (1892): 200.

52. See Olaf Blaschke and Aram Mattioli, eds., *Katholischer Antisemitismus im 19. Jahrhundert: Ursachen und Traditionen im internationalen Vergleich* (Zürich 2000).

53. Manfred Böcker, *Antisemitismus ohne Juden: Die zweite Republik, die antirepublikanische Rechte und die Juden, Spanien 1931 bis 1936* (Frankfurt 2000). For Poland see Viktoria Pollmann, "'Ungebetene Gäste im christlichen Haus': Die Kirche und die Juden im Polen des 19. und frühen 20. Jahrhunderts," in *Katholischer Antisemitismus im 19. Jahrhundert,* 259–86; idem, *Untermieter im christlichen Haus: Die Kirche und die „jüdische Frage" in Polen anhand der Bistumspresse der Metropolie Krakau 1926–1939* (Wiesbaden 2001). See also the review of Heidemarie Petersen, in H-Soz-u-Kult [Humanities—Sozial- und Kulturgeschichte], 12 May 2004, <http://hsozkult.geschichte.hu-berlin.de/rezensionen/2004-2-099>.

54. Urs Altermatt, *Katholizismus und Antisemitismus: Mentalitäten, Kontinuitäten, Ambivalenze:. Zur Kulturgeschichte der Schweiz 1918–1945* (Frauenfeld 1999). Although Altermatt's "new" approach was quickly identified as plagiarism (See Willy Spieler's review, *Neue Wege* 94 [2000]: 3), this does not affect the empirical valency of his observations. See also Michael Meier, "Hat Historiker Urs Altermatt abgekupfert?" *Tagesanzeiger,* 11 Mar. 2000; Josef Lang, "Ein trübes Kapitel Schweizergeschichte," *Israelitisches Wochenblatt* (Zürich), 3 Mar. 2000; idem, "Lernfeld der Judenfeindschaft: Urs Altermatt: 'Katholizismus und Antisemitismus,'" *Die Wochenzeitung,* 6 Jan. 2000; idem, "Kontroverse um Olaf Blaschkes und Urs Altermatts Antisemitismus-Thesen: Die Wörter übers Kreuz gelegt," ibid., 3 Aug. 2000: 13; Armin Owzar, www// http://hsozkult.geschichte.hu-berlin.de (3 July 2000); Otto Weiss, "Beim Lesen zweier Bücher über den katholischen Antisemitismus," *Traverse* 7 (2000); Olaf Blaschke and Urs Altermatt, "'Katholizismus und Antisemitismus': Eine Kontroverse," *Schweizerische Zeitschrift für Geschichte* 50 (2000): 204–36.

55. Hubert Wolf, "'Pro perfidis Judaeis': Die 'Amici Israel' und ihr Antrag auf eine Reform der Karfreitagsfürbitte für die Juden" (1928). Oder: Bemerkungen zum Thema katholische Kirche und Antisemitismus," *Historische Zeitschrift* 279 (2004),

611–58, esp. 614, referring, with the phrase "better, Christian antisemitism," to Altermatt, *Katholizismus,* 55, without noticing that exactly the same argument and terminology can be found already in Blaschke, *Katholizismus,* 87–117, 125–26, 316, whom Wolf wants to contradict. For the ambivalence towards antisemitism there are unequivocal arguments in ibid., 86, 319. For the original "Ambivalenzthese" see Lill, "Die deutschen Katholiken," 392 (ambivalence towards Jews), which Altermatt and Wolf seem to ignore against their own findings. Unfortunately, history can be very complicated sometimes as can be the politics of historiography. While apologetic historians try to "occupy" the term "thesis of ambivalence" within the field in a way that leaves Catholics in a good light, their own evidence and the original meaning (ambivalence towards Jews) has hardly anything to do with it. When I introduced the term "Ambivalenzthese" in 1997 I referred only to Lill, nothing more and nothing less, and my intention was to show that there was no "middle," balanced, or ambivalent attitude. When apologists use the term today they suggest that Lill was right thirty five years ago, notwithstanding historiographical progress since then. Logically, the term opposing the thesis of ambivalence is "aversion" but this seems too strong for their liking. For the strategies of academic politics and of occupying and re-occupying territories within the scholarly field see Robert K. Merton, *The Sociology of Science: Theoretical and Empirical Investigations* (Chicago 1973).

56. About the growing divergence of opinions within Catholicism during the Weimar Republic see Blaschke, *Katholizismus,* 325–27.

57. Wolf, "'Pro perfidis Judaeis,'" 656.

58. Ibid., 654–58.

59. "May, therefore, the father of the family remember his divine mission above everything else." He must be aware of and fear the "dangers of the anti-Christian world" for his family: "Upbringing, books, journals, theatre, and society will often act as traps for his children's beliefs and virtues," but "if all fathers fulfil their holy duties, then the future is saved." Who was supposed to save the suffering family? "Who other than the Church—which has been determined by the great, divine doctor to be a loving, healing mother for all the illnesses in our society—will indeed help and heal, if one [i.e., the state] does not bind its hands to do so." This was an allusion to the metaphorical strangling of the Catholics by the Kulturkampf. See "Die christliche Familie und ihre soziale Bedeutung," *Neue Mosel-Zeitung,* 10 Mar. 1875 (successor to the *Mosel-Zeitung,* which was founded by Georg Friedrich Dasbach among others).

60. See Thomas Nipperdey, *Deutsche Geschichte 1866–1918,* vol. 1: *Arbeitswelt und Bürgergeist* (Munich 1990), 476–79.

61. For anti-Catholicism, anti-clericalism, and anti-ultramontanism, see Norbert Schloßmacher, "Antiultramontanismus im Wilhelminischen Deutschland: Ein Versuch," in *Deutscher Katholizismus im Umbruch zur Moderne,* ed. Wilfried Loth (Stuttgart 1991), 164–98; Michael B. Gross, "Anti-Catholicism, Liberalism and German National Identity, 1848–1880" (Ph.D. diss., Brown University, 1997 [published as *The War against Catholicism: Liberalism and the Anti-Catholic Imagination in Nineteenth-Century Germany* (Ann Arbor 2004)]; idem, "Kulturkampf and Unification: German Liberalism and the War against the Jesuits," *Central European History* 30 (2001): 545–66; Róisin Healy, "Anti-Jesuitism in Imperial Germany: The Jesuit as Androgyne," in *Protestants, Catholics and Jews in Germany,* 153–84. Particularly for Protestant anti-Catholicism, see Claudia Lepp, *Protestantisch-liberaler Aufbruch in die Moderne: Der deutsche Protestantenverein in der Zeit der Reichsgründung und des Kulturkampfes* (Gütersloh 1996); Armin Müller-Dreier, *Konfession in Politik, Gesellschaft und Kultur des Kaiserreichs: Der Evangelische Bund 1886–1914* (Gütersloh 1998); see also Richard Millman, "Jewish Anticlericalism and the Rise of Modern French Antisemitism," *History* 77 (1992): 220–36.

62. For a more detailed examination see Olaf Blaschke: "Das 19. Jahrhundert: Ein Zweites Konfessionelles Zeitalter?" *Geschichte und Gesellschaft* 26 (2000): 38–75; idem., "Das Zweite Konfessionelle Zeitalter: Ein Deutungsangebot für Katholizismus- und Sozialhistoriker," in *Konfession, Milieu, Moderne: Konzeptionelle Positionen und Kontroversen zur Geschichte von Katholizismus und Kirche im 19. und 20. Jahrhundert,* eds. Johannes Horstmann and Antonius Liedhegener (Schwerte 2001), 27–78; and Olaf Blaschke, ed., *Konfessionen im Konflikt: Deutschland zwischen 1800 und 1970: ein zweites konfessionelles Zeitalter,* (Göttingen 2002). For a critical review of *Konfessionen im Konflikt,* see Helmut W. Smith, German Historical Institute London, *Bulletin* 25 (2003): 101–106. For some fine polemics, summarizing the critical arguments which are already in the book, but unfortunately offering not a single new argument, see Carsten Kretschmann and Henning Pahl, "Ein 'Zweites Konfessionelles Zeitalter'? Vom Nutzen und Nachteil einer neuen Epochensignatur," *Historische Zeitschrift* 276 (2003): 369–92. A well-thought-out critique can help to improve the concept. In sharp contrast to the article by Kretschmann and Pahl, Anthony Steinhoff, in his most recent critique of the approach, offers a very productive contribution to the discussion; see Anthony J. Steinhoff, "Ein zweites konfessionelles Zeitalter?: Nachdenken über die Religion im langen 19. Jahrhundert," *Geschichte und Gesellschaft* 30 (2004): 549–70. He is certainly right that the criteria of uniformization and clericalization can hardly be applied to Protestantism, which was becoming ever more pluralistic by the time,

though even if neither Protestantism nor Catholicism were uniform this would not diminish the role of confessionalism. I would also subscribe to his argument that the interconfessional competition and the perceptions of believers and their practices should be emphasized and studied more deeply. There obviously should be more research into why neo-confessionalism was unleashed. See, as a preliminary attempt (overlooked by Steinhoff who criticizes the lack of explanation), Olaf Blaschke, "Die Inkubationszeit konfessioneller Intoleranz im frühen 19. Jahrundert," in *Intoleranz im Zeitalter der Revolutionen. Europa 1770–1848,* eds. Aram Mattioli et al. (Zürich 2004), 189–209. See also the classical study by Christel Köhle-Hezinger, *Evangelisch-Katholisch. Untersuchungen zu konfessionellem Vorurteil und Konflikt im 19. und 20. Jahrhundert vornehmlich am Beispiel Württembergs* (Tübingen 1976); Alfred Wahl, *Confession et comportement dans les campagnes d'Alsace et de Bade 1871–1939: Catholiques, Protestants et Juifs,* 2 vols. (Strassbourg 1980).

63. Hans Kohn, *The Age of Nationalism: The First Era of Global History* (New York 1968).

64. Gabriel Motzkin and Jens Mattern, eds., *Welt ohne Gott: Jüdisches Denken im Zeitalter der Säkularisierung: Festschrift für Stéphane Mosès* (Amsterdam 2000).

65. The literature suggests that since the mid-seventeenth century the Christian religion was replaced by secular forces. The church is either *between* something or *in* something important. Christian belief has lost its central position. It is no longer a major player but only a minor player in the age of Enlightenment, in the age of Liberalism, etc. The Churches in the "age of Liberalism" or in the "Industrial Age" often appear like a small fish, desperately trying to adapt to the ever-changing water in the aquarium. See *History of the Church,* vol. 8: *The Church in the Age of Liberalism,* ed. Hubert Jedin (London 1980); vol. 9: *The Church in the Industrial Age* (London 1981). What if we try to turn the tables? If we see liberalism as struggling its way through an age of conservative religious forces and of resisting piety? If we regard nationalism, which was bound to unify the national in-group, as the major bone of contention between people of different beliefs, as another occasion to split the in-group in the period of confessionalism? What if we take into consideration that modernity in an age of confessional revival was deeply contested alongside religious preferences?

66. See Hartmut Lehmann. ed., *Säkularisierung, Dechristianisierung, Rechristianisierung im neuzeitlichen Europa: Bilanz und Perspektiven der Forschung* (Göttingen 1997); Hugh McLeod, ed., *European Religion in the Age of Great Cities 1830–1930* (London 1995).

67. Buisson is quoted by Daniel Mollenhauer, "Symbolkämpfe um die Nation: Katholiken und Laizisten in Frankreich (1871–1914)," in *Nation und Religion in*

Europa: Mehrkonfessionelle Gesellschaften im 19. und 20. Jahrhundert, eds. Heinz-Gerhard Haupt and Dieter Langewiesche (Frankfurt 2004), 202–230, quote on 205; Mollenhauer tends to view laicism as a confession. In contrast, Steinhoff, "Ein zweites konfessionelles Zeitalter?," 562, would find this usage "too elastic" while at the same time refusing to reduce the term as referring to Catholics, Lutherans, Calvinists, and Jews alone. See also Johannes Koll, "Die Reformation in der Kontroverse: Nation und Protestantismus bei belgischen Katholiken und Liberalen im 19. Jahrhundert," in ibid., 99–134, who demonstrates that even in a mono-confessional society (Belgium: 99 percent Catholic) Catholics, in order to consolidate their identity, instrumentalized the Reformation and Protestantism inside and outside Belgium, and made use of anti-Protestant polemics. Steinhoff, "Ein zweites konfessionelles Zeitalter?," 561, declares this to be impossible. The most recent critique that the confessional age fits to multiconfessional countries but not to monoconfessional countries can be found in Christopher Clark and Wolfram Kaiser, eds., *Culture Wars. Secular-Catholic Conflict in Nineteenth-Century Europe* (Campbridge 2003).

68. "De negentiende eeuw was de eeuw van de neostijlen," claim Tom Verschaffel et al., *Neostijlen in de negentiende eeuw* (Leuven 2002).

69. In some countries historians talk about subcultures, in others about pillars, as in Belgium and the Netherlands; in Austria the term *Lager* (camp) is favored, while in Spain they talked about the "true Spain" against the secular one, and France was divided into "les deux France." For a brilliant international comparison, see Tom Buchanan and Martin Conway, eds., *Political Catholicism in Europe 1918–1965* (Oxford 1996); and Clark and Kaiser, *Culture Wars.* See also Armin Owzar, *"Reden ist Silber, Schweigen ist Gold." Konfliktmanagement im Alltag des wilhelminischen Obrigkeitsstaates* (Konstanz 2006). Protestants and Catholics tried to avoid each other; Christians and Jews didn't communicate with each other if it was not necessary, but also workers and artisans, men and women didn't share the same public places.

70. This is what Smith in his review suggests (n. 62 above) as an alternative.

71. See Heinz Schilling, "Confessional Europe: Bureaucrats, La Bonne Police, Civilizations," in *Handbook of European History 1400–1600: Late Middle Ages, Renaissance and Reformation,* eds. Thomas A. Brady, H. A. Oberman and J. D. Tracy (Leiden 1995), 2:641–81, esp. 642; Heinrich Richard Schmidt, *Konfessionalisierung im 16. Jahrhundert* (München 1992); Heinz Schilling, "Die Konfessionalisierung im Reich. Religiöser und gesellschaftlicher Wandel in Deutschland zwischen 1555 und 1620," *Historische Zeitschrift* 246 (1988): 1–45, esp. 13; idem, "Konfessionelles Zeitalter, I–II" *Geschichte in Wissenschaft und*

Unterricht 48 (1997): 350–70, esp. 360; 618–27. See also Wolfgang Reinhard, "Gegenreformation als Modernisierung? Prolegomena zu einer Theorie des konfessionellen Zeitalters," *Archiv für Reformationsgeschichte* 68 (1977): 226–52; Harm Klueting, *Das Konfessionelle Zeitalter 1525–1648* (Stuttgart 1989). For the comparison see Blaschke: "Das 19. Jahrhundert."

72. Franz Schnabel, *Deutsche Geschichte im neunzehnten Jahrhundert,* vol. 4: *Die religiösen Kräfte* (1937; Munich 1987), 270–71. On the other hand, Schnabel maintains that "in spite of all renewed religious impetus" the nineteenth century had gone extremely badly for Christianity and Catholicism. It remained very secular and political passion had replaced "the old religious fervor." Manfred Klug, *Rückwendung zum Mittelalter? Geschichtsbilder und historische Argumentation im politischen Katholizismus des Vormärz* (Paderborn 1995), 96, also speaks of the development of a "new denominational age" since the anniversary of the Reformation in 1817.

73. Ansgar Albrecht, "Konfessionalismus," in *Sacramentum Mundi: Theologisches Lexikon für die Praxis* (Freiburg 1969), 3:1–5, who claims that denominationalism mostly means "valuing a restricted ecclesiastical tradition over the general Christian heritage which exists in other churches, and consequently isolating oneself from these other churches." See also Erwin Fahlbusch, "Konfessionalismus," in *Evangelisches Kirchenlexikon,* 3d ed. (Göttingen 1990), 2:1360–65. Cf. the important study about the semantics of confession and confessionalism in the nineteenth century by Lucian Hölscher, "Konfessionspolitik in Deutschland zwishchen Glaubensstreit und Koexistenz," in *Baupläne der sichtbaren Kirche. Sprachliche Konsepte religiöser Vergemeinschaftung in Europa,* ed. Lucian Hölscher (Göttingen 2007), 11–52.

74. Heinz Fleckenstein, "Konfessionalismus," in *Staatslexikon,* 6th ed. (Freiburg 1959), 4:1206–208.

75. See Altgeld, *Katholizismus, Protestantismus, Judentum*; Dieter Langewiesche, "Nation, Nationalismus, Nationalstaat: Forschungsstand und Forschungsperspektiven," *Neue Politische Literatur* 40 (1995): 190–236; Helmut Walser Smith, *German Nationalism and Religious Conflict* (Princeton 1995).

76. Gross, *War,* 186, 175.

77. Margaret L. Anderson, "Living Apart and Together in Germany," in *Protestants, Catholics and Jews in Germany,* 319–27, quote on 320. However, Anderson is skeptical about the notion of a second confessional age since there were signs of cooperation.

78. Quoted by Heinrich Graetz, *Volkstümliche Geschichte der Juden* (Vienna 1888; rprt. Cologne 2000), 2:977.

79. "Die Rückschritte," *Israelitische Wochenschrift* 1 (1870): 149.

80. "Wider den Strom," *Israelitische Wochenschrift* 3 (1872): 107.

81. C. Burger, *Antisemitenspiegel: Die Antisemiten im Lichte des Christentums, des Rechts und der Wissenschaft,* 2d ed. (Danzig: Verein zur Abwehr des Antisemitismus, 1900), 282.

82. Adolf Hitler, *Mein Kampf,* 170th ed. (1924; Munich 1936), 629–32; "Jüdisches," *St. Paulinusblatt für das deutsche Volk,* 15 Aug. 1880. For an examination of the isolating effect of nationalism, see Helmut W. Smith, "Nationalism and Religious Conflict in Germany, 1887–1914" (Ph.D. diss., Yale University, 1991).

83. Franz Overbeck, "Gegenwart; Confessionalismus," in *Werke und Nachlaß,* vol. 4: *Kirchenlexicon Texte,* ed. Barbara von Reibnitz (Stuttgart 1995), 290–93; 354–56.

84. Joseph E. Jörg, "Wie das alte Jahr dem neuen die Judenfrage vermacht," *Historisch-politische Blätter* 87 (1981): 1–18, quotes on 14, 16–18.

85. See Goldhagen, *Hitler's Willing Executioners*; idem, *Moral Reckoning.*

86. See Aram Mattioli, "Das letzte Ghetto Alteuropas: Antisemitismus im Kirchenstaat bis 1870," in *Katholischer Antisemitismus*; Olaf Blaschke, "'Non comprare dagli ebrei': Il Vaticano, l'ultramontanismo e l'antisemitismo: Proposte per una comparazione europea," *Ricerche di storia politica,* n.s. 4 (2001): 147–64.

CHAPTER 2

Jewish Attitudes toward Catholics

Is there a "Jewish reality" behind any of the claims directed against them? Did Jews do anything which helps to "justify" antisemitism or to understand or at least explain it? How did they behave towards Catholics?

EXPLAINING ANTISEMITISM WITH REGARD TO A "JEWISH OFFENDERS"

Let us take up the question which Konrad Löw asked in all seriousness, namely, "whether the criticism" of Jews by Catholics couldn't possibly "have somehow been justified."[1] It should definitely be answered, but on an appropriately analytical level. To do so, it is necessary to differentiate further between the different antisemitic patterns of blame. We have already come up against the distinction between realists and nominalists. While the nominalists regard all antisemitic reproaches as pure fiction, the realists suspect that certain facts are actually a point of reference for anti-Jewish accusations. Thus, to those researchers who believe in the theory of prejudice, antisemitism seems to be an *Ersatzkonflikt,* an attempt to distract from and provide a solution for tension other than that between Jews and non-Jews.

To those authors who support the *Konflikttheorie* (conflict theory), on the other hand, there appears to be real tension between Jews and non-Jews. After all, the prejudices between Germans and French, between Catholics and Protestants, fascists and communists, or men and women have also been based on real social differences, conflicts, and divergence of interests. Though socially constructed, they are, nonetheless, concrete. Why should it be different in the case of antisemitism? For radical realists such facts are the cause of antisemitism: without the Jews and their specific patterns of behavior, they believe, there would not be any antisemitism, just as there would be no anti-Marxism without Marxism and no anti-feminism without women. Moderate realists, in comparison, see the success of Jews as a reason for envy and resentment by non-Jews.

A third approach would distinguish between various levels: although the antisemites' accusations were exaggerated, they might actually have been right about certain points. However, it is crucial to bear in mind that prejudiced people perceive certain facts selectively and then interpret them negatively. They observe certain acts of individuals and generalize their observation for the group to which the individual belongs.

Continuing along this line, it is possible to distinguish three different levels. They allow us to compare the respective Catholic attitudes towards Jews with the phenomena to which it is claimed they are related. The categories proposed by Gavin I. Langmuir in 1987 (which, unfortunately, are seldom taken into account) are of interest here. He differentiated between three types of view: chimeric, xenophobic, and realistic.

1. "Chimeric assertions are propositions which grammatically attribute with certitude to an out-group and all its members characteristics which have never been empirically observed."

2. "Xenophobic assertions are propositions which grammatically attribute a socially menacing conduct to an out-group and all its members but are empirically based only on the conduct of an historical minority of the members; they neglect other, unthreatening characteristics of the out-group; and they do not acknowledge that there are great differences between the individuals who compose the out-group."

3. "Realistic assertions about out-groups are propositions which utilise the information available about an out-group and are based on the same assumptions about the nature of groups and the effect of membership of individuals as those used to understand the in-group and its reference group and their members."[2]

All three kinds of claims can be used to justify hostility towards out-groups. Langmuir's categorization serves as a stimulus for our present investigation as his model is exceptionally applicable to the question of what is concealed behind Catholic antisemitism and how this is to be explained. Yet all three levels must be checked against empirical material, since not all of Langmuir's basic assumptions can be adopted here. His actual aim was to provide a definition of antisemitism and to establish a way of differentiating between it and all other kinds of resentment. He believed antisemitism to be something specific, not because it was racist or more intense than other resentments, but because he thought that in this case the chimerical factor was shown to its fullest advantage. Moreover, he claimed that it is important to be able to distinguish between the antisemitism of the Final Solution and the reproaches against Jews in Antiquity and the Middle Ages, not for moral reasons or because of the technical capacities for extermination of humans in the twentieth century, but because hardly any out-group has been the subject of so much chimerical reproach as the Jews.[3] "Chimeric assertions have no 'grain of truth.' This is the contrast which distinguishes the hostility that produced Auschwitz from that manifest against Jews in ancient Alexandria." This hostility serves as one criterion under which all members of the group are to be understood, as, for example, the Nürnburger Gesetze attempted to do with their racist definitions.[4]

If one defines antisemitism very narrowly on the basis of chimerical assertions, the character of antisemitism as a generalization (i.e., xenophobia) and even as a group conflict (i.e., as realistic views) is completely invalid. As a historian it is possible to argue, on the other hand, that all three categories of prejudice had a harmful affect on Jewish contemporaries. The three levels were included in the term antisemitism, which was created in 1879. In contemporary terminology they already counted as "antisemitism." It is up to the historical philosophers and those affected to decide whether antisemitism was necessarily something peculiar and incomparable, but the "Holocaust" was without doubt a genuine crime in the history of the world.[5] As far as antisemitism is concerned, it is important that Langmuir's categorization opens up the prospects of coming closer to a solution to the question, whether realistic or fictitious causes of the anti-Jewish attitude of Catholics in the nineteenth century predominated. Strauss and Kampe evidently followed a similar model in 1985, suggesting that the relationship between a real social object and its perception could now and again prove to reflect reality (if not, we could not write any book about Catholics). Since perception, however, is always selective and reality is absolutely complex, the forming of prejudices represents the normal case. The production of chimerical reflections without reference to any object represents the rare, extreme case.[6]

The parallels in both three-part models are evident. The pattern of chimera, normal case, and optimum correlate to Langmuir's three steps of chimera, xenophobia, and realism and can also be illustrated through the terms "conspiracy," "construction," and "conflict." It is possible to sort the antisemitic stereotypes in this useful framework. Another advantage is that they can be simultaneously questioned in their social-ideological contexts.

Conspiracy: The Chimerical Attitude

A prominent and obvious example of the chimeric view is the ritual murder myth (*Ritualmordlegende*). It originated in Catholicism and was especially popular among Catholics. Catholic professor of theology August Rohling, based in Münster, "proved" in various works from 1871 onwards that the Jews abducted Christian children, abused them, and even killed them for religious purposes.[7] Soon this legend, which dates back to the Middle Ages and was "rediscovered" in the early nineteenth century, began to have an affect on Catholic believers, of course, but also on some Protestants and radical antisemites. Various legal proceedings gave unbiased observers an opportunity to take note of the atrocity of the ritual murder myths and *Antitalmudismus*.[8] It could be argued that these accusations were simply strange phenomena which could easily be disproved. Yet this chimera, which caused Jews to be seen as ritual murderers and the Talmudic commandments as hostile towards the "Goyim," was very widespread. Catholic magazines and newspapers helped to circulate this myth, which sometimes aroused panicky reactions in devout Catholic mothers on Easter Day.

The Catholic world-view held further opinions of Jews, which were as widespread as they were far removed from reality. A fundamental topos was the heaping of collective guilt on the Jews for the crucifixion of Christ, whereas the idea that Jews were unproductive and incapable of creativity was more secular. Later, Hitler in *Mein Kampf* also discussed such topoi in great detail. Moreover, both of the macro stereotypes of Jewish "world domination" and of the "Jewification" of society could be included here. They were stereotypes at a macro level because single prejudices could be easily subsumed under them, for example, that of "Jewish freemasonry" or that of the alleged dominance of the press by the Jews.[9] After the First World War the myth of a Jewish worldwide conspiracy was spread to a large extent by the *Protocols of the Elders of Zion,* which purported to document the secret meetings of leading Jews and their plan to take over the world. This fabricated "document" was immensely influential and is still reprinted today in some Arab countries. There is no doubt that this fundamental "source" of antisemitism is far removed from any "reality." Lindemann, therefore, probably "forgot" to mention it at least once in his 568-page book, for it would have driven his argument (that antisemites are prudent people reacting to real experiences) too easily into absurdity.[10]

Any world conspiracy, however, needed an organized center to hold everything together. Therefore the antisemites were particularly pleased about the existence of the Alliance Israélite Universelle (AIU). This organization was founded in 1860 in reaction to hostility towards Jews—which, in this case, came from Catholics—and it remained a mouthpiece against growing antisemitism and for Jewish interests. In numerous countries it coordinated charity work and educational efforts for poverty-stricken and persecuted Jews.[11] In spite of its aims, the AIU suffered from an antisemitic propaganda campaign against the supposed Jewish power. The enemies of the AIU made it out to be some sort of super-lodge which they claimed coordinated the entire conspiracy. It served as obvious "proof" of Jewry's worldwide organization and centralization. The assertion that the Jews still considered themselves to be the Chosen People was an important prerequisite for this "proof," for it could lend plausibility to the idea that they possessed a manic desire for power. "The whole mass of Jews, which is dispersed and yet connected," the *Kölnische Volkszeitung* declared in 1880, is "possessed by one single belief: that they are the Chosen People, that they are to inherit the treasures of this world." In Catholicism the macro stereotype of "world domination" was based on this religious premise and then oscillated between theology and politics, resulting in anti-Judaism being transformed into antisemitism.[12]

Freemasonry, regarded as one of the foremost enemies of ultramontanism, could be conveniently linked to the AIU. Freemasonry was seen as being centrally run and led by Jews, and the AIU served as perfect proof of this. According to Mainz-based Canon Ludwig Erler, its existence proved the power of the Jews, which was spread "across the entire globe." In his (falsified) speech, President Adolphe Crémieux, "Grand Master of the French Lodge" and a minister in the French government (in 1848 and 1870), allegedly proclaimed to the AIU that "a new Messianic empire, a New Jerusalem must rise in place of the Emperor and the Pope." Ludwig Erler's terrible series of antisemitic articles were published in the renowned canon law periodical *Archiv für katholisches Kirchenrecht* between 1879 and 1885.[13]

The "shady, wheeling and dealing" Jews supposedly governed the "membership of an illegal secret society." In 1872 parish priest Johannes Sigl's Catholic *Bayerisches Vaterland* angrily accused the AIU of being a "Semitic" Freemason's Lodge with the aim of attaining world domination. Left-wing liberal MP Eduard Lasker belonged to this Lodge, claimed the paper:

> Since the Talmud says, "All people, the Earth and all that fills it, belong to Israel." To this purpose, as an *elimination* "of the Emperors and the Popes," *Judaism* is fundamentally connected to the *Freemason's lodge* and vice versa. The *Jews* are the most eager Freemasons; they are to be found in all lodges. The president of the Jewish world power *Alliance Israélite,* Crémieux, is also the Grand Master of the French Lodge! Every day it is evident to us that Jews and Freemasons also . . . work hand in hand in Munich, we see this particularly in the imperial, state parliament and local government elections [emphases in original].[14]

The idea of the Freemason–Jewish world conspiracy, which was invented by Catholicism to a considerable extent, fueled the propaganda of national socialist and nationalist circles, especially that of General Ludendorff. Adolf

Hitler also commented not long after the First World War that Freemasonry was a "magnificent propaganda and supporting organization" of the AIU, which for its part controlled Marxism.[15]

But was this a mere chimera? The AIU really existed and the stereotype was therefore related to a "reality." Yet the distorted image which the Catholics held of it had nothing in common with its true nature. What is more, one should not forget that Jews in the German Empire were increasingly excluded from the Freemason lodges and that all claims about world conspiracy by the "Jewish Freemasonry" are therefore incorrect.[16] We would be able to safely ignore such an edifice of ideas, were it not for the fact that, first, Catholic historians claim even today that only a conventional, theological anti-Judaism dominated Catholicism and secondly, that this chimera was so fraught with consequences for those affected Jewish contemporaries. The *Israelistische Wochenschrift,* a Jewish weekly newspaper, openly expressed its disappointment about this development in 1882: "Poor Alliance Israélite Universelle! Is there anything for which you are not now blamed? What strange ideas, what fantasies your existence generates in the heads of our enemies! If we affirm and prove by means of tangible facts that the Alliance only serves the purpose of working for the moral and intellectual improvement of the Jews" and to help them wherever they suffer as Jews, this only results in derisive smiles from the enemies. Catholicism too was criticized by the *Israelistische Wochenschrift*: "Year in, year out, the ultramontane and conservative papers announce to their readers that the Alliance is a movement of all Israelites in the world, founded for the purpose of subjugating and fighting against the Christian world, of establishing a Jewish empire."[17]

It would be quite strange to once more set out to disprove such categorical insinuations as world domination or ritual murder. Yet they are proof that a large part of Catholic antisemitism is completely independent of Jewish realities and Jewish provocations. In fact, an extremely large proportion of antisemitism is chimeric.

Construction: The Xenophobic Attitude

The field of xenophobia in antisemitism is more complex. In a narrow sense xenophobia means fear of the unknown, whereby, however, the definition of "the unknown" or that which is "strange" depends upon the individual perception of the observer. In the definition presented here, which is based on Langmuir, the term suggests that single phenomena are observed, that these are classified as being the characteristics of individuals (men, Germans, dealers, Jews etc.), and finally the characteristics of the group which is considered "strange" are classified as a whole. It may be possible that there is a kernel of truth in these assumptions.

What is more, this type of idea shows that it is assumed that the "strange" group has certain affinities to phenomena which the in-group rejects, such as Marxism or prostitution. According to Langmuir, a third characteristic exists in the fact that the Jews are not actually the problem anymore, but rather that "the subject of a xenophobic assertion is not the out-group; it is a felt social menace."[18]

Catholic antisemitism was actually aimed primarily at liberalism, modernism, emancipation, etc. When labeled as "Jewish," these seemed to be twice as bad. This ties in with the observations of Shulamit Volkov, who described antisemitism in the German Empire as a "code," the key to other patterns of attitudes at the time. In the words of the *Israelistische Wochenblatt* over ninety years ago, everything had become part of a "Jewish Question": "Every problem is blamed on the Jews and then an antisemitic solution is very easily found."[19]

A classic example of this generalization is the so-called "profiteering question." It is a fact that in some areas of Germany the cattle trade and money lending in the countryside were in fact mainly administered by Jewsy.[20] In order to have a minimum income, they naturally had to earn some profit from this, yet many Jews in the countryside remained poor. When a farmer considered himself to be the victim of a bad deal, the first thing he noticed was that he was dealing with a Jew. He did not ask himself whether Christian traders would have acted similarly under similar conditions, especially since the stock of anti-Jewish interpretations made stereotypes readily available to him which generally classified the Jew as an exploitative, profit-hungry "creature." The "reality" on which these stereotypes were based was reduced to rumor and individual experiences, which were seldom attributed as such. What is more, the historical conditions of the Jewish situation as a whole, and their need to earn a living, were not taken into account.[21] He who "profiteered" deserved to be punished.

However, despite the complaints of conservatives and Catholics, from November 1867, the North German government actually left the level of interest charges open to free agreement between the parties, and in 1872 the anti-profiteering laws which still existed were repealed in all the individual states. The Center Party and Catholic spokesmen fought long and hard to reinstate certain anti-profiteering laws, using antisemitic ammunition in their struggle. In a pamphlet published in Breslau in 1879 it was claimed that the Jews owed their dominant position to profiteering, and especially to the lifting of the anti-profiteering legislation in 1867. This was, however, a call to the Catholics, since—the pamphlet proclaimed—there was also a "certain contingent" of Christian "sharks" who were assisting the Jews. All profiteers were to be excluded from Christian organizations.[22] Finally, the liberal era came to an end. The long awaited first anti-profiteering law of May 1880 once again restricted the credit profiteer, and any transgression was punishable by high fines or imprisonment. The supplementary law of 1893 made predatory *Sachwucher* ("commercial profiteering") illegal as well.[23] Nevertheless, this did nothing to quell resentment. Hans Rost, who continues to be used as a source by many experts on Catholicism today, still took the Jews severely to task. The Görres Gesellschaft edited his contribution to *Moralstatistik* ("criminality figures") in 1913. "The Jews have caused the increasingly sharper intensification of the capitalist speculative economic system; they have established the odious business of *large department stores* . . . ; the *brothel business* is partly their monopoly . . . their *criminality* predominates to an alarming extent in the offences of profiteering, deceit, bankruptcy, dishonoring Sundays [emphases in original]."[24] For many the word "Jew" became synonymous with "profiteer." Yet for a long time a minority was aware that the claim that Jews in particular were liable to risk prosecution for profiteering was not really true. In 1900, statistics in the *Antisemitenspiegel* put the relationships straight. According to the sixteen official volumes of crime statistics in the German Empire, the following sentencing figures relating to the so-called "profiteering question" became apparent, as in Table 1, below.

The *Antisemitenspiegel* conceded that, if one went by the proportional representation of the population alone, then only eight Jews (ca. one percent), not 131 Jews, should be among those sentenced. No far-reaching conclusions could be drawn from these figures, since profiteering was certainly more widespread than the statistics were able to show. With regard to the distribution of jobs, the figures were relatively "normal." In general, though, the publication suggested that Christians were involved in profiteering to a far greater extent than were Jews, so a profiteering "business" controlled mainly by Jews was therefore out of the question. Jews were above all more likely to be suspect of usury than non-Jews and made their way more easily into the criminal statistics.

The issues surrounding a further accusation, however, are more difficult to tackle. Assumed and genuine affinities played a large role in shaping the profile of antisemitism. One cannot systematically list and disprove all of the prejudices, for there must have been hundreds of them. Some prominent examples are the alleged proximity of "the Jews" to revolution and socialism

TABLE 1

SENTENCING DUE TO USURY

ACCORDING TO GOVERNMENT CRIME STATISTICS

Year	Total	Jews
1882	98	21
1883	93	16
1884	61	12
1885	37	10
1886	42	3
1887	36	8
1888	36	8
1889	41	4
1890	22	5
1891	44	7
1892	37	6
1893	31	6
1894	40	5
1895	57	10
1896	56	7
1897	39	3
in 16 years	770	131

Source: C. Burger, *Antisemitenspiegel: Die Antisemiten im Lichte des Christentums, des Rechts und der Wissenschaft*, 2d ed. (Danzig: Verein zur Abwehr des Antisemitismus, 1900), 189.

and their affinity to liberalism and capitalism. Much of this was hardly compatible—how could the Jews, thought of as a collective unit, be capitalists and anti-capitalists at the same time?

Moreover, accusations that the Jews controlled the anti-Christian and therefore "Jewish" press and that Jews had supported or even initiated the Kulturkampf were of prime importance for the Catholics. In 1880 Joseph Edmund Jörg wrote in his journal that the "Jewish press"

> had for years persecuted that which is holy to the Christian, without any shame or inhibition, and dragged it through the mud. As MP Stöcker [court chaplain and antisemitic leader] quite rightly said in the Prussian Chamber, up until now we have been "hunted like a wild animal by the Jews." Everything that is related to Catholicism has been treated in an even more poisonous way by this press, where possible. At every ill treatment that we have had to suffer, the Jew has stood by smirking. Therefore, he must have been sure that he had nothing to fear; he was convinced that in this way he was promoting his own interests.

Jörg thought that a large part of Christendom was already "led by the spirit of modern Judaism." He claimed that left-wing liberal MP Eugen Richter said that in hitting out at the Jews one was really attacking liberalism as a whole.

> He is right; and there is no way that it can be any different. Modern liberalism is nothing other than a denationalized Judaism—it is the knave, and the open lodge are the masters. All three share the common aim of founding the kingdom of so-called humanity on the ruins of the Christian world-order, and when they pray, they pray to the Golden Calf. The Jews have breathed strength and life into this idol through their capitalism. The antisemites may not be mistaken—the three of them are closely connected and therefore fearsome enemies, against whom they raise their weapons.[25]

Jörg's remarks were aimed at the emerging antisemitic parties and related to the *Antisemitenpetition,* a petition which, with its quarter-of-a-million signatures, demanded the withdrawal of certain rights from Jews. His observations demonstrate the typical mixture of macro stereotypes and chimeras, such as a new world-order and the leadership of the Jewish spirit, with concrete stereotypes, e.g., the Jewish press and attacks on Catholics. These were so deeply rooted that some historians, as we have seen, are still convinced of their validity today and speak of Jewish *Kulturkämpfer* and the Jewish press.

Is there any truth behind these xenophobic attitudes? One could argue that many Jews allegedly devoted themselves to liberalism and became loyal members of the National Liberal Party, which led the Kulturkampf, in which case they would have certainly supported the persecution of the Church. As for the "Jewish Press," one could assume that it attacked Catholicism because of its affinity with liberalism and because of the large number of Jewish journalists.[26]

Both topics should be treated separately. Let us first look at the Kulturkampf. Mazura claimed that "a large proportion of Jews and their press supported the *Kulturkampfgesetzgebung*."[27] Lindemann shares this view: "A number of liberal Jewish journalists, writing in support of Bismarck, gained notoriety for the virulence of their attacks on the Church."[28] This idea is still prevalent in the literature until the present. It serves Lindemann's general argument about Jewish misdeeds. Other authors simply repeat this claim because they have found it somewhere in the literature. Italian historian Massimo Ferrari Zumbini, for example, who in 2003 published a very balanced book about German antisemitism, reproduced this tale without further research into it: "The Jewish public" during the Kulturkampf "took sides with the anti-Catholic legislation."[29]

The truth is that many Jewish journalists and Jews were generally unhappy about the Kulturkampf. Jewish MPs, in particular, behaved in an extremely restrained and cautious manner, since, as members of a recently emancipated minority, they disapproved of the discrimination against other minorities. Furthermore, the liberals among them were especially mistrustful of the omnipotence of the state. National liberals Eduard Lasker and Ludwig Bamberger did, however, become targets of an antisemitic hate-campaign: the *Fränkischen Volksblatt* wrote of "the conceited Jew Bamberger." The Paderborn priest Josef Rebbert held "the Jew Lasker" with his "loyal comrade" (Bamberger) responsible for the Kulturkampf and the *Gründerkrise* (economic crisis). In this business, the paper reported, Jews and national liberals had shaken hands "like brothers." As a solution to the "Jewish question" Rebbert recommended voting for the Center to "eliminate the Jewish National Liberal Party."[30] Can it be proven that Bamberger, Lasker, and other Jews subsequently supported the *Jesuitengesetz* (Jesuit Law)?

Lindemann correctly assesses that liberals favored a limitation of the influence of religion in public life. "Historically, Jews had ample reason to fear Catholic influence. Most recently, Church spokesmen had been among those in Germany who opposed Jewish emancipation." But then Lindemann states that the proscription of the Jesuit order was a measure "that found especially warm support among Jews, given the long-standing reputation of the order as hostile to them." Although this sounds plausible, Lindemann does not bother to give any examples to support this argument. In fact, he ignores the proof that prominent Jews were struggling hard against the Jesuit Law. He refrains from giving any proof for the "virulence" of the Jewish attacks on the Church. Not a single German book or other resource is consulted. Lindemann is not aware that Jewish attorneys opposed the Jesuit law. In fact, the ostracized Lasker and Bamberger were secular Jews who distanced themselves from the religious practice of Judaism while remaining loyal to their Jewish identities. Both, even though voting for some other Kulturkampf laws, belonged to the few liberals who refused to accept the law which outlawed the order in 1872 and compelled many Jesuits to leave Germany. All Jewish deputies in the Reichstag refused to vote for the Jesuit bill, either abstaining or voting against it. These included national liberals Lasker, Bamberger, and the deputy from Hamburg, Isaac Wolffson, as well as Leopold Sonnemann among the democrats.

This law, which dealt a severe blow to the Catholics, was not demanded by the Jews but by anti-ultramontane Protestant groups as well as Old Catholics—those Catholics who had distanced themselves from Roman Catholicism after the first Vatican Council. Not only Old Catholics such as

Eduart Windthorst, the nephew of Ludwig Windthorst, opposed the Jesuits, but also Catholic national liberals and Catholic progressives. Like Eduard Windthorst, most of them paid the price for their opposition; the Catholic electorate did not re-elect them, and they were replaced by Center Party politicians. Even though Catholic deputies in liberal parties were in favor of the Jesuit Law, one finds no mention in the literature that Catholics were responsible for this law. However, the charge that Jews supported it keeps cropping up in the literature without comment, even though they did not. The Kulturkampf laws were the initiative of the national liberals. If Protestant liberals promoted them, they did so because they were Protestans and liberals. If Jewish liberals voted against the Kulturkampf legislation, they did this although they were liberals and because they were Jewish, being torn between two identities. For many ultramontane Catholics this context was too complicated. They preferred to regard the Jews as those pulling the strings where the Jesuit Law was concerned; they preferred to see Jews as those standing behind the liberals. This topos was not only widespread during the Kulturkampf; it continued to exist up until the Weimar Republic.[31]

The comparison between the persecution of Jews and the persecution of Jesuits also persisted. It still played a role in the National Socialist regime: Catholics expressed their fear that persecution of Catholics could arise out of persecution of the Jews, which is why they believed that the latter should not be supported. It had nothing to do with protecting the Jews as such. When Jewish businesses were boycotted on 1st April 1933, Munich's Cardinal Faulhaber was much more worried "that the fight against the Jews" could transform into "a fight against the Catholics" and "the anti-Jewish hate campaign" could change into an "anti-Jesuit hate campaign." This is the clearest possible example of the long and fatal continuity of Catholic fear between the Kulturkampf of the 1870s and the so-called *Kirchenkampf* of the 1930s.[32]

Journalist Joseph Eberle, who made a name for himself in 1912 with his anti-Jewish book *Großmacht Presse* (The imperial power of the press), exploited this comparison between Jews and Jesuits in the *Allgemeine Rundschau,* in order to win the Jesuits back to Germany. He asked why the nationalists had only banned the Jesuits: "Why is there only a fight against the German Loyolites . . . and not against the completely foreign Jewish race, for example, against a certain modern Jewry, whose obsession with criticism and subversive negation, whose materialism and . . . internationalism and strict tribal solidarity is also foreign to the national feeling? Why are the Jesuits detested and the Semites beloved children?" Eberle was surprised that the nationalists feared the Jesuits to such an extent, instead of doing something against the "Jewification [which was] already occurring." This "corruption by Jews" is described in order to finally answer the question: "Why so much interest for the Jesuits and none for the Jewish problem?" The answer, Eberle offered, was simple—it lay in the process of "Jewification" itself. Religious and political questions were studied from the daily press, the "oracle of the average people," so public opinion was therefore controlled by the Jews. Considering this, how was one supposed to be able to judge the Jesuits justly?

The weekly *Israelitische Wochenblatt* confessed that it had not expected such attacks from a "serious Catholic newspaper" and in 1912 published the following text, stating its view on the Jesuit question once again:

> We have never made any secret of the fact that we are very uncomfortable about the Jesuit-law and that we do not hold it to be compatible with the principles of justice and liberalism. We always speak out against every *Ausnahmegesetz* . . . and are therefore also in favor of the lifting of the Jesuit-law. But we must ask how an honest, respectable author can bring himself to combine Jews and Jesuits one with the other? What does this matter have to do with us Jews? The writer seems to have raised the whole issue simply in order to be able to curse and stir up hatred against the Jews.

Such a battle tactic, it was concluded, contradicted the rules of religion and of literary decency.[33]

Jewish abstention from participation in the Kulturkampf is also confirmed by the *Mitteilungen aus dem Verein zur Abwehr des Antisemitismus*. After the chairman of the Catholic Bürgerverein of Liegnitz delivered an election campaign speech for the Center Party in 1893 in which he determined that "primarily Jews and the Jewish press" were to be counted among the "enemies" in the Kulturkampf, the Abwehrverein reacted in the usual manner: "It is entirely untrue that 'Jews and the Jewish press' have played such a predominant role in the ranks of the '*Kulturkämpfer*,' no matter how often the opposite is claimed. MPs of the Jewish faith have mostly held themselves back from the Kulturkampf and, for example, voted against the decision about the Jesuit-law." This did not only apply to Eduard Lasker, Ludwig Bamberger, or Ludwig Löwe: "The Jewish MP Sonnemann has not voted for a single Kulturkampf law." In some constituencies, therefore, Catholics later went so far as to give the Jewish candidates preference over others, in recognition of these facts. "Considering these circumstances, one will not be able to claim that the Jews occupied a leading place, so to speak, in the Kulturkampf. It is high time that this myth was dissolved."[34]

Yet even today the myth still seems to persist. It may be based on the entirely logical, basic assumption that Jews were not supporters of ultramontanism. They consequently reacted to the Church's claim to certain privileges and, similarly, to its power and anti-liberal stance, with concern and distrust. The drawn-out suffering and legal oppression of Jewry at the hands of the Christians had, indeed, already been eliminated at the time of emancipation. Yet their memory remained present. Furthermore, one must not forget how indescribable were the living conditions of the Jews in the Papal States itself, the very center of world Catholicism, before its residents, including Catholics without civil rights, were liberated by the Italian unification movement in 1870. Until then the Papal States were a "repressive police state," as Aram Mattioli states in his research into the miserable living conditions in the last ghetto of Ancient Europe. Since the Counter-Reformation, Jews had been forced to eke out their wretched existence in the ghetto. The growing ultramontanism under Gregory XVI was accompanied by an increase of anti-Jewish policies. Pius IX did indeed have the wall of the ghetto razed to the ground in 1848, but, worn down by revolution and exile, he turned back to a restrictive policy in 1850 and the wall was promptly reerected. Jews forfeited all rights and all properties; they had to pay heavy "special taxes" and were not allowed to engage in any trades or independent professions. They were supposed to convert to the true faith, even if this happened by force, as in the secret baptism of children. In 1858 the baptism and abduction of the Jewish child Edgardo Mortaro provoked outrage in the enlightened world.

Clerical fanaticism contributed to the fact that the worn-out absolutist Papal States was finally left without international support and then captured in 1870. Catholics in all countries immediately complained that it had been a victim of Jewish-Freemason machinations, and Pius IX (who was beatified in September 2000 by Pope John Paul II) did not hesitate to hold the Jews responsible for this and other misdeeds. Did the Papal States, with the contemptible, inhuman manner in which it treated Jews, look like an ideal model for a Catholic society? Indeed, this was the frightening perspective, if we consider the tearful complaints of the "Prisoners in the Vatican" about the destruction of the Papal States which continued to be heard until well into the twentieth century, before the concordat with fascist Italy finally brought a little comfort in 1929.[35]

Legal equality, established in France as early as 1791, was reluctantly and gradually passed in the German states in the decades before 1870, yet even then did not grant full social equality. This was a very fragile process, with many Jews fearing that there could be a setback. Their concern about the progress of emancipation could not really be dispelled, a state of affairs which was not helped at all by the fact that certain circles within the clergy attempted to undermine Jewish emancipation. The Church's entitlement to truth and power was highlighted time and time again, including in 1864 in the *Syllabus Errorum*. The encyclical *Rerum Novarum* of 1891 frankly expressed the Church's interest in leadership. It claimed to possess the special gift of "manipulation" of the people, who are first and foremost defined as "sinners." "The whole working" of the Church

> has the effect of reorganizing and educating humankind in accordance with its doctrine and its spirit. Through the episcopate and the clergy, it sends its holy teaching down into the widest circles of the people, as far as its influence can go. It seeks to penetrate the innermost being of the people and to guide their will, so that they will aim to follow God's commands in all aspects of their lives. Over this inner effectiveness, the point around which everything revolves, the Church wields a victorious power, which is exclusively its own."[36]

The "power of the priests," seen by some as a polemical catch-phrase and by others as a function derived from the mastery of Christ,[37] remained a latent threat to civil society and its postulates of freedom.

Considering this hostile framework and the affinity of most Jews for liberalism, it would not be surprising if a few among them had gravitated towards the widespread anticlerical and anti-ultramontane stereotypes. In fact, if one looks long and hard enough, such statements can be found. How were the Jews alone supposed to have been able to resist adopting an anti-Church stance, when it was regarded as a matter of course? Abraham Geiger, for example, harbored extremely unfavorable ideas about Catholics. In June 1858 he wrote a letter to his wife from Breslau, where he had been officiating as a rabbi since 1838. She was ill and had gone to Karlsbad, in Austria, to convalesce. Geiger first asks her to write him, then goes on to complain disparagingly about the Catholic postal service and Catholicism in general:

> I wonder whether I'll hear a few loving words from you tomorrow? I can hardly believe how the Austrian postal connection continually disappoints me. Everything's done the Catholic way. Don't the Holy Joes have any idea of speedy transport? It would make the people more sensible and less liable to be bossed about. Pilgrimages, prayers to the Virgin Mary, stupidity, ignorance are their domains; advancement and development are their enemies. We must be able to control ourselves well and be aware that we will not experience much of what we hope and wish for, but I'd like to see Catholicism completely and utterly overthrown. I know that it will happen, but

> until it does, I'm not going to receive your letter a single hour earlier.[38]

If this quote is not amusing, then it is disturbing. At first glance the figure of classic anti-Catholic prejudice is recognizable. It consists of stupid Catholics who are spoon-fed by the powerful clergy and willfully refused access to information. Non-Catholics saw Catholics as pious and ignorant, as superstitious and mendacious, as internationalist and loyal to Rome at all costs. What is more, they were supposedly slovenly, lazy, and dirty.[39]

Such topoi caused Geiger to yearn for the collapse of Catholicism. Did ultramontane groups therefore have realistic grounds for suspicion that the Jews wanted to destroy Catholic Christendom? The factual and temporal contexts of the quoted passage lead us to view Geiger's note in a somewhat different light. It is not a religiously intolerant statement, but rather a criticism of the political and social power of Catholicism, especially in Austria, a country in which, at the time Geiger wrote his letter, Catholicism was once again highly influential. Since the failed revolution of 1848, the Church had presented itself to the State as a power representing order during the Restoration. Both State and Church aspired to elevate Austria to the position of a "protective power" of all German Catholics, of the ultimate "Great Catholic Power," and together they took action against liberalism. With the concordat of 1855 the success of the Church reached its zenith: it received extensive privileges and a power of disposal over believers which it had not enjoyed for a long time. Mixed marriages were outlawed, strictly segregated areas in cemeteries were to be assigned to different confessions, and even the papal Primacy of Jurisdiction, which the first Vatican Council did not proclaim until fifteen years later, was anticipated here. Appointments to offices no longer needed to be approved and the freedom of the episcopate was recognized, as were the jurisdiction of the Church (including matters relating to marriage), the local immunity and general protection of the Church, the autonomy of law of monastic orders, and the Church's property rights. Moreover, its influence in the education and publishing sectors was guaranteed, which meant that the bishops supervised teachers and could decide which books were to be read in schools, and the government helped by banning improper reading matter.

This was an incomparable triumph of re-Catholicization. The Church's power was to decrease again during the years of the liberal era and the State terminated the concordat in 1870. Yet in 1858, when Geiger was writing his letter and the Mortara Affair was causing public outcry in Europe, horrified liberals had begun to realize the extent of the Roman Catholic Church's stubborn attitude and of the liberties it was taking with the Jews. At the same time, the heights of power to which Catholicism, with its anti-emancipation stance, had climbed in the mid-nineteenth century had become worryingly evident.[40]

It is not the threatening presence of Catholicism which is crucial in interpreting Geiger's words, but the fact that he was expressing his thoughts in a purely private manner. He didn't engage in public anti-Catholic propaganda. In this case a major difference between the behavior patterns of Catholics and Jews can be discerned. While anti-Jewish stereotypes had not only been internalized but were also publicly expressed and exploited for Catholic purposes, liberal Jews like Geiger were certainly not completely free of some anti-Catholic thoughts. Yet it seems as though they generally behaved calmly and diplomatically in public, because as a minority they did not want to launch a polemical attack on the majority.

Are there no exceptions? Occasionally attention is drawn to the observations of Jewish historian Heinrich Graetz (d. 1891). In 1879 Berlin-based historian Heinrich von Treitschke pointed to Graetz in order to prove, by means of his writings, that Judaism was arrogant and that it inveighed against Christianity and German culture. This led to a separate sub-controversy within the so-called *Antisemitismusstreit* which was fought out between the followers of Treitschke and the disciples of Theodor Mommsen, a historian and supporter of emancipation.

Heinrich Graetz is regarded as one of the most important historians of Judaism and Jewry. Between 1853 and 1876 he published his eleven-volume *Geschichte der Juden von den ältesten Zeiten bis zur Gegenwart,* the bone of contention between Graetz and Treitschke. As far as Jewish attitudes to Reform are concerned, Graetz fluctuates between the liberalism of Abraham Geiger's stormy obsession ("*Stürmerei*") and the orthodoxy of Samson Raphael Hirsch ("*Mumienverehrung*"), representing a self-confident kind of Judaism. His total account covers an enormous historical sphere. Shulamit Volkov described it as "the most important intellectual event in connection with German-Jewish culture of the nineteenth century."[41] A widely read popular edition of his work was finally published in 1888.

Graetz's history of the Jews does not skirt around the topic of their oppression, but details it century after century. For example, he severely took to task Pope Innocent III (1198–1216)

> who was the first to place the iron yoke of the Church upon princes and peoples that led to the enslavement and the brutalization of the human spirit, who was the first to persecute liberal thinkers, the father of the Inquisition and the stake for heretics, that is, for such who dared question the infallibility of the Roman bishop; this pope was also an

> inexorable foe of Jews and Judaism, and inflicted upon them more serious wounds than all the adversaries who preceded him.[42]

It was easy to make the text about medieval figures bear upon the second half of the nineteenth century. This may not have been entirely coincidental, since epithets such as "enslaving and dulling the spirit," "infallibility," and "enemy of the Jews" characterized Pius IX for Graetz's contemporaries as well. From a democratic point of view, it was just as difficult to understand the superior strength of the Church (and ultramontane policy) as the suppression of Jews under Innocent III or Pius IX.[43] On the other hand, Graetz also reports how Innocent III opposed the persecution of the Jews.

As his history approaches the nineteenth century, Graetz's aversion to the Papal States and to the "medieval smoke" of Jew-hatred becomes increasingly frank. He accuses Joseph Görres, Friedrich Schlegel, and Adam Müller, who had converted to Catholicism in the early nineteenth century, of having wanted to "re-erect the empire of the Jesuits and the Inquisition." "The fantastic Christian *Deutschtümelei* [a jingoistic emphasis on all things German] was the armed ghost which, over several centuries, robbed the Jew of peace, honor, and enthusiasm for his work." He claimed that German scholars, such as Friedrich Rühs, spoke "the language of the Fathers of the Church." "In their hatred of the Jews they competed with ultra-Catholicism. Pius VII, who, owing to the Restoration, became ruler of the Papal States once more and reinstated the Inquisition, decreed that the Jews were once again to lose the freedom which they had enjoyed under French rule." Sadly, Graetz was speaking the truth in this case—the Jews actually had to clear out of their houses in Rome and return to the cramped, unhygienic ghetto. "The Middle Ages were reintroduced into the Papal States. The Jews had to report to the conversion preachers for punishment, just as they had done in the seventeenth century." Considering how his own religious contemporaries were humiliated, is it really surprising that Graetz's tone is rather harsh?[44]

He uses the term "Middle Ages" repeatedly, almost on every page, and in the negative sense, as a contrast to the nineteenth century. He reports that all Jews in Europe were absolutely horrified that, faced with the alleged ritual murder case in Damascus in 1840, they "still had to fight against the dark spirit of the blood libel (*Blutanklage*) in the bright days of the nineteenth century."[45] The Damascus blood libel was set off by the rumor that two Capuchin monks had been killed by a group of Jews. It occupied politicians and newspapers throughout Europe. Graetz, who was born in 1817, had been able to consciously experience this scandal as a contemporary, as well as the kidnapping of Mortara in 1858. Once again he takes a stand against the "terrible after-effect of the Middle Ages." "The entire European press, including the Russian, excepting the ultra-Catholic, were unanimous in their condemnation of such a crime."[46] However, the term "Middle Ages" was regarded as extremely positive among Catholics who therefore considered negative judgments about their retrogressive ideals to be raw materialism.[47]

Graetz's work does not only target the enemies of the Jews. It contains several critical observations of Jews, rabbis, and even "Jewish profiteers." He reports that during the Napoleonic era Jews tried to recover their money from Alsatian farmers who had got themselves back on their feet with the help of loans. Since the farmers did not want to pay cash, they had to settle their debts by making over fields and vineyards to the Jewish creditors. "Some Jewish profiteers may well have used a large degree of force in ensuring that the loans were settled," writes Graetz. "The enemies of the Jews made use of this. In order to prevent equal rights being given to the French Jews, they generalized the misdeeds of individual Jews, exaggerated the suffering of the Christian debtors who were forced to pay, and labeled all Jews as profiteers and leeches."[48]

One has to give Graetz credit for the fact that he always keeps both sides in view, not forgetting also to mention those Christians who supported the Jews, such as Abbé Grégoire during the French Revolution, or the Catholic preacher Veith in Vienna, during the Damascus Affair of 1840.[49] He criticizes conservatism and *Deutschtümelei* just as much as he does Catholicism or Lutheranism. The Jews, he writes at the end of his work, were particularly "hated by a party that desired to see the restoration of medievalism with its enslavement and obscurantism. Its prophet was Friedrich Julius Stahl (1802–61), a Jewish apostate." Graetz was referring to the Conservatives, whose central paper was the *Kreuzzeitung*.[50] It is not surprising that the nationalists were annoyed by the term *Deutschtümelei,* that Conservatives were indignant at being accused of wanting to return to the Middle Ages, and that Catholics were angered by the faultfinding with the Papal States. All of these reproaches sprang from the desperate condition of a small minority, faced with premodern authorities which were becoming enormously powerful. On the other hand, Graetz always remained cautious with his judgments, which are certainly harsh but not as severe as those of non-Jewish socialists or dissidents, Freemasons, Old Catholics, or deserter monks. Each of these groups suffered at the hands of Catholicism to some extent, but none of these cases were at all comparable to the plight of being ghettoized, discriminated against, and persecuted.

This brief examination of Graetz's historical work leads us to ask whether "Jewish literary figures" or "the Jewish press" were involved in anti-papal acts and engaged in the Kulturkampf hate campaign. Even today this has not been proven to be true, despite the frequent claims by Catholics in the past and by present-day pro-Catholic historians. First, a fact which is often forgotten, but that should be taken into consideration, is that not one Jewish daily newspaper existed in the nineteenth century. The central question is this: How does one define the "Jewish press"? Many antisemites regarded every paper which did not share their own views as being Jewish. We do not need to examine these papers for our purpose. What is important is that the term "Jewish paper" was by this time used in an inflammatory manner. Ultramontane Catholics even classified the dissident Catholics, who called themselves "Old Catholics," as Protestant and Jewish.[51] What is more, ultramontane Catholics who did something of which their comrades disapproved were accused of being "Jews."

An incident which took place in Munich in 1901 is one amusing example. In July of that year a monk with a large string of rosary beads stopped passers-by on the Isar Bridge and asked them whether they read newspapers. "Of course," was the answer. "To which newspaper do you subscribe, then?" "The *Bayerische Kurier.*" "But that's a Jewish one!" "I didn't know that!" "Oh come on, you can't read the *Bayerische Kurier* if you're a Catholic, it's not a Catholic paper. Look, the *Neue Bayerische Zeitung* is coming out right near here in Herrnstrasse. If you came with me now and subscribed to it for the new quarter, the editor would be overjoyed. Come on, come with me." But the passer-by in question refused and instead reported the incident to the *Bayerische Kurier,* the so-called "Jewish paper," which a few days later announced with pleasure that the over-zealous brother had been recalled by his superiors. Center Party circles found this "advertising campaign" embarrassing. Catholic papers dissociated themselves from it, whereas the ultramontane paper, for which the brother was also canvassing door to door, praised him for his success up to that point. The exaggerated, aggressive form of his engagement was strange, more so the fact that a newspaper like the *Bayerische Kurier,* which had never shown the slightest hint of being a "Jewish" paper, could be discredited in this manner. The *Kurier* was actually *the* Catholic paper in Munich. Its considerable reputation was attested at various times by guardians of the milieu press (Leo Woerl, Clemens Löffler, Heinrich Keiter). In the case before us, it is evident that Catholics could make good Catholic papers appear "Jewish" without any basis of reality in order, for example, to meet certain economic targets. This came about because the competition between Catholic papers was growing alongside the increasing tensions inside the milieu, as the memory of the Kulturkampf began to fade.[52]

It is no wonder that the works emanating from the Mosse publishing house were regarded as "Jewish" no matter whether Mosse acted predominantly as a Jew or as a publisher.[53] In any case, the suggestion that the famous *Frankfurter Zeitung* or the cynical weekly journal *Simplizissimus* were Jewish appears plausible to some historians today. Indeed, with reference to Jewish publishers or journalists, papers were labeled as "Jewish" a century ago, just as supermarkets were called Jewish if they were owned by Jews (but they were not called Protestant supermarkets if they were owned by a Protestant). Probably inspired by this sort of logic, Heinz Hürten concludes that the concept of a Jewified and Jewish press had "realistic grounds," since Heine and Sonnemann were Jews.[54] In former times, statements about the "Jewish press" sounded much harsher. The ultramontane paper *Oberschlesische Volkszeitung,* from Upper Silesia, fumed against the "tyranny of Israel, which would like to build its world imperialism on the ruins of the world created by Christendom." Behind the "rage" of the *Simplizissimus* stood the "subversive Jew, the Ahasverus, or 'eternal Jew' of vengeance, with a desire to rule the world." In August 1910 the *Jüdische Volksblatt,* referring to this article, refuted these "attempts to antagonize" and declared that this kind of behavior was hardly going to help the Center win the trust of the Jewish citizens.[55]

Was the much-cursed *Frankfurter Zeitung* a Jewish paper? It certainly never regarded itself as such. If it criticized Catholics, it did so not from a Jewish point of view but from a liberal, or more precisely, a democratic standpoint. The *Frankfurter Zeitung*, moreover, did not subject only Catholicism to critical analysis, but also conservatism and Protestantism, liberalism and militarism, and any other general issues which came to its notice. There is just as little proof that Heine and Sonnemann acted as "Jews" as there is of their anti-Catholic behavior.

Of course Sonnemann was a secular Jew and a democrat. It is also true that in 1856, together with others, he established the *Frankfurter Handelszeitung,* later called the *Frankfurter Zeitung,* which he also edited. As of 1867 he was the sole owner of the paper. Sonnemann, of course, was in favor of the separation of church and state, a condition which had already been achieved in so many other countries by that time.

Yet, first of all, Sonnemann was a secular Jew and a democrat. He purposefully refrained from leading the *Frankfurter Zeitung* along lines based on tradition and heritage, preferring to follow civic and democratic lines. Second, a close inspection of the *Frankfurter*'s position in the German empire makes one wonder where the idea of an anti-Catholic tendency, which so many people believed and still seem to believe, came from. Reading the *Frankfurter* (which can be found in the Dortmund Newspaper Archive, for example) reveals no evidence of pronounced anti-Catholicism or support for the Kulturkampf. It is true, of course, that the paper could not agree with demands that corresponded with the *Syllabus Errorum,* which had condemned the modern age in 1864. That is understandable, because otherwise the paper would have been strongly ultramontane. The *Syllabus* condemned freedom of opinion and of the press, to which the *Frankfurter Zeitung* would have been unable to subscribe.

The *Frankfurter* participated of course in combatting superstition and oppression. Critical, almost derogatory observations about those who opposed science, enlightenment, and progress can be found in its pages. During the obscure affaire of Leo Taxil, who fooled Catholics with his stories about devils and flying Freemasons, the newspaper took the side of reason and enlightenment. "It goes without saying," it maintained in 1899, "that people who have no idea about scientific thought and who are unfit for serious intellectual work go to the Pope, who has declared himself to be infallible, for their even greater comfort; they are in suitable company with Miss Vaughan and the devil Bitru." This is a reference to the two characters created by Taxil: Diana Vaughan, who had unveiled the "evil machinations" of the allegedly satanic Freemason organization, and the devil Bitru, who was connected to the lodge. Leo Taxil, a French con-artist, could spin the most terrifying yarns to the Catholics and the Pope even blessed him for it. This story, which was remembered for a long time as the "Taxil affaire," exposed the naïveté and gullibility, as well as the unenlightened consciousness, present in Catholicism. Obviously, those who held liberal views saw this as dangerous. But that did not make the *Frankfurter* a staunchly anti-Catholic paper.[56]

Third, the *Frankfurter Zeitung* even frequently assisted Catholicism against the Kulturkampf. If it had been driven by the same liberalism which motivated the National Liberal and Protestant *Kultukämpfer,* it would have, like these groups and like Bismarck, relied on the fresh hope of Old Catholicism, for instance. Yet it actually spoke about the Old Catholic movement in a derogatory tone, which sounded exactly as though it could have come from an ultramontane paper. "It is not enough that the state should regard the handful of professors as the real Catholic Church," reported the *Frankfurter* in September 1872, in an article about the demands of Old Catholicism. "They are also calling for the introduction of state salaries for Old Catholic parish priests." At this point in time the Old Catholic movement, which had split off from the Catholic Church, had not yet been recognized as a Church in its own right. Its bishop's office, which was first filled by professor of theology Joseph Hubert Reinkens and whose seat is still in Bonn today, was not established until August 1873. Ultramontane groups always put this “bishop” in quotation marks and rejected this institutionalization. Yet the *Frankfurter Zeitung* also observed this process with derision from the very beginning: “To not want to separate from the Catholic Church and to demand recognition as the true Catholic Church at the same time, to hold onto Catholic hierarchy and simultaneously let themselves be paid by the state—only Old Catholicism could fail to notice the contradictions here.” The paper declared that the Old Catholic movement would not get any further. The *Frankfurter Zeitung,* though attacked by liberals, had since 1875 run a fortnightly Kulturkampf Calendar which documented the state’s repressive measures against Catholics.[57]

If the *Frankfurter Zeitung* was therefore not anti-Catholic, Sonnemann’s “being Jewish” would have been of no relevance to our question, yet the concept of the anti-Catholic “Jewish paper” was believed to have a real basis. If Sonnemann did not act as a Jew, did he then, perhaps, at least stand out as a *Kulturkämpfer*? This question would also have been easy to answer if one checked the 1898 edition of the *Brockhaus* general encyclopedia which succinctly states that “he opposed the Kulturkampf,”[58] indicating beyond doubt that his behavior was known to his contemporaries. Jewish journalist August Stein, a friend of Ludwig Windthorst, worked for Sonnemann as a Berlin correspondent at the same time and frequently allowed the leader of the Center Party to use the *Frankfurter* as a mouthpiece for Catholic interests.[59]

The extent to which the *Frankfurter* was unhappy about the Kulturkampf and to which it very often took the side of the Catholics became evident when the Kulturkampf laws were discussed and issued or when a scandalous breach of rights was revealed. When the Paderborn-based bishop Konrad Martin escaped to Holland just in time to avoid serving a jail term in 1874, he addressed a moving farewell message to his supporters in order to encourage solidarity with their spiritual leaders. Like all ultramontane circulars, the *Germania* printed it word for word. The *Frankfurter,* however, picked up the message from *Germania* and printed it as well, reproducing the extremely appellative text without commenting on it.[60] One of the most important guiding intellectual forces of lay Catholicism, Joseph Edmund Jörg, could therefore have easily himself discovered how neutral a stand the *Frankfurter Zeitung* had adopted on internal Church issues and how often the newspaper, as well as many Jews, in fact disapproved of the Kulturkampf. Yet Jörg adhered tightly to his antisemitic insinuations, claiming that the leading Jews had established a “hate campaign directed at Christians” and, especially during the Kulturkampf, had “fought a thousand more times against the loyal Catholics, in the same way in which they are now attacking us with accusations of antisemitism and are ever ready to fight. . . . Their intention was to help Protestantism to sweep away the Catholics from German territory." Previously, however, he had himself quoted a few lines from the *Frankfurter Zeitung* of 28 November 1880:

> For years we have predicted that, with a policy like the one which has been introduced against the Catholics and socialists, nobody's rights, least of all those of a minority, can continue to exist and we have quietly issued a warning on more than one occasion. Yes, as the Kulturkampf climbed to new heights, we even repeatedly asked what would happen if the Jews, regarded as a threat to the state and an enemy of culture, were treated similarly—what would be ruled out if one unlawfully gave every majority the power to restrict the rights of the minority?[61]

The conclusion of our research is quite evident: Despite tireless claims by antisemites of various faiths and by some present-day historians, it is obvious that they are thrice mistaken: it remains obvious that the *Frankfurter Zeitung* was neither anti-Catholic nor Jewish; nor did it support the Kulturkampf. Considering the decades of research and the wealth of contemporary sources which should have made this clear over and over again, it is alarming that one is still forced to repeat the basic mechanisms of the formation of stereotypes in order to contradict incorrigible revisionists or Church historians, who consider the *Frankfurter Zeitung* to be a Jewish paper and therefore pretend that the Catholic reproaches are justified. The *Jüdische Volksblatt* described this depressing experience over ninety years ago. In September 1910 that weekly, published in Breslau, reacted to antisemitic attacks on the "Jewish press" by the ultramontane *Oberschlesischen Volkszeitung*. The *Jüdische Volksblatt* demonstrates to today's contemporary historians just how truly absurd is the conceived idea of the all-embracing "Jewish press." "It is a dishonest and insincere battle tactic—we repeat this for the thousandth time—to pretend that liberal or democratic comments in the press represent the public voices of Judaism. The *Oberschlesische Volkszeitung* should also be aware that the German Jews do not own any daily paper which they would be willing to turn into an official channel of Judaism."

Yet, despite all the factual evidence, politically liberal and democratic newspapers were frequently described as being just that: Jewish. The article went on to say that this "rubbish" must be stopped once and for all. Those who deploy "such dishonest tactics" should "at least have the courtesy to admit that they are genuine antisemites, from whom we do expect such behavior. We are gradually becoming used to them blaming us for every kind of misfortune, such as bad weather at harvest time, epidemics during the Middle Ages, and so forth, but it is not permissible to make a show of being the objective 'upright citizen' while secretly blackening the reputation of the Jewish population with the mud of unadulterated antisemitism." The "*Oberschlesische Volkszeitung* is increasingly treading on antisemitic ground. . . . It is continuing to hold Jews responsible for things . . . in which they are most definitely not involved and it keeps discussing Jewish newspapers and Jewish humorous magazines, even though it knows it is a fact that there are no such things." The *Volkszeitung* had ignored "the thousands of recriminations from the real Jewish press" and was well aware "that the newspapers which it is talking about are either liberal or democratic party papers."[62]

Hence, refusing to recognize non-Jewish papers as Jewish is not tantamount to a "cheap gag," as Heinz Hürten claimed. The antisemites attempted to prove non-Jewish papers to be "Jewish" or "Jewified." Anyone even casually examining the topic of antisemitism using nineteenth-century sources can easily gather this. However, there were indeed papers for which Jews were writing and which published jokes about Catholicism. How did matters actually stand vis-à-vis the supposedly "Jewish" satirical comic papers, which were strongly condemned? How did genuine Jewish papers deal with this? In 1875, for example, a "humorous paper" (*Witzblatt*) carried an advertisement for a market "selling relics from Plunderweiler," indicating that relics are junk (Plunder-Weiler is a fictitious village whose name means Junkhamlet). Catholics did not find this funny. In contrast to the sovereignty and the ability to see things with humor which characterizes non-dogmatic positions, Catholics reacted very severely: "The local garlic farmers and matzo bakers should count themselves lucky that the Catholics prefer neatness and tidiness. Otherwise they would have had the living daylights beaten out of them by now."[63] The *Israelitische Wochenschrift* took up the Catholic complaints in an article about ultramontane antisemitism: So much is imputed to Jews, "however, we are not merely imagining it; these are stern, pressing reminders. The Jewish people should not want to pour oil on the fire," the weekly stressed.

> We wish this for the sake of our own religion, which means nothing to those we are talking about. . . . We quoted a passage from a humorous paper from Berlin, which is bound to make Catholics really angry. Everything else that the political smear-sheets have said about the Jews is pure fantasy with an obvious invention, good only for those who regularly believe everything they're told. One thing is true though. There are actually some Jews among the people who publish

> injurious outpourings of scorn towards all religions—particularly towards Christianity, especially towards the Catholic Church and, most oddly, towards ultramontanism. Jews?! Now admittedly, the only people who can and do still refer to them as Jews are those who want to vent their spleen on Jewry as a whole. Many of them ceased to be Jewish in name a long time ago, but that is seen as irrelevant. It is the corrupt and harmful writers who first directed their jibes at Jews and Jewry, when it was not yet possible to criticize Christianity or the Pope without ending up before the public prosecutor; it is the people who mock our Torah, ridicule our "Jewish God," our festivals, our statutes . . . it is those who were born Jewish who, by taking part in all this, either try to forget their descent or want to prove that they are free from religious prejudices. Or they complain bitterly that they had been forced to adhere to certain principles when they were Jews. After they have demonstrated that they are not bigoted Jews, they can then pour scorn on Christian things.

The author claimed that there had been enough of laughing. Now the "nonsense" must be stopped.[64]

Between 1870 and 1872 the *Israelitische Wochenschrift* still expressed hope that the conflict between the state and the Church would bring about emancipation, but the paper finally confined itself to reporting on ultramontane antisemitism. It was not afraid of evincing understanding for Catholic sensitivities, though. Above all, the weekly was self-critical of supposedly "Jewish" faults. It got to the bottom of the myth of "Jewish" satirical papers and "Jewish" misdeeds.

There was a substantial amount of evidence against this myth. In 1912, when the *Kölnische Volkszeitung* once again sneered at the "Jewish press" because of its "furious hate campaign against the Catholics," the *Israelitische Wochenblatt* considered it its duty to openly state its thoughts about this accusation. It claimed that it was able to certify that the *Kölnische Volkszeitung* had always held an objective attitude towards the "Jewish Question." During the "'Dreyfus Affair,' the *Kölnische Volkszeitung* was the only exception among the Center papers." Yet now it instrumentalizes the term "Jewish press" to refer to "liberal papers, whose owners happen to be Jews. These papers are not organs of Judaism and the Jewish religion has absolutely no influence on their attitudes or positions." The *Israelitische Wochenblatt* asked whether people would seriously expect the allegedly Jewish *Berliner Tagesblatt* to change at all if its ownership were tomorrow to be passed into the hands of a Protestant or a Catholic.[65]

Thus, those who today conveniently adopt the notion of the "Jewish press," taken from the nineteenth-century antisemitic stock of ideas, for the sole reason that some papers were owned or edited by Jews, would, according to the same logic, also have to maintain that Hitler founded a Catholic empire in 1933, and that his long-term aim was Catholic world-domination. After all, Hitler was a Catholic, never left the Catholic Church, and was never pronounced excommunicate. Applying facts in this way is not a cheap gag, since some Catholics did in fact expect Hitler to fulfill the Catholic *Reichsidee*.[66] A hundred years ago Jews were already desperately trying to use similar comparisons to make it clear just how nonsensical it was to lay the blame upon them just because of their religion. The paper *Im Deutschen Reich* sarcastically illustrated what it meant to carelessly use the terms "Jewish companies" or the "Jewish press" when it had to defend itself against another such insinuations in 1900. "Most of the members and councilors of the *Grosse Karnevalgesellschaft* [a Carnival Society in Cologne] are of Catholic faith; does that, then, make it a Catholic organization? No, a Catholic association is one which is based on Catholic principles, which specifically represents Catholic interests. Shouldn't the same principle apply to Jews? My God, it is so simple for every clear-thinking person to grasp that we are almost ashamed to discuss such things in these advanced times."[67] Should there not be reason enough to be ashamed even more a century later, considering that there are still incorrigible gentlemen today who make inaccurate references to the "Jewish press"?

There is hardly any genuine proof, then, of Jewish MPs and the "Jewish press" (which was not actually Jewish) harboring pro-Kulturkampf ambitions. Faced with the myth of the "power of the Jewish press," the few genuine Jewish papers tried desperately to explain how small was their sphere of influence. "The only publications that count as Jewish are those which are exclusively dedicated to serving Jewish interests," wrote M. Mannheimer in the *Israelitische Wochenschrift* in 1882. Whereas the antisemites alone had over 150 newspapers at their disposal, only half a dozen papers could be described as Jewish, "none of which would dream of disparaging Christian institutions." "There are papers and periodicals whose owners or editors are indeed Jews, but which deal with general political and social issues rather than being exclusively dedicated to Jewish affairs. It goes without saying that these publications are definitely not part of the 'Jewish press.'" If, by way of exception, an "Israelite" vilified Christianity, Mannheimer wrote, he had certainly left Judaism behind him a long time ago and was holding it up to ridicule.[68] The *Israelitische Wochenblatt,* referring to the allegedly Jewish *Berliner Tageblatt,* the *Vossische Zeitung,* and the

Frankfurter Zeitung, also stressed in 1912 that it was "blatantly unjust to blame the Jews for whatever may or may not be written in them."[69]

What kind of opinions did Jewish authors and the "genuine" Jewish papers and magazines express about Catholics? To ascertain this, one must examine only "real" Jewish papers, like the *Israelitische Wochenblatt* or the *Jüdische Volksblatt*. This is how such an analysis should be performed, despite Hürten's claims that the papers he mentioned, the *Frankfurter Zeitung* and *Simplicissimus,* were Jewish and controlled by Jews. After having studied several "genuine" Jewish newspapers, as well as other publications, we can conclude that the notion of an anti-ultramontane ambition is completely out of the question.

Even during the Kulturkampf the few Reform and Orthodox Jewish papers behaved very diplomatically. Liberal papers such as the *Allgemeine Zeitung des Judentums* had to criticize the farreaching demands of the *Syllabus* of 1864 several times, if they wanted to defend humanity and civil society standards. But even though they kept observing the dangers deriving from ultramontanism, they were more occupied with stemming Jewish Orthodoxy than with anti-Catholicism. In this context, however, ultramontanism and Orthodoxy were in a parallelogram, compared with each other and set into the respective relationship to true Catholicism and true Judaism. Their aim was to combat fanaticism and reactionary ideas in each religion; this was neither anti-Catholicism nor anti-Judaism.[70] Even when liberal or Orthodox Jewish journals came across fierce anti-Jewish polemics, their reaction was neither concealed nor over the top. The Orthodox *Israelit* did not have the slightest intention of attacking Catholicism. The *Jüdische Literaturblatt,* edited by Rabbi Rahmer, avoided every provocation, but naturally opposed Rohling in 1883, taking the side of the defenders of Jewish integrity: the critical Protestant theologians Friedrich Delitzsch and Hermann Strack.

The attitude of the *Israelitische Wochenschrift für die religiösen und socialen Interessen des Judentums,* also edited by Rahmer from 1875 onwards, can, in any case, be studied more exactly because it is occasionally cited as evidence for Jewish support of the Kulturkampf and hostility toward Catholics, against which, it is claimed, the Catholics then simply reacted.[71] The paper was founded in 1870 in Stettin and was edited until 1875 by Rabbi A. Treuenfels. It certainly includes a few texts that could have appeared as being hostile to sensitive ultramontane temperaments, but from a Jewish point of view they were born of legitimate concern about a relapse into the oppression of the pre-emancipation period. As early as April 1870, this weekly dedicated its leading article to the retrograde steps recently taken, referring to the "progress" of both Lutheran orthodoxy and ultramontanism.

It was the Vatican Council that triggered the article. For three centuries, the paper claimed, not one important decision had been made by Rome and everyone had become used to receiving rulings from Paris, London, Vienna, and Berlin. Suddenly Rome had regained some authority. "How frightened the Jew must be by the possibility that Rome's attempt at victory, if only just a temporary one, could succeed!" Why were there ultramontane and Protestant "steps backward," asked the paper, presenting various explanations, including the power of the *Zeitgeist,* the alliance between throne and altar, and the Jesuits. "We should not allow the Jesuits to control the present anymore." Their disgraceful dirty tricks had been sufficiently revealed, the paper announced. "Why are the sinister characters not swept away by our moral outrage?" Clement XIV had dissolved the Order of Jesuits—"how is it that they managed to return and rule half of the world?" The weekly went on to comment that retrograde steps had been precipitated by a renunciation of "true," valid religion and a change of direction towards Church orthodoxy. "We must not underestimate or overlook the power of the parties who have a bitter, hostile attitude towards Judaism; it is necessary to understand that only religion, rather than lack of faith, can fight ultramontane fanaticism and the Protestant yes-men." Yet the paper also proved capable of criticizing its own side, suggesting that the behavior of the Jews had paralleled that of its adversaries in some cases: "One extreme has provoked the other; we would have made progress long ago if we had not encouraged fanatical resistance by rushing into things."[72]

The *Israelitische Wochenschrift*'s bitterness seems more understandable if we consider the fact that the Jesuits were significantly involved in antisemitic agitation in the 1870s, in the *Stimmen aus Maria-Laach,* for example. Traditionally, the Jesuits had established a clear borderline between themselves and the Jews. The Fifth General Assembly of Jesuits in 1593 had decided to not admit any "Marrano [pejorative term for converted Jews] members" and to exclude candidates of Jewish extraction up to the fifth degree of descent. The Jesuits did not relax this restriction until canon law dropped its discriminatory "Jew laws" in 1918. In 1923 the Jesuits decided that the fourth degree of descent became the cut-off point for admission.[73]

At the beginning of April 1872, as a unique exception to the rule, the *Israelitische Wochenschrift* commented on the Kulturkampf, which did not yet have an official name. "Everyone is very carefully following the struggle which the Imperial Chancellor has taken up with the ultramontanes and their allies and their followers." In fact, reported the paper, this "matter" was not really within its field of interest, but it admitted that there was no doubt as to "which side we Israelites must support, with our warmest sympathies and wishes. It is evident to us that the struggle taken up by the government is a struggle of the light and the law against its enemies, and that it is simultaneously aimed at the ancient, bitter enemies of Jewry and Judaism. Consequently we should rejoice at this uplifting triumph, together with those involved in the beginnings of the struggle . . . we have found an ally more powerful than any other we have ever known." Such explanations always refer to the awful experience of discrimination, for which the Churches were responsible. The last ghetto in the Papal States had only just been liberated, after Pius IX had persistently held onto it.

The *Wochenschrift* also stressed that the Jews "had the concepts of humanity and tolerance and the ideas of the French Revolution to thank for their liberation from medieval oppression," the same concepts, then, which ultramontanism fiercely rejected. "But we mustn't gloat," stressed the paper, since nobody could be certain what damage religion in general was going to suffer. "We should not celebrate our enemies' defeat; we must not overlook the danger. In any case the matter does not concern the Jewish religion as such, but, as Horace once said, 'the neighbor's house is on fire' and therefore 'it is our business.'"[74]

A little later the *Wochenschrift* went on to explain that "the new turn of events is leading to attempts to separate the State from the Church and to remove religious education from school." What was the attitude of the paper itself? The Church and Catholics were eager to cling to their privileged position. Any sign that the Church and state authorities were becoming independent of each other was therefore quickly labeled an example of "de-Christianization." Why should Jews have encouraged a "Christian society"? In fact, the *Israelitische Wochenschrift* wrote:

> We wish, admittedly, the separation of the State from the Church. The German state has never had any connection to Judaism. Therefore there is nothing for us to separate. The state will never guarantee the Jewish people what it guaranteed the Churches, even those in the minority. We cannot expect the state to introduce religious parity, so the more completely this separation [of Church and State] be carried out, the more secure the equal position of our religion would be.

Yet, it continues, this security should not be put at stake. "We would therefore be pleased just to see [the state's] exclusive confessionalism eliminated, to see teaching and learning no longer 'tarnished' by the dogmas of Christianity, and devoutness; in contrast, [to see] the religions preserved, protected, and cultivated."[75] In July 1872 the paper appealed once more for the right to equality and against the "power of the Church": "Vote for and appoint your teachers and clergymen as well, just as we do; do not demand that the state give them privileges and preferential treatment," and then the state will not interfere in religious affairs.[76]

There were few articles in which the *Israelitische Wochenschrift* felt compelled to express its position, one that cannot stand for "Jewry as a whole" and was not understood to do so. Even during the escalating Kulturkampf the paper had already ceased to publish its views on this matter and begun to once again exercise its usual caution. Yet the *Israelitische Wochenschrift* still fought repeatedly against sweeping judgment by the ultramontanes. In 1882 it assured Catholics that they were not as anti-Jewish as the Protestants.[77]

Jewish opinion during the Kulturkampf was divided. It is true that many Jews felt threatened by clerical fundamentalism and the anti-emancipation climate present in ultramontanism. Many also wished for a modern separation of Church and State. On the other hand, none of the four Jewish Reichstag MPs voted for the Jesuit-law, though Lasker and Bamberger later voted for the *Maigesetze* (May Laws), which imposed serious restrictions on the Church. But again: Lasker and Bamberger were not practicing Jews and whatever they did, their example can count neither in showing Jews to be supporters of the Kulturkampf, nor in resisting it. Notwithstanding this, Catholics branded Jewry as the main trigger of the Kulturkampf.[78]

Incidentally, Jewish voices have continued, even into the present, to speak cautiously with regard to other religious communities and minorities. When Rolf Hochhuth published his *Stellvertreter* in 1963, in which he accused Pius XII of being aware of and keeping silent about the extermination of the Jews, there was hardly any genuinely German-Jewish participation in the heated debate. The reason for this was clear, especially among those who held official Jewish positions—in order to avoid endangering the weak beginnings of a real integration into West German society. In 1963 there were just 30,000 Jews living in the Federal Republic. Heinz Galinski, head of the Berlin Jewish community, and committed to integration, said that it was up to others and not to the Jews to take up a definite position on the issues raised in the *Stellvertreter*. The Jewish *Allgemeine Wochenzeitung* deliberately avoided publishing any positive reviews.[79]

If the "Jewish press" offered no reason for Catholics to condemn it, did not Catholics at least have reason to complain about the anti-Catholicism displayed by Jewish authors? In any case, Heinrich Heine and Ludwig Börne had the doubtful honor of being the authors most hated by Catholics. In 1836 the Catholic Church banned Heine's works. In 1891 alone, several papers on Heine appeared simultaneously, including an antisemitic pamphlet by the influential Viennese priest Sebastian Brunner as well as a biography by

Heinrich Keiter. The Jesuit *Stimmen aus Maria-Laach* warmly recommended both books to its readers, emphasizing that Brunner proved that Catholics should mount a resistance against Börne and Heine, the "shameless and characterless detractors of everything that is holy." Until now, the paper continued, Heine "had set the tone in the Jewish press—today he is still the author of choice of the playboy set and . . . of the happy-go-lucky, fairer sex. . . . Hopefully people will finally realize now, at least in Catholic circles, that every woman and every girl should be ashamed of herself if she even touches the works of a poet like this . . . [and] that the miasma of intellectual decay which contaminates his works" is a serious danger.[80]

Biting irony runs through Heine's works. In fact, he wrote a few precarious anti-Catholic sentences which would have been interpreted as being anti-Jewish if a non-Jew had directed them towards a Jew. "Those who are familiar with my satirical talent, my wantonness, and my need to parody will certainly testify that I was always kind to the clergy's human weaknesses," he writes in his *Confessions* of 1854. On the other hand "in my later years the devout, but nonetheless very vicious rats who rustle around in the sacristies of Bavaria and Austria, the rotten clerical vermin, often irritated me so much that I turned to resistance."[81] Elsewhere he accuses people who go to Holy Communion of "eating their God." He sees Catholicism as a systematic dulling of the mind. "In order to be Catholic, one does not need to know anything at all, one only needs to believe."[82] It must be borne in mind that Heine's childhood experiences in his Catholic hometown of Düsseldorf were not all pleasant. It had a population of 12,700 Catholics, 2,000 Protestants, and just 300 Jews. After a short flirtation with Catholicism, he converted to Protestantism in 1825—or rather, he was forced to convert in order to receive the degree of recognition he deserved. The anti-Jewish attitude prevalent in Christianity makes his aversion to it understandable. When considering the hatred and derision he showed towards Christian virtues, we must take into account the ghetto situation, the notorious experience of discrimination, and then the anti-Jewish "Hep-Hep" riots in 1819. "The Rabbi of Bacharach" is an attempt to come to terms with the Damascus Blood Libel of 1840 and the ritual murder legend (about Werner von Oberwesel who was allegedly killed by Jews, which originates from the thirteenth century).[83]

However, it is just as important to note that Heine did not shrink from any ironic observation, whether it concerned the nobility, the Germans, or any kind of orthodox religiosity. Heine held a cynical view of any kind of sanctimonious act or dogmatism. He also criticized Judaism, to which he certainly felt connected, but without a sense of belonging. He supported its fight for equality but showed little commitment to the religion, whether Orthodox or Reform. According to his individualistic point of view, Heine was suspicious of every institutional union, be it in the Jewish denomination with its customs, or in the Protestant Church. This was not obvious, however. Heine's criticism was regarded much more as a firm "Jewish" attack against the Catholic Church. It was not only Catholics who shared this view, but also Conservatives and later the National Socialists who, paradoxically, quoted Karl Kraus, the Viennese Jewish critic, to support their case. In the attacks on Heine, criticism of the modern age, education, and *Ortlosigkeit* (the feeling of not belonging) were reduced to a personal level and intensified. By reducing Heine to his Jewishness, his views could immediately be labeled as mistaken, instead of being understood.[84]

With his "blasphemy against Christ, Heine has manifested himself a Talmud Jew completely saturated with hatred," wrote Brunner. He was much afraid of the seemingly powerful "literary Jews" who, as a consequence of Heine's example, destroyed every critic. "The antisemitic bias which completely saturates Brunner's book, is . . . justified," acknowledged the *Historisch-politische Blätter,* commenting on Brunner's *Buschmänner.* Joseph Lerique's *Das Judentum in der deutschen Literatur* was just as fiercely critical. The author, a priest, condemned Heine and Börne as well as Moses Mendelssohn, Lessing, a few "brilliant Jewesses" (Dorothea Veit, Henriette Herz, Rahel Levin), Berthold Auerbach, and other writers, in addition to journalism and the book trade, which "is completely in the hands of the Semites." He wrote that the "corrosive" influence and the "superior power of the Semites" in society must be curbed. Antisemitism was, he believed, nothing more than a justified reaction to "Reform Judaism, which is cosmopolitan and anti-Christian to its very core."[85]

An analysis of anti-Catholic belles-lettres, especially from the period of the Kulturkampf, proves these accusations to be unfounded. It was by no means Jews, but rather Protestants and disloyal Catholics, who stood out as anti-Catholic authors. The contemporary historical novel purposefully incorporated contemporary issues and was unstinting in its mockery of priests. Felix Dahn's *Kampf um Rom,* for example, incidentally exposed the Donation of Constantine as a forgery and thus contested the legitimacy of the Papal States, whose loss was mourned by the Catholics after 1870. Between 1859 and 1878, 427 historical novels were written by 156 authors, the majority of whom were Protestants. Only 45 were Catholics, while there were no Jews evident among them. The contents of more than 90 percent of these novels were anti-Catholic.[86]

This denominational polemic was based on reciprocation. Protestants, Catholics, and those who were removed from the Church attacked each other vehemently. Thus the nineteenth century in Germany, the second confessional age, was characterized by the conflict between Protestants and ultramontanes which culminated in the Kulturkampf. It was not characterized by an imaginary Christian–Jewish conflict, as is also evident from literary sources. Those contemporaries who paid close attention to literature would have easily been able to refute the accusation that anti-Christian attitudes were a product primarily of Jewish literature, as was claimed. At the end of the nineteenth century Heinrich Keiter, editor of a Catholic newspaper, meticulously put together a list of works of literature in which priests, monks, Jesuits, or nuns—i.e., Catholicism as a whole—were attacked or mocked. Even the title is informative: "Confessionelle Brunnenvergiftung" [literally, Confessional Well-poisoning]: The True Ignominy of the Nineteenth Century." Keiter was referring directly to a remark made by Emperor Friedrich III (1888) who, when he was still the crown prince, had described antisemitism as "the ignominy of the century." Keiter contradicted the liberal-minded emperor's statement by claiming that the true ignominy of the century was anti-Catholicism. "Feelings of hatred towards Rome are being systematically cultivated. They are swelling and forming an avalanche, and antisemitism remains just a tiny ball in comparison." Keiter dramatized anti-Catholicism in comparison with antisemitism. His own book contained antisemitic insinuations.

In this context his phrase about anti-Catholicism being the true ignominy of the nineteenth century has a certain meaning, downplaying antisemitism and dramatizing anti-Catholicism. Yet, completely unaware of Keiter's insinuations in 1896, Michael B. Gross recently developed a similar comparative argument: Even though "anti-Semitism"[!] has undeniable importance for the history of Germany and indeed of Europe, "the nineteenth century in Germany with its particular confessional divide, modern rationalizing culture, and secularizing social currents was arguably more a century of anti-Catholicism." Gross certainly doesn't want to downplay antisemitism, and his observation about a "century of anti-Catholicism" certainly is based on evidence. On the other hand, he ignores anti-Protestantism among Catholics and confessional conflicts among Protestants, while anti-Jewish prejudices hardly play any role in his book. Because resentments were manifold, not just against Catholics, it would seem that the framework of a second age of confessionalism is able to cover more of the phenomena in the period after 1830. The Jesuit *Stimmen aus Maria-Laach* highly recommended Keiter's book with emphasis on its anti-Jewish attitudes: "A Jew only has to have a single hair harmed and there are immediately complaints about brutality, intolerance, an obsessive desire for persecution, and the ignominy of the century. If Catholics are ridiculed, slandered, and persecuted, then those same people who speak out against antisemitism are often the ones who say nothing, who gloss over it, approve it, or even join in."[87]

In fact, Keiter's blacklist includes just a few Jews or Christian converts of Jewish descent. Strangely enough, Heine, Börne, and Auerbach are missing; Fanny Lewald and Jacob Wassermann appear instead. The authors of many titles were anonymous and Keiter refrained from including further Jewish authors. Lewald (who died in 1889) had already converted to Christianity by the age of seventeen. She is reproached for having a "loving" monk commit suicide in her novel *Benedikt*. "The Jew Jacob Wassermann glorifies his racial comrades in the novel *Die Juden von Zirndorf*. In this work Agathon, a gifted youth and the personification of Jewish honor, takes revenge through murder on his torturer for the dishonor inflicted by a brutal Christian." Keiter also complains that in Wassermann's *Der Moloch* the poor young Jewess Jutta Elasser is kidnapped by nuns and never found again. "The degree of objectivity which the author shows towards the Catholics is evident from the fact that he writes of a priest: 'He had a mighty head, as large as that of an ox.' What would the Jews say if one were to. . .compare. . .a rabbi to an ox?"

These, however, are among the most harmless passages which Keiter cites. He quotes far more reprehensible passages from other, definitely non-Jewish authors, including Adolf Bartels, Felix Dahn, Gustav Freytag, Ludwig Ganghofer, Rudolf Gottschwall, Paul Heyse, Gottfried Keller, Luise Otto, and Emile Zola, whether about lecherous monks, violent priests, or sly Jesuits. It is significant that there are so few "Jewish" authors among the approximately 300 provocative titles cited and analyzed by Keiter in 1896. If there would have been more, certainly he would have found them. In the second edition of his collection, when he had by then (1908) come up with more than 420 titles, he succeeded in almost exclusively quoting Protestants.[88]

Accusations of antisemitism were in no way related to reality. In the second confessional age there were real and painful conflicts—between Catholics and Protestants, between the Catholic Church and the state, between Catholicism and liberalism, between Protestants and Protestants. But the claims that there was a Christian–Jewish conflict and a Catholic–Jewish conflict are based on imaginary phenomena. This conflict was one-sided: it came from Christians, was aimed at Jews, and was not reciprocated. The allegation that the Jewish people welcomed the Kulturkampf and that the

"Jewish press" or "Jewish literature" fought against the Church does not stand up to any thorough analysis of the Kulturkampf and the Jewish press.

Conflict: The Realistic View

The realistic approach offers a final opportunity to discover something "concrete" behind Catholic antisemitism. Yet how should realistic antisemitic views be defined?[89] Was Arnold Zweig's description realistic? In 1934, as a Jew faced with the National Socialist terror campaign, he emphasized in *Bilanz der deutschen Judenheit* the loss which Germany would suffer if it excluded the Jewish people:

> The German Jews are very much involved in the intellectual and social development of German life, in the useful elements just as much as in the harmful ones, in those which are beneficial just as much as in those which get in the way. The German Jews are merely human, they are not angels, and the things that people do when they are forced to merge together and socialize into modern ways can be unsettling and destructive.[90]

Descriptions of one's own group as well as of other groups can be both realistic and unrealistic. However, a different standard is applied more frequently to the out-group than to the in-group. Most judgments about groups contain positive or negative misjudgments which make it difficult to define "prejudices" and their relationship to "correct" judgments. Nevertheless the following question arises: Was there, in fact, a real group tension, a case of rivalry, or a correct observation hidden behind some of the descriptions of the Jews by the non-Jewish side, even if the non-Jews were occupied with negative emotions? As long as certain authors continue to maintain that antisemitism conceals a "kernel of truth," this question must be taken seriously and examined analytically. The topoi of the "Jewish" Kulturkampf and of Jewish anti-Catholicism in an allegedly "Jewish" and an actual Jewish press have already proved to be untenable. What about the theory that Jews were over-represented in the socio-economic and cultural spheres? We should avoid the premature dismissal of such arguments as "antisemitic" and instead present them as strongly as possible before offering counter-arguments. After all, there were statistics that showed where and how Jews were over-represented in certain areas.

It is true that antisemites frequently exaggerated these figures. In 1901, in a meeting of the parliamentary coalition, Georg Heim, leader of the Bavarian Center Party, complained that "we Catholics are becoming increasingly worse off. The judges always seem to be Jewish and their numbers are increasing alarmingly. Jewry always counts on the destruction of everything." He wanted to limit the number of Jews in the legal administration (*Justizverwaltung*) so that it would be proportionate to the Jewish population. This was important, he claimed, since soon a third of all judges would be Jewish. "If this trend continues, then all judges could be Jews in six years' time, and then we Catholics can pack our bags, adieu, Catholicism!"[91] Heim has outrageously dramatized the real figures, especially since there should have actually been more Jewish judges when we take the number of Jewish law students into account.

The issue is more complicated when the numbers are correct. Antisemites often complain about the large number of Jewish bankers, for example. In actual fact, in Prussia in the year 1855 there were 513 bankers of which 385 were Jews, writes Jewish historian Arthur Prinz. In 1862, 550 out of 642 bankers were Jewish. "Due to their large numbers, they [the Jews] had already left their mark on the German banking profession and it was to have a lasting effect for decades afterwards."[92] German Jewry's rise to social and economic success is indisputable. Whereas most Jews accounted for a large part of the marginal and lower classes around 1830, the number had decreased to only 10 percent by 1870. About two-thirds of the Jews now belonged to the financially secure and educated middle class.[93] This is not the place to recount the history of the German Jews before and during their emancipation and the problems of their German-Jewish identity. Yet it is true that the average Jewish tax payment around 1900 was approximately seven times as high as that of the Catholics and more than three times the amount of the Protestant equivalent.[94] However, such statistics are worthless in this respect, since they give the impression that the Jews were overrepresented as a group. In fact, every person reached his goal in his own way and as an individual. Any cohesion, any presence of Jewry as a group, is a static projection. It was Gentiles and non-Gentiles who believed in these projections.[95]

Jewish author Jakob Wassermann, for example, proudly proclaimed in 1898 that he was able to confirm that "Jews control all aspects of public life. The banks, the press, theater, literature, and social organizations, everything is in Jewish hands." This claim is just as exaggerated as the antisemites' distorted views. Wassermann overlooked Jewish under-representation in other areas, for example in parliament, where just ten out of 512 MPs were Jewish.[96] Then again, there were a very great number of Jewish solicitors and doctors compared to the proportion of the Jews in the population. Less successful groups saw such discrepancies as cause for complaint. The Catholic milieu was actually one of the most underdeveloped groups whose members complained bitterly of discrimination, inequality, and inferiority.

This also applied to the lack of symmetry in the cultural sector. Jewish journalists were indeed very prominent. "The Jews," writes Prinz, "were among the pioneers of this profession from the beginning."[97] But why were others, such as the Catholics, unable to keep up with them? Even today Catholic historians use secularization to explain the difference between Jews and Catholics, the former being, on average, far better educated than the latter. They claim that this development deprived the Catholics of an equal chance. The secularization of 1803 should not be underestimated, yet the Catholics' lack of education goes back much further. In the nineteenth century it was encouraged even more by the Church, which preferred young men to be trained for the priesthood rather than for an academic profession. In 1897 Catholic MP Georg Hertling mercilessly accused his fellow-believers of being too "*afraid* of science" [emphasis in original] and for taking pleasure in "pronouncing all . . . scientific progress a threat to traditional Christian doctrine." In rural and lower middle-class circles the lack of interest in grammar school and university education was, he said, depressing. "From the outset people have little or no interest in young men becoming officials or even secular scholars." Parents, he claimed, were only proud when their sons entered the priesthood.[98]

As far as Protestants (and Jews) were concerned, their familiarity with and attachment to their "holy books" was greater than that of the Catholics, who relied on traditions, rites, and images of holy phenomena, as well as the mediating function of the clergy. Long before Jews were emancipated, they held education (at first considered to be simply knowledge of the Talmud) in high regard. Increasingly, they took their children away from Jewish schools and attempted to establish contacts with grammar schools and universities. Education proved to be socially open and, therefore, something to which they could aspire. Out of all groups "in the empire, the intellectual lifestyle was most strongly pronounced among . . . the Jewish educated bourgeoisie [*Bildungsbürgertum*]." In comparison, the "anti-intellectualist structure of the Catholic education system"[99] opposed this kind of lifestyle. Catholics suspected education of distracting people's attention from their religion and leading them to question the Church's divine authority. Harry Graf Kessler's recollection of the 1880s may apply to Protestants and Jews: "Describing someone as 'uneducated' [*ungebildet*] was the equivalent of describing an Englishman as 'ungentlemanly.' There was no greater insult."[100] Catholics saw things somewhat differently: describing somebody as "educated" was a sign of their contempt. They accused the Staatskatholiken and the Old Catholics, who had changed direction and gone over to Bismarck's nation-state, of "thinking they're educated" and said that such people were hardly likely to wear out the benches in church. The Deutsche Verein für die Rheinprovinz, comprised of Old Catholics, Protestants, and a few Jews, was described by ultramontanes in a deliberately offensive manner as "an educational organization."[101] According to Rudolf Vierhaus, the term "education" (*Bildung*) had become the "preferred, principal term" in nineteenth-century Germany.[102] Catholics felt differently about that.

This is proof that even the German language was divided along denominational lines. The *Syllabus* had rejected "modern" education, in the belief that all that counted was superordinate truth, which was dictated by the Church. The Jesuit Theodor Mönnichs described the Church as the only true educational establishment, since it made the people moral and godlike. Its "education does not cost anything and does not demand that we attend a higher school. In the school of our own hearts everyone should and can satisfy their desire for education through self-cultivation."[103]

Time and again, in spite of these different connotations, Catholicism proved to be, structurally as well as intellectually, a latecomer where education was concerned. Hermann Cardauns, in 1912, reported candidly (and with significant quotation marks), on the founding of the Cologne Center Party: "It [the Party] didn't match up to the liberal rival initially, neither in representatives of 'education' nor in 'estate'. . .there was nothing the Cologne people found more intolerable than arrogant contempt or self-satisfied pride about education and property." With its claim that it was the sole legitimate representative, Protestantism divided the bourgeoisie because it demanded more from the Catholics than they could give, namely an anti-ultramontane denomination. In fact, Protestants combined education (which was held in high esteem and was almost a "substitute religion") (Wehler) with an anticlerical sentiment, which only increased Catholic mistrust of "educational piety" [*Bildungsfrömmigkeit*]. While Jews saw education as a means of advancement and a chance to approach the central Protestant culture, Catholics regarded it as an instrument of alienation from Christian educational ideals. Of course, there were also Catholic highbrow intellectuals and scholars, some of whom shared the anticlerical attitudes or even turned their back on the Church, and others who invested their spiritual assets in their work for the Church. However this does not change anything as regards the general skepticism evinced towards education, which continued well into the twentieth century.[104]

The statistics highlight the differences between the denominations with regard to their views on education, which did not escape the notice of contemporaries. Prussian university figures for 1887 show that Catholics were the eldest students and took the most time to complete their studies, whereas

Jews were the youngest and graduated most quickly. The Catholic paper *Stimmen aus Maria-Laach* bemourned the fact that in the universities there were only 20.12 percent Catholics (compared to 34.1 percent in the entire population) and 64.24 percent Protestants, but 9.58 percent Jews (instead of 1.3 percent). "In all matters" in which allowances are made for the "diversity of the religious denominations, the result for the Catholics appears to be extremely unfavorable; in comparison it is most flattering to the Jews."[105]

The effects of the second confessional age were visible in every school and university, but also in reading habits outside the educational system. Protestants did not go near Catholic books or newspapers. The "unwritten ban on books" went: "Catholica non leguntur." In their turn, Catholics made a point of not reading any "non-Catholic" texts.[106] Jews did not fear such contact. They read both Jewish and liberal papers. Protestants derived a feeling of superiority from their "educational religiousness" (*Bildungs-religion)*, to which the Catholics were only able to surrender or to emulate at great expense. While Jews gave a variety of new forms to civil society ideals in literature, art (also as patrons), science, and politics, and were regarded as "pioneers," almost "a paradigm of becoming bourgeois" (Volkov), Catholics lagged behind. Through their abstinence, they caused the middle class ("*bürgerlich*") way of life to appear essentially un-Catholic.[107] This, and not Jewish success, is one reason for Catholic resentment of Jews.

In the field of political ideology there was a further accusation, which crystallized in the phrase "Jewish National-Liberal Party." Indeed, Jews and liberalism demonstrated a significant proximity to one another. Their opponents claimed that the former controlled the latter. In actual fact, the majority of Jewish voters and MPs were inclined towards National Liberalism until 1878, when most swung round to left-wing Liberalism. The fact that social democracy was considered "Jewified" was not only based on the prominence of Karl Marx, Ferdinand Lassalle, Karl Kautsky, and later Karl Liebknecht and Rosa Luxemburg, but also on the increasing number of MPs in the Social Democratic Party who were Jewish or of Jewish descent. The accurate picture of Jewish MPs and their party affiliation is given in Table 2.

It could seem paradoxical that antisemites offered the same data and names to support their arguments as did contemporary Jews—such as Wassermann or Arnold Zweig—or modern historians, who want to demonstrate Jewry's "contribution" to German social history.[108] Therefore the figures alone, whether political or social, cannot explain antisemitic claims. Two other factors are much more decisive if antisemitism is formed by any "reality."

TABLE 2:

JEWISH MPS IN THE GERMAN PARLIAMENT BETWEEN 1867 AND 1918

Party	1867–78[1]	1881–92[2]	1893–1914[3]
Center	-	-	-
German Conservatives	-	-	-
Free Conservatives	4	1	1
National Liberals	12	1	3
Left-wing Liberals	5	8	5
Social Democrats	3	5	17

[1] Zollparlament, Reichstag, and Bundesrat.

[2] Reichstag and Bundesrat.

[3] Only Reichstag.

Source: Jacob Toury, *Die politische Orientierung der Juden in Deutschland: Von Jena bis Weimar* (Tübingen 1966), 124, 193, 229–30.

1. The data alone do not reflect the historical and social factors on which they were founded. Centuries of discrimination excluded Jews from various professions. Ironically, restrictions introduced by the Christians forced them into specific occupations in the fields of trade and finance. Agriculture was the declining sector in the nineteenth century, a decline that occurred side by side with Jewish emancipation. It is no wonder that Jews did not enter into this profession, although antisemites demanded it and some Jews tried to convince other Jews to do so in order to improve the Jewish image in society.

Emancipation opened up new possibilities for Jews. The desire to acculturate and gain social recognition led many to take up an academic career, but further obstacles were put in their way. It was rarely possible for a candidate of Jewish origin or Jewish faith to become an officer, judge, or university professor, let alone an official. In 1875, only 1.4 percent of full professors were Jewish, and in 1917 they still accounted for only 2.5 percent—25 professors in all. It is no wonder that there was a huge backlog of *Privatdozenten*—lecturers who were not members of the salaried university staff: in 1875, 13.5 percent of them were Jews and another 5.3 percent were baptized Jews, while in 1910 11.9 percent were Jews and 7.3 percent were baptized Jews. In professions such as high-school teaching (either with permanent civil servant status or in non-Jewish schools) Jews were excluded to an even greater extent. They were completely barred from becoming public prosecutors. Many Jewish people therefore turned to the professions that were still open to them, becoming lawyers, doctors, journalists, bankers, or industrialists.[109]

2. We have presented some data. But the crucial question is, how does perception select certain data in order to present them as facts which are subject to evaluation? Sartre hit the nail on the head when he said that people did indeed complain that there were many Jewish lawyers, "but is there any complaint that there are too many Norman lawyers?"[110] In this respect it is actually antisemitism that creates negative facts out of "correct" data. This invalidates even the strongest revisionist-apologist argument, which is based on real group tensions, on rivalry and conflict. There was certainly tension between groups. Jews sought emancipation and Christians of all denominations tried to prevent it. However, we cannot blame Jews for having longed for equal civil rights, whereas the Christians can be criticized for having let this provoke such fear in them. The real conflict did not emanate from the Jews in the socio-economic sphere. It had not been their objective to reach their position in the economy and society "as Jews" but rather as trained lawyers and doctors or successful industrialists, who did not compete with Catholic or Protestant rivals but with other members of the same profession. Therefore we are dealing with a question of an "imagined" conflict by the Christian side which is not the cause, but the product, of antisemitic prejudice.[111]

In contrast to Jewish conduct, many Catholics actually behaved and worked *as Catholics*. While they took refuge in a "milieu" in the battle against the modern age and developed an exclusive ghetto mentality, Jews, in contrast, were released from their ghetto. They took advantage of the opportunities offered by bourgeois civil society, and certainly did not intend to seal themselves off from society. Contrary to the opinion of some researchers subsequent to David Sorkin, they did not create a "subculture." Catholicism, on the other hand, formed an entire sub-society, with its own political party, organizations, literature, and so on. It was not until the end of the nineteenth century that the process of dissimilation began among many Jews—as a desperate reaction to antisemitism, which was becoming increasingly radical.[112] Three conclusions can be drawn from this significant difference.

First, it renders the naive comparison between anti-Catholicism and anti-semitism invalid, since Catholicism, a minority compared with Protestantism but a majority in comparison to Judaism, had willfully and consciously built up a counter-culture. Its members, who behaved firmly as Catholics, were thereby endowed with a claim to universal truth and hoped to shape "Christian" society according to Catholic ideals. The Jews had no intention of constituting an alternative culture. Their tendency was to become acculturated Germans who did not try to behave overtly as Jews when engaging in their various occupations. This is especially evident in patronage, for example. Jews were overrepresented in this area, supporting artists and collectors, yet the patrons did not behave primarily as Jews but rather as citizens who had experienced exclusion as Jews and particularly wanted to prove themselves in civic society.[113]

Second, this discrepancy between Catholicism and Judaism distorted Catholic perceptions of Jewish behavior. Catholic journalists, as loyal Catholics upholding the traditions of Catholicism, were obliged to write for Catholic media. It is not surprising that they expected the same from Jewish authors.[114] They often could not comprehend that a Jewish editor of a non-Jewish paper did not write as a Jew, for Jewry, or to safeguard the principles of Judaism, but out of political interest or simply from a desire to instruct and inform. Of course, the journalists who wrote for explicitly Jewish newspapers did write first and foremost as Jews; however their number was so small as to be insignificant. As is evident, they did not attack Catholicism at all. Their spectrum of opinion was certainly not as homogeneous as that of the Catholics, but was divided between orthodox and liberal positions. The percentage of Jews in journalism was always exaggerated. It was claimed that they dominated the press; in fact, they accounted for less than 8 percent of all German journalists.[115]

Third, the asymmetry between the relative, intentional Catholic unity and Jewish heterogeneity suggests that the popular view of "Jewry" was biased. Some Jews viewed this in a similar way, refusing to be seen as a group. In 1912 the *Israelitische Wochenblatt* discussed this topic, this at a time when some Jewish "dissimilation" had already begun as a response to German society, which prevented Jewish integration. The weekly admired German Catholics' "military display" [*Heerschau*] at a "Catholic day" in Aachen. "The Catholics of Germany constitute a minority, even if it is not as small as the Jews, and its power does not originate from the mass, but from cleverness and unity. Even though the Catholics differ on many issues, they stand as a closed phalanx whenever they have to defend their ideals, as a force for protection and shelter. And they created an admirable organization," which, notwithstanding their values, aroused respect among Jews. "What a lot we Jews could learn from these Catholics!" If this minority was united, it could achieve great things. "Yet we are distracted and split up into different parties and groups. German Jewry seldom appears to be united. It seems that the party spirit is stronger than any religious sentiment." In addition, the paper claimed, many Jews were too shy to admit to being Jewish. These times were serious, but the "awful fragmentation of the Jewish powers" was obvious. "What we lack above all is unity."[116]

The *Israelitische Wochenblatt* had a normative vision, but was pained by the fact that it was not reality. There was neither Jewish unity nor, logically, one Jewish press. While the non-Jewish periodicals in which Jews or people of Jewish origin were involved certainly covered a wide political spectrum, reaching from the far left to the extreme fringe of conservatism, even the "truly" Jewish press stretched from a national-Zionist position, through an Orthodox one, to Reform Jewish and left-wing liberal stances. Whatever was visible on all levels—in the community, in Jewish organizations, and in student associations—was also clearly reflected in the Jewish press, as well as among the practicing Jewish journalists who were employed in the non-Jewish press, not to mention assimilated Jews.[117]

Although the claim that the Jews were responsible for the Kulturkampf has been refuted, some people may still insist that antisemitism was related to a certain reality. How far is it necessary to go in order to prove wrong certain anti-Jewish stereotypes? Anyone who continues to cling to the notion that a Jewish "reality" existed behind the antisemitic curtain, even when faced with these findings—Catholic self-exclusion and Jewish inclusion, the very different roles of Catholic and Jewish journalists, as well as of the heterogeneity of Judaism—would have to go as far as to say that the SA men were "right" in scrawling the word "Jew" on shop windows. As long as the owners of the shops were actually Jews, then this act was connected to a "reality." This example shows how little the search for "realities" is able to contribute to the explanation or even justification of antisemitic actions or patterns of interpretation. Labeling such shops as "Jewish" (as was done across the length and breadth of Germany on 1 April 1933) emphasized a single group characteristic—one that was obviously considered particularly negative—and made it solely responsible for other things (for the proprietors' supposed faults or for the economic conduct of Jews outside of Germany). Those whose goods were very cheap were regarded with just as much suspicion as those who set their prices high, but this was irrelevant. Discrimination depended entirely on the construction that the antisemite made of the Jew, on the values that he rejected, and on those that he defended. In the figurative sense, the same thing also applied to the "real" involvement of Jews in liberalism, socialism, or capitalism, in the modern age, and in the project of a civic society in general.[118] Despite the fact that rejection of these phenomena had preceded antisemitism, they continued to be rejected in any case, and such rejection was reinforced by the tendency to condemn things as "Jewish" by simply calling them "Jewish." Antisemitism functioned as a partial element of a dichotomy of values in which the positive values were labeled as Christian (or German) and non-Jewish, and the negative ones as Jewish.

This context, which makes it possible to explain the antisemitism of individual groups, also contradicts those who regarded antisemitism in itself as a complete "ideology," as a "Weltanschauung," the preferred German term at the time. Sartre called it a "passion" and a "conception of the world."[119] It is also often considered a "world-view" in modern antisemitism research, a world-view which "appears well-rounded, logical" to the antisemites.[120] With this approach it is easy to lose sight of the context in which antisemitism was bred. There was a latent antisemitism, which was not organized and not a coherent ideology. A person may have various views on a wide variety of different subjects. But if he grew up in the "age of ideologies" he usually had but one world-view in the sense of an entire system that controls his interpretation of reality.

If antisemitism is supposedly a world-view, what, then, is the place of other ideologies such as conservatism, Catholicism, Protestantism, socialism, or liberalism? Catholics understood the system which accompanied them from the cradle to the grave, structured their day, and determined their company and thoughts, feelings, and perception as being a world-view. Their resentment of others, which is built into the encompassing system, can only be considered a partial world-view.[121] This ideological and social context enables determination of the character of antisemitism.

The term "Jew" in itself could be ambiguous. If a non-Jew hurled it at a Jew with an insulting tone of voice, then it was anti-Jewish. If, on the other hand, a Jew used it himself to describe other Jewish people, it was possibly a positive signal of his affiliation to them. On a complex level this means that a combination such as "Jews and Liberals" cannot be interpreted correctly without taking into account the speaker and the situation in which he uses the phrase. If a Catholic were to use it he would be putting together two terms that already had negative connotations, forming a distinctly negative combination. If Jews or liberals were to utter the very same words, they would be combining positive elements to produce a generally positive phrase. Thus it is impossible to categorize individual stereotypes without taking into account the contexts of each respective world-view. This is what has earlier in this volume been termed speaker-ideology dependence, in contrast to semantic dependence. The negative usage of "Jews and liberals" alone lets us draw conclusions as to the ideology of the speaker—in the context under discussion it was Catholicism, which was obviously both anti-Jewish and anti-liberal. Antisemitism says more about its agent than about the object of its hate.

What is the consequence of this argument? It means that rather than examining particular instances of antisemitism on the basis of Jewish "realities," we must attempt to relate it to the attitudes of the group in question. We need to thoroughly understand an individual's ideology and values in order to be able to establish why that person described certain phenomena as "Jewish" and whether he or she was degrading these phenomena by doing so. Social democratic laborers, for example, targeted not only Jewish employers but also non-Jewish ones as being "Jewish," yet were hardly antisemitic otherwise and were not at all interested in the Freemason networks. Catholics, however, were terrified by them: they believed Freemason lodges to be extremely Jewish.

To summarize, then, it is apparent that all three levels—conspiracy (the chimerical attitude), construction (the xenophobic attitude), and conflict (the realistic approach)—are certainly useful. They are necessary for arguing against revisionists and apologists, but in the final tally do not provide a sufficient explanation for the phenomenon of antisemitism on the basis of its target group. The chimerical, xenophobic, and realistic attitudes have already been examined often enough, at least implicitly. What has been lacking until now is a critical examination of the accusations that were leveled mostly by Catholics. Until recently, apologists, untroubled by better insight, have therefore been able to maintain that the "Jewish press" and many Jews had led hate campaigns against the Catholics during and after the Kulturkampf. That charge is based on the uncritical acceptance of Catholic antisemitic complaints. Empirically, this has been shown untenable. On closer inspection, it has proven necessary to examine the antisemites rather than the role of the Jews. The thesis of a real conflict is the weakest explanation of all. In contrast to the *Realkonfliktthese,* the argument of a substitute-conflict has been favored. It is the superior explanation since there were real conflicts; these, however, were not between Catholics and Jews but rather between Catholics and other opponents. In the broader context of the *Ersatzkonfliktthese,* various other approaches can be identified, which, in contrast to the *Realkonfliktthese,* offer superior alternatives in the search for the causes of Catholic antisemitism.

Explaining Catholic Antisemitism without Jews

Academic attempts to unearth the real causes of modern antisemitism have clearly intensified since 1945, especially since the 1960s. A wide range of disciplines have been involved, including research of stereotypes and prejudices, social psychology, history, sociology, and—of course—the newer discipline of antisemitism research. They all support various main emphases and tackle the issue from a wide variety of perspectives. In fact, antisemitism cannot be explained monocausally, just as Auschwitz cannot be traced back to a specific aspect of "German" behavior (Goldhagen). Combining various approaches definitely helps, though this approach is not as easy to sell as are simple explanations. Yet, as we have seen, not all approaches are valid. Some are more convincing than others, since a few prominent theses contribute little to the explanation of antisemitism within Catholicism. Other models of explanation prove to be totally inaccurate on closer inspection, because they do not seem to have moved beyond the conceived horizon of antisemitism. Antisemitism in its own right was indeed successful because it offered a simple explanation, and whenever researchers offer simple explanations for the causes of antisemitism—for example, that all Germans were to blame (Goldhagen) or that it was the fault of the Jews (Lindemann)—they are simply repeating antisemitism's complexity-reducing mechanism.

In the following examination twelve theories will be identified as important. That is not to say that there are not many more variables which have been responsible for the development, expression, and varying intensity of antisemitism, such as gender, descent, occupation, education, personal experience, life circumstances, situation, and more. To begin with, the central, non-mutually exclusive theses and approaches will be listed briefly.[122]

1. The *thesis of a real conflict (Realkonfliktthese)* is based on the belief that tensions exist between Jews and Christians. It attempts to demonstrate that antisemitism originates from genuine group tensions.

2. In comparison, the *thesis of a substitute conflict (Ersatzkonfliktthese)* supports the notion that Jews serve as scapegoats for a different conflict, which might be a real one. It explains antisemitism as having derived from conflicts other than those between Jews and Gentiles.

3. The *tradition theory* refers to the idea of eternal antisemitism. It implies that antisemitism stems from an unreflecting observance of tradition.

4. The *local tradition theory* refers to specific local traditions, which can date back as far as the High Middle Ages. It suggests that antisemitism was rooted in local traditions.

5. The *urban-rural discrepancy* takes as its starting point the hypothesis that prejudices are more pronounced in the countryside and are neutralized through urbanization. It cites an anti-modernist backwardness as the cause of antisemitism.

6. The *socio-historical theory* examines the antisemites themselves and attempts to prove that antisemitism was triggered by the social and political interests of identifiable individuals and groups.

7. The *economic crisis theory* suggests that periods of economic decline trigger waves of antisemitism. It explains antisemitism as having economic roots.

8. The *socialization theory* assumes that upbringing and school are ultimately responsible for antisemitic attitudes. It argues that antisemitism is the product of education.

9. The *authoritarianism theory* denotes a school of thought that recognizes the influence of authoritarian views in certain collectives. It suggests that antisemitism originates from certain collective psychological dispositions.

10. The *minority theory* is the name given to the claim that the quantitative status of a group within a society influences the extent of its xenophobia. It attempts to demonstrate that antisemitism is triggered by the pressurized situation of a minority group.

11. The *ultramontanism theory* suggests that this specific fundamentalism, the dogmatic, ultramontane stiffening of attitudes towards all aliens, is responsible for hostility towards the Jews. It specifically cites ideological-religious guidelines as the cause of antisemitism.

12. The theory of *functionalism* examines the advantages of anti-Jewish stereotypes. It explains antisemitism as a product of the functions that it can perform.

Conflict Theory

Because it is so prominent, the *Realkonfliktthese* (conflict theory) has become the focus of the present study. There is no need for a detailed repetition of the arguments that speak for and against it. The term which is often used to explain the theory—the "Christian–Jewish conflict"—suggests a mutual feud, as though Jews had attacked Christian society just as Christians attacked Jews. Sure enough, there was Jewish resistance to antisemitism, but this can not be interpreted as aggression. What is meant by Jews attacking Catholics is aggressive, anticlerical, or anti-Christian behavior from the Jewish side. The *Lexikon für Theologie und Kirche,* which was republished without revision in 1986, complained in 1961 about "anticlericalism, which, promoted by liberal Jewish newspapers, especially *Die Neue Freie Presse,* caused Christian thought to become completely extinct in many people."[123] In his classic 1954 study *The Nature of Prejudice,* Gordon W. Allport talks of "the assessment of the stimulus object," but only after having first dealt with five other explanatory models (the historical, socio-cultural, situative, etc.).

The *Realkonfliktthese* takes the "well-earned reputation" and the notion of a "kernel of truth" as its starting point, as though the minority being assessed actually exhibited some characteristics ascribed to them. Allport took great care in preparing his report on this assessment, unlike those historians who try to pass off Jewish practices and views as cause for Catholic reaction.[124] Lindemann's view is particularly striking: "The most obvious material factor" for the "growth of modern antisemitism—though not of course its deepest origins—is the rise of the Jews. It was not a fantasy but rather a perfectly real, measurable, and understandable development."[125] This looks very much like a monocausal explanation. But Lindemann has other things to offer, which unfortunately turn out to be basically rhetoric: "It is far too simple to say that the rise of Jews in Germany, and particularly in the Weimar Republic, 'explains' the triumph of Nazism, but it verges on the absurd to insist that the presence, activities, or nature of Jews in Germany had nothing whatsoever to do with the success of the Nazis."[126] It shows absolute ignorance of the results of any research into German history and the Nazi movement to claim that it was the Jews who were responsible for their persecution.

Certainly, antisemites did instrumentalize the presence of Jews in business and society for their own purposes. But to make Jews responsible for the rise of the National-Socialist movement would be to ignore hundreds of reasons which, in a clever combination, explain this in a much more satisfactory way: the German special path [*Sonderweg*], Versailles and the feeling of being suppressed and exploited, the myths of the "stab in the back" (*Dolchstoß*) and of an international conspiracy against Germany, deep-rooted and rising nationalism, the wide acceptance of antisemitism and the weak acceptance of democracy, the economic disasters of Weimar, charismatic leadership and the longing for a *Führer,* the role of the elite in the 1930s, the attitudes of the "lost generation" (born around 1900) which had confidence in Hitler, etc. Instead of presenting a distinguished hierarchy for the reasons which led to the Nazis' success or antisemitism, Lindemann concentrates on the Jews. He concedes that the rise of Jews does not explain everything, leaving his reader expecting him to cite a further reason. But what other reason does Lindemann put forward? "The absolute number of Jews, whether Jews are rising or not in other regards, also needs to be taken into account. It is simply untrue that the number of Jews in a given area is irrelevant to the Jew-hatred in that area." Finally he presents another explanation: "The nature of the Jewish population, whatever its numbers, in a given country is also important in influencing that country's attitude for Jews." So, if we sum up Lindemann's approach, he comes up with three reasons for antisemitism, all of them resting on the shoulders of the Jews. Lindemann cannot be blamed for basing his explanation of antisemitism merely on the rise of the Jews in modern times. There are other factors, the second reason being the number of Jews. But the rise and the number of Jews are not sufficient. There is a third reason that explains antisemitism: the nature of the Jewish population, what Jews believed and how they behaved.[127]

Compared with those three major reasons all the other explanations Lindemann offers (prejudices, antisemitic traditions, nationalism, crisis, etc.) have the function of a fig leaf, concealing the monocausal dilemma of his approach. In the end, all blame is put on the Jews. Lindemann vehemently defends the argument that there were "tensions between Jews and non-Jews in the 1870s and 1880s." "Since the aversion of Gentile to Jew and Jew to Gentile is deeply embedded in their respective traditions, the two groups are unlikely, without fundamental changes in their identities, to arrive at a lasting harmony in the foreseeable future."[128] If this mutual aversion really existed, then why did so many Jews integrate into German society and participate in its national projects? Why do we not find evidence for this tension in the Jewish sources? Why did more than 10,000 Jews voluntarily report for military service in 1914? How is it that 78,000 Jews fought bravely for their German fatherland, of whom 30,000 were awarded medals for bravery and 12,000 were killed in action? Most German Jews saw the war as a chance to finally prove that they felt themselves to be, and were, "good Germans." There is no evidence whatsoever to support Lindemann's notion of mutual aversion. There was only one-way aversion.

For analytical rather than moral reasons the *Realkonfliktthese* is the most unsuitable of the twelve assessments listed above. It is much more useful as a way of steering away from the actual causes instead of getting to the bottom of them, not to mention the fact that its implications are antisemitic.

Substitute Conflict Theory

For a long time the theory of a substitute conflict, the *Ersatzkonfliktthese,* has been the standard, and it still is. Ultimately, all of the following theses introduced here can be subsumed to it, insofar as they start out with the assumption that animosity against Jews offered an outlet for other conflicts: a scapegoat was sought in moments of crisis. Socialization gave birth to the concept of the enemy and constructed imaginary conflicts. The advantage of the *Ersatzkonflikthese* consists in its making the antisemites themselves responsible for antisemitism, rather than the Jews. Yet this approach is just the first step in the right direction. Its weakness lies in its vagueness, for it does not clarify which conflicts require an alternative solution and why the

Jews in particular came under fire. Therefore further steps must be taken and other theses must be analyzed and refined in conjunction with this one. Above all, the world-view of the group in question must be examined in detail, in order to identify the role it assigns to the negatively labeled Jews. The world-view of the group examined in this study was determined by ultramontanism, which was attached to particular traditions.

Tradition Theory

The *tradition theory* is based on the assumption that antisemitism is a phenomenon of *longue durée*. This theory represents one of the oldest attempts to explain antisemitism among Catholics in the nineteenth century. It is quite rightly reminiscent of the long lines of continuity of Christian antisemitism. Until quite late into the twentieth century the Catholic view of Jews was characterized by traditional stereotypes, above all the accusation that they murdered Christ, and God's threat to disperse the Jewish people. Medieval myths about sacrilege of the Host and ritual murder were regarded with particular horror in pious Catholic circles, while the stereotype of the Jewish profiteer, which is hundreds of years old, remained one of the stock prejudices of every denomination. Goldhagen, in his recent work, concentrates on the 2000-year-old tradition of Catholic antisemitism and maintains that even the New Testament should be rewritten, since he detected hundreds of antisemitic proclamations there.[129] There is no doubt that the survival of these traditions formed the basis of modern antisemitism. Their long duration supports the tradition theory and has led to the exaggerated expression: "eternal antisemitism."

The weaknesses of this approach has been vigorously exposed by Hannah Arendt, who demonstrates that it loses all power of distinction with regard to the innovations of modern antisemitism. The distinctive feature of modern antisemitism is not racism alone. Modern antisemitism targeted the emancipated Jews, whereas the traditional form of antisemitism was embedded in a Christian society in which Jews were not emancipated. The latest form of antisemitism in the nineteenth century suggested that the Christians now had to emancipate themselves from the Jews. The idea was put forward that the Jews strived for financial might, world power, and prestige, and in addition attempted to achieve cultural dominance by "Jewifying" society. Many of these modern elements had been inconceivable in earlier times. All this notwithstanding, the theory of eternal antisemitism has found its particular niche in popular scientific accounts. "Eternal Jew-hatred" has been the topic of many books.[130] Gerhard Czermak claims that the antisemitism of the first century, "changing in detail, yet without ceasing . . . led . . . to the ovens of Auschwitz."[131] The tradition theory errs about more than just the changing features of antisemitism. It is also too simple to encapsulate all the facets of modern post-emancipatory antisemitism. It does not explain why certain groups proved to be especially susceptible to this syndrome at specific points in time. It overlooks the fact that many traditions did not simply survive, but had to be reinvented in the nineteenth century. The phenomenon of inventing traditions in nationalism is well documented.[132] The traditionalization of anti-Talmudism and of the nearly forgotten ritual murder legend, which turned up again in Germany for the first time in Dormagen in 1819, corresponded to an act of transformation, in the same way in which Neo-Scholasticism changed Scholasticism, or that nationalists picked out suitable events and personalities from history to serve as a constructed continuity of their own nation.

Local Tradition Theory

Unlike the previous approach, the *local tradition theory,* according to which specific local traditions are responsible for an anti-Jewish climate, manages to at least consider regional differences. Ascribing national or regional differences in the degree of antisemitism to the presence of Jews is in no way satisfactory. "The size of the Jewish community is an element of the explanation," Lindemann claims. The countries of "happy exile," like England with its low level of antisemitism, had a small Jewish population of 2 percent or less. When the number rose above 5 percent, Lindemann calculates, there was a significant expression of antisemitism; when it neared 10 percent, as in Poland, the likelihood of severe antisemitism was high. Lindemann explicitly rejects the idea of antisemitism without Jews.[133]

There is a plethora of examples proving the opposite. In Austria severe antisemitism could be observed in the Vorarlberg region, even though few Jews were living there.[134] The same phenomenon applies to Baden. Most petitions against Jewish emancipation came from areas with few Jews. The French example, of which Lindemann should have been aware, is very striking. Though France had fewer Jews than the city of Berlin, antisemitism was as widespread there as in Germany. In Bretagne, Normandy, royalist Vendée, Poitou, Anjou, and Maine antisemitism was remarkably higher than elsewhere—but virtually no Jews lived there. The reason for antisemitism—as usual—lay elsewhere, in an aversion to the principles of 1789, combined with the newly revived Catholic ideology, defending itself against laicism.[135]

Analyses of elections and, most recently, the study by Stefan Scheil, show how core zones developed from the 1890s onwards in which the antisemitic parties could be sure of their success. In the constituencies of Hessen, Kassel, and Saxony, for example, several times they received more than 50 percent of the votes. But, they met with distrust in areas with a Catholic majority. The Center Party, which rejected the rowdy antisemitism of these single-issue parties, was active there. Nonetheless, the Center promised its voters a "better" solution to the problem associated with the "Jewish Question." The scale of anti-Jewish propaganda in use in Catholic regions depended, as with the antisemitic parties, on talented demagogues. The antisemites, for example, employed Ernst Henrici and Hermann Ahlwardt, whereas the Center put forward men such as the journalist and chaplain Georg Friedrich Dasbach from the Mosel area. Karl Lueger and Adolf Hitler are further examples of "charismatic people" who successfully exploited antisemitism. "Great men" are always just one of several causes, but this is usually not over interpreted in the literature. Lindemann presents us with a veritable travesty of literature: "The tendency [where?] to dismiss antisemitism as a bizarre hallucination, a fantasy of diseased minds, is undoubtedly justified in some instances but has also often been overdone and has thus hindered understanding, for Jews have been disliked for many reasons by a very wide variety of normal people."[136] It is rather Lindemann's portrait of the literature which has a hallucinatory quality. In fact there are hardly any studies that depict antisemites as having "diseased minds." Most of the literature actually tries to implement various sophisticated approaches in order to explain antisemitism. But it is true that most researchers are aware that it does not aid our understanding of antisemitism if it is explained primarily with the notion of Jews being disliked for good reasons.

The argument that antisemitism depends on local traditions is enlightening with regard to certain regions such as that of the lower Rhine. Its inhabitants had been living off antisemitic resentment for centuries. There are certain places where an anti-Jewish tradition and memory was cultivated. Prominent examples of such "memories" were the small town of Bacharach, where it was claimed that Werner von Oberwesel was murdered by Jews in 1287, and the local veneration (until very recently) of Anderl von Rinn, who was allegedly slaughtered by Jews in 1462. Such "memories" were rather popular in Bavaria and Tyrol. The Deggendorf myth about the desecration of the Host is proof of this until this very day.[137]

The local tradition approach is less effective when it has to explain the functions as well as the uniformity of Catholic antisemitism, which was similar everywhere, from Silesia to the Rhineland and from Bavaria to the Münsterland.[138]

Urban–Rural Discrepancy

The *urban-rural approach* is linked with the regional-historical perspective. It is frequently suggested that the rural population, which regarded modern achievements with skepticism, would have been particularly susceptible to anti-Jewish propaganda. Thousands of peasants added their names to petitions against equal rights for Jews during the first half of the nineteenth century. These petitions often were preformulated by priests. The success of the propaganda by the *Bund deutscher Landwirte* (German Peasant's League) in the 1890s, as well as by various Catholic farmers' organizations, also supports this assertion.[139]

Was the lack of urbanization responsible for a greater degree of antisemitism? This idea is contradicted by an obvious counterargument, namely the fact that it was cities such as Adolf Stoecker's Berlin or Karl Lueger's Vienna, not rural areas, that became centers of the antisemitic movement. Yet this approach is helpful in highlighting the differences between urban and rural antisemitism.

Socio-historical Approach

The *socio-historical approach* is especially valuable. It takes into consideration the factors already mentioned—tradition, region, differences between village and city—but in addition it focuses on the perpetrators of antisemitism and their interests. It does not regard antisemitism as the protagonist but specific people, who wanted to have their politics carried out by parties and organizations. In fact, identifiable agents contributed to the varying severity of antisemitism. Ahlwardt, Henrici, Stoecker, and Lueger have already been named. Some of them were regarded as charismatic propagandists. Wherever Ernst Boeckel, the "Farmer-King of Hessen," made an appearance, garlands were strung up in his honor and the farmers flocked to see him, calling him "their arouser and redeemer."[140] Boeckel was the first Reichstag MP to register himself as an "Antisemite." His Catholic counterparts were Georg Friedrich Dasbach, a Center Party MP who even disseminated ritual murder propaganda before the parliament in 1893; Burghard von Schorlemer-Alst; and Alban Stolz, a popular writer of folk tales from Baden whose traditional works, bursting with anti-Jewish sentiment, were still being read well into the twentieth century. The Catholic clergy can be clearly identified as a supporter of antisemitism. They produced most of the antisemitic writings, and in their sermons from the pulpit on Sundays were able to lend Divine authority to the anti-Jewish opinions they spouted.[141]

However, the socio-historical approach of the agent leads us to regard the "people" as a seduced mass, just as does the Marxist idea of clerical fraud [*Priesterbetrugsthese*]. Were the officials and the recipients of antisemitism, then, not convinced by the anti-Jewish insinuations? Notwithstanding the breadth and plurality of social history, which is quite prepared to embrace and incorporate those approaches that are still to come, it often has not taken seriously enough the autonomous power of ideas, the details of discourses, and the sophisticated complexity of mentalities and religions. Without considering the topoi and their mental breeding ground, it is difficult to identify the effects of the development of antisemitic prejudice. It would not be satisfying to resort to a hasty explanation of everything as an outlet for social circumstances and socio-economic crises.[142]

Economic Crisis Theory

A very prominent socio-historical approach, typical of the 1960s, is the *economic crisis* model. In 1967 Hans Rosenberg produced a prototype which has since been very influential. According to Rosenberg, the rise and fall of antisemitism was "inversely proportional to the long oscillations of the economy and social tensions." The first of the three "long oscillations" was due to the "great depression" between 1873 and 1896. In the next phase of high industrialization, between 1896 and 1914, antisemitism had retreated. It increased again during the period of economic crisis between 1919 and 1939. This model also relates the short-term growth of antisemitism to falling stock prices.

Overall, however, this theory remains too reductionist. Rosenberg himself admitted that in 1879, when the career of political antisemitism across Germany started, the economy had only just begun to recover. The incubation phase was not a consequence of the stock market crash of May 1873. For much too long, historians have overlooked the fact that Catholicism had already begun its antisemitic revolt earlier.[143] There are several reasons for this: the First Vatican Council, the occupation of the Papal States, the founding of the "Protestant" empire, and the formation of Old Catholicism—but not the economy.

On the basis of the "Hep-Hep" riots in the village of Weisweiler (near Aachen) in 1834, Stefan Rohrbacher and Michael Schmidt proved that neither a social nor an economic crisis was their cause, but a rumor of ritual murder that had been circulated. Catholic superstitions and religious patterns of thought must therefore be brought into focus.[144]

Socialization Theory

Much time and energy was required to identify *socialization* as a "key factor" for the genesis of antisemitic attitudes. A higher level of education correlates with a smaller degree of antisemitism.[145] In any case, parents definitely influence their child's bias. "Children who can as yet hardly even talk learn to detest the name Jew like an evil demon," observed a Christian mother in 1847. The secondary instances of socialization then follow, first and foremost the primary school. Here children were acquainted with the "pettiness and exclusiveness of the Jewish law," admitted the Mainz-based journal *Katholic* in 1877, and the "rigorous particularism" of the Jews who, the pupils were told, despised all non-Jews. Antisemitic sentiment in young adults then became more firmly established at the university or in the theological seminary. There is no doubt that socialization—and the earlier the more successful—forms the basis of every long-standing resentment. We only need to examine the biography of a historical figure to identify what stirred up his or her antisemitism.[146]

On the other hand this very obvious approach does not explain why so many members of one group are afflicted by such socialization. Why are there behavioral differences in adulthood? Above all: Why did antisemitism appear especially vociferous at certain times and not at others? Studying the socialization of people in order to understand their prejudices is an important perspective. But this approach does not provide us with a clue about the content of these prejudices and about their significance in a given ideological context.

Authoritarianism Theory

For a long time many researchers saw in *authoritarianism,* as a structuring of personality, a solution for the explanation of prejudices. Here again, socialization plays a central role, this time not as the passing on of certain stereotypes but as the development of an "authoritarian personality." Scholars suggested that exaggerated discipline forced the individual to suppress physical needs, and he therefore had to direct his aggression at other, weaker objects. Sigmund Freud was clearly the inspiration for this concept, which was largely developed by Theodor W. Adorno in the 1950s. The individual who is servile to his parents, the Church, and the state is openly hostile towards members of alien groups. This theory was empirically supported by means of the F Scale (Fascism Scale), which measured democratic and fascist personal characteristics. Antisemitism is therefore just one component in a complex web of attitudes.[147] For Catholics, for whom one cannot produce an F Scale post factum, it would follow that their antisemitism was just one element of a whole inventory of views. This is correct. It was only one building block in the whole ultramontane complex and not even the fundamental one at that, unlike the belief in the Resurrection, for example. In addition, obedient serfdom towards bishops and priests formed a basic principle of ultramontanism. Christoph Weber not unreasonably interpreted ultramontanism as "fundamentalism."[148]

According to more recent studies, members of orthodox and fundamentalist denominations are more likely to develop a concept of Jews as the enemy than are supporters of a liberal religion. In any case, this is not generated by orthodoxy alone, but in conjunction with three of its basic principles: its particularism (its claim to divine truth), traditional anti-Jewish attitudes (such as "the Jews" killed Jesus), and religious hostility (God will punish the Jews).[149]

Adorno's studies of authoritarianism were controversial from the outset. They put entire societies at the risk of being pathologized. His approach can only account for individual differences in attitude within a society. It does not explain why prejudices came into being and passed, why it was Jews who were specifically targeted, or why antisemitism occurs in specific phases of intensity. Moreover, antisemitism was not always directed towards support for authority, but also against the authorities. At times antisemitism was a means of criticizing the ruling power and therefore destabilizing the system. The cultural norms that antisemites supported provide more information about the causes of their prejudice than does the psychoanalytical authoritarianism approach. Yet we must not lose sight of this important clue to the close connection between extreme dogmatism and marked aversion to foreignness.

Minority Theory

The *minority theory* can be helpful in explaining why Catholics, who made up only 36 percent of the population in Germany, perceived themselves to be a threatened group. They believed that the empire, dominated by *kleindeutsch,* Protestant, and Prussian powers, wanted to challenge their privileges and even their rights. When the Catholics were banned as "enemies of the empire" in the Kulturkampf they became even more united. At the same time they sought an explanation for this fierce conflict, whose traumatic aftereffects were still discernable as late as the 1950s. The Jews, it was soon concluded, were responsible (or at least partly responsible) for the "annihilation campaign" against Christendom. From their disadvantaged minority position the Catholics attacked the smaller Jewish minority, which they believed to be more powerful.

Yet, on the other hand, why are majorities or hegemonic groups antisemitic or racist, like German Protestants against Jews or American Protestants (WASPs) against black people? The minority theory can even be used to explain the opposite case. For the very reason that Catholics possessed much smaller resources and less power and were struggling for parity, they could not discriminate against another minority if they wanted to remain credible. If we apply this model to regional levels, it throws light on the fact that in areas where Catholics formed the majority, such as Bavaria, their antisemitism was all the more fierce. It appears that their minority status in Germany had a constraining function. In countries that were almost entirely Catholic, such as France or Austria, the bishops and priests competed with each other unrestrainedly in fanatical Jew-hatred, while Catholic politicians in Germany, led by Ludwig Windthorst, tried to curb the anti-Jewish demands of their fellow MPs and voters with the very egotistical minority argument.

Ultramontanism Theory

The *ultramontanism theory* has proved and confirmed in several investigations why Catholics supported the notion of "dual antisemitism." Few of them really condemned antisemitism and few, in turn, defended even more radical, also racial-ideological, positions. It is evident that ultramontanism, as a kind of ideological straightjacket, prefigured many views from the mid-nineteenth century onwards, whether they applied to saints or miracles, socialists or Jews.[150] Every day the cliché-filled ultramontane papers published the same auto-stereotypes about the pious flock and the same hetero-stereotypes about the terrible enemies outside the Catholic milieu. Anybody who "went astray" weakened the strong structure of the Catholic bloc. Mocking the Catholic "obsession with miracles," missing confession frequently, becoming a Freemason, reading a liberal-"Jewish" newspaper, marrying a Protestant, or defending the Jews too vehemently—all of these were forms of behavior which were likely to arouse suspicion in the milieu. Anyone found guilty of these "transgressions" risked being excluded or disciplined by his fellow Catholics or by the Church. Even Karl Bachem, a leading Catholic figure, had to put up with such trouble. In 1894 he dared object to a speech by the "Jew-eater" ["*Judenfresser*"] Liebermann von Sonnenberg, whose description of a "plague" of Russian Jews in the middle of a debate had nothing to do with the matter in hand—the trade agreement with Russia. The ultramontane *Gladbacher Merkur* attacked Bachem fiercely, accusing him of having behaved like an "unappointed 'Protector of the Jews'" in the Reichstag. How could a Catholic take sides against an antisemite? The paper condemned Bachem for having stabbed all respectable Catholic antisemites in the back. After all, it protested, Catholics did, at the very least, still have the right "to be allowed to speak out openly and honestly. . .about the ancient, cancerous element of destruction, against which the Catholic Church and the popes are constantly fighting, employing all possible preventative measures. . . : the parasitic Jews." With the obvious aim of exerting influence over Center Party MPs and isolating Bachem, the paper confessed that it must "hold Bachem's concern for the Jews against him." So "many men in the Center" would not "shrink from discussing the Jewish question openly and without unnecessary hesitation." It was high time, the *Merkur* proclaimed, that something was done. In view of the affinity between loyalty to the Papacy, piety, and xenophobia, it was certainly risky to ignore ultramontane pressure and express support for the Jews, even in passing. A second article, also on the front page, propagated the notion that to be "resolutely Catholic" one must also be firmly antisemitic.[151]

But why should the dualism of ultramontanism promote antisemitism? Did not other ideologies operate in a similarly dualist manner? The proletarian movement, for example, divided the world into two classes. It regarded employers, capitalists, and the military as the enemy of the oppressed. Antisemitic attitudes were also present here, but were mainly limited to "Jewish" bankers and entrepreneurs. Social Democrats were not interested in the countless other stereotypes. They actually rejected antisemitism as a diversionary tactic that was thwarting the revolution. "Antisemitism is socialism for idiots," declared August Bebel. Ultramontane dualism was differently formed. It was more extensive, it was based on a long Christian tradition, on its traditionalization, as well as on dogmatism and piety. This extensive dualism had to serve the various levels within the milieu and therefore had to produce many more enemies than did the workers. Antisemitic dualism was highly compatible with ultramontane piety, fundamental dogmatism, and universal dualism. They all offered a "dual schemism."[152] Judaism functioned as an "antithesis" of all positive values and as a label for all phenomena of which the ultramontanes disapproved. "Jewish" capitalism opposed Christian economic ideals, the "Jewish" obsession with criticizing things opposed Catholic obedience, and so on. "Christianity and Judaism are opposite poles, to the same extent as are German culture and Judaism," explained the best-selling ultramontane author Hans Rost in 1907. "The modern Jewish world-view emphasizes the earthly existence; Christianity lays emphasis on the next world. Because of this essential, conflicting difference, all advances and attempts at assimilation fail completely."

The correlation of the two dualisms, of ultramontanism and antisemitism, was significant. The only debatable issue was to what extent a minority group such as the Catholics should be allowed to identify themselves as such. Whereas radical voices in the 1890s, such as the "Catholic German" Philippikus, declared that it was necessary "to simply and officially confirm the antisemitism of Catholic Germany, which, to all intents and purposes, has been around for a long time," most played it down. Hans Rost recognized that antisemitism was implicit in the Catholic party and so did not have to be expressly written into its manifesto. Rost even likened the Center to the Antisemite Party and the German Conservatives. All three, he claimed, had suitable agendas against Judaism. In comparison, he accused the Social Democrats of not being "anti-Jewish": "The social and economic program of the Center Party in particular has no need to hoist a new antisemitic flag; it contains a denial of everything which is revealed to be harmful on the Jewish side."[153]

This correlation theory is confirmed by a comparison with other Catholics and societies. In France, for example, the tendency to antisemitism grew with the ultramontane denomination, but liberal, laical France—although it was also Catholic—categorically rejected superstition and antisemitism. The Old Catholics in Germany, who were National-Liberal, undogmatic, and opposed the pope, regarded "Jesuit" antisemitism as medieval. Later, many reform Catholics also turned against this propaganda, while others turned out to be enthusiastic about modern racism. It is certain that the great degree of dogmatism promoted antisemitism, whereas the very small extent of dogmatism among the *Kulturkatholiken* permitted various individual options.

Thus, it is evident that the ultramontanism theory is incomplete. First, it only applies to Catholicism and second, it has to be combined with other theories. It can be enhanced by the authoritarianism theory, but it must of course also take anti-Jewish national and local traditions into consideration, and furthermore take seriously the functions of antisemitism as an *Ersatzkonflikt*.

Functionalism

Functionalism is an approach that is concerned with the benefits and functions of antisemitism, in this case for Catholicism. Five advantages which Catholics expected from antisemitism can be distinguished:[154]

a) Counter-modernization: Catholicism openly confessed its hostility towards modernity, which the *Syllabus Errorum* had programmatically proclaimed in 1864. In order to defend this manifesto, the ultramontane followers of this anti-modern catalogue of vices branded its enemy "modern." The Jews in particular were suspected of being part of the modernizing process. Catholic steadfastness was "the most unbearable cruelty to the Jewish spirit," according to Albert Stoeckl, capitular at the Eichstatt cathedral (*Domkapitular*). In his 1886 book about the many "modern errors" he explained why the Jewish spirit was once again calling out the phrase "*Crucifigator!*" ("Crucify him!"). The word "Jewish" served as an insult, just as did the adjective "modern." Anything that was seen as modern, such as the "modern" press or the "Jewish" press, was stigmatized and must be boycotted. Antisemitism among Catholics was therefore a sign of their anti-modern attitude. At the same time it was a signal of counter-modernization, of active participation in the program to thwart the development of the modern age, to curb "de-Catholization" as they called it, and to introduce re-Catholicization. Therefore it was never reduced to a universal panacea, as with the antisemitic parties, because only the return to the Blessed Sacrament promised the desired effect. It focused not on the "Jewish question" but the "Catholic question." In 1881, the ultramontane *Augsburger Postzeitung* stated its case regarding the "antisemite petition" which called for annulment of parts of emancipation in 1880–1881. In an article concerning Christian home rule (*Hausrecht*), the newspaper declared that "only constitutional Christian authorities in the Christian state" could "give credit to this law and show it to its best advantage again, indeed by standardizing anew the emancipation of the Jews on the basis of the most generous . . . right to hospitality (*Gastrecht*)." It added that the Jews should, of course, not be granted "any authoritative position at all in the Christian family of people and nations."

This function of antisemitism was specifically Catholic. It motivated people to put their trust in the counter-modern utopia of re-Catholicization. Nonetheless it is true that antisemitism also functioned as a sign here, as a "code" for the rejection of the modern age in other conservative circles, whose utopian visions were different. Antisemitism as a "cultural code," a notion convincingly developed by Shulamit Volkov, divided society into two groups—those who stood up for emancipation, like many Liberals and the Social Democrats, and those who did not want to come to terms with it.[155]

b) Minimization of complexity: Stereotypes are an effective means of dealing with intellectually demanding, complicated problems and reducing their complexity. Reality was shaped as if there was only a single conflict which was raging between God and Satan, between the Church and the world. The Jews were among the enemies who attacked the bastion of Christ. "The founders and promoters of Social Democracy are primarily Jews," revealed Philippikus in 1893. The Jews were always trying "to get to the top." He compared the relationship between the Social Democrats and the Jews to that between a dog and its master. It was certain, he claimed, that the only solution to the present crisis existed in the "return to true Christianity." This mechanism also served as election propaganda which had certainly been picked up by the Christian Socialists in Germany and Austria. The following was published in the *Christlich-sozialen Blätter* in 1880: "If we treat the Jewish Question as a 'socio-ethical' scientific problem, we will not have much success with the majority of the population. . . . Such subtleties and abstractions have little effect on them. 'Don't vote for Jews,' everyone can understand that." Simple recriminations, which could also be reduced to a personal level, to "the Jews," or to "the Rothschilds," brought "light" into the dark machinations of a rapidly transforming world. These recriminations were a means of overcoming the great difficulties of the present—secularization and the Kulturkampf.[156]

c) Maximization of coherence: One of the main concerns of the milieu-managers,[157] the priests, and the professional Catholics (*Berufskatholiken*) was to maintain the idea of a unified Catholic community. This not only guaranteed the success of the Center Party but also boosted the sales of Catholic newspapers. This idea was flanked by the dualistic message that Catholic Christianity was surrounded by external enemies, a notion which was continually repeated. In 1880 the readers of Breslau's ultramontane *Deutsche Volksfreund* were informed that "the Jews" had realized that the press was a "world power" and had sneaked into it everywhere, "so that at present it is swarming with Semitic newspapers," including the *Frankfurter Zeitung* and the *Breslauer Zeitung*.

> It is difficult to conquer such a superior strength. . . . What is the point of the Christians fighting against the Jewish power when the Jews won't release their hold on the Semitic press? Those who are serious about the fight against Jewish domination should choose a Christian-Conservative circular as their personal newspaper; there are enough of them to choose from, after all.[158]

It is a well known fact that convincing images of the enemy increase the integration of the in-group. The Jews were perceived as an opponent, along with Liberals, Freemasons, Old Catholics, Social Democrats, and other godless people. A relatively unified sub-society generally has a relatively uniform subculture, a discourse that is based on common premises. The priests were well aware of how to keep their flock together and knew what they were doing when they branded their adversaries and Catholic trouble-makers, such as the Old Catholics, as "friends of the Jews." Center Party propagandists sensed what a deterring effect it had when they labeled their political opponents "Jews," and the editors of the Catholic newspapers noted carefully how sales increased when they reviled the "Jewish press." The homogeneity of the milieu was cemented by the exclusion of the "Jewish" enemies, the wish for a "pure" milieu free of Jews, the election to Parliament of the Center Party and the belief that it held the solution to the "Jewish Question," and the antisemitic, ultramontane press. The homogeneity of this milieu discourse can also be gauged with the help of the discussion about antisemitism. Everyone was aware that there were definite boundaries: racism, for example, was off-limits. Nobody had doubts about the existence of the "Jewish Question." And nobody doubted the accusation that the Jews had murdered God.

d) Compensation: The theory of the function of consolation and exoneration is very close to the *Ersatzkonfliktthese*. Both real conflicts, such as the Kulturkampf between the state and the Church, as well as over-dramatized crisis scenarios—particularly de-Catholicization—needed to be explained. There was suffering, and this provoked attempts to compensate for the suffering. Jew-hatred exposed the guilty party. It suggested a temporary half-solution; above all it raised the Catholic sense of self-esteem, which had been attacked. The tables could even be turned: Rost saw in Catholicism "the definitive culture ideal," in comparison to the "frightening moral inferiority of Judaism." The priest Georg Ratzinger, complaining about "Jewish" materialism, said that what appeared to be a success there arose simply from the "inferiority of the Jewish view and doctrine towards the Christian faith."[159] The utopia of re-Catholicization was held out as a means of release from the real experience of deprivation. It denounced concrete enemies like the Jews. Because of their blatant social inferiority and resistance to higher education, Catholics remained especially susceptible to the compensation function, an explanation for antisemitism.

e) Coming to terms with competition: The priests, professional Catholics, journalists, and politicians who constituted the guardians of the milieu had the difficult task of constantly flattering their believers, readers, voters, and fellow club members. Not only was the corpus of milieu members socially heterogeneous, but other world-views, interest groups, and parties were also being promoted here and there. In order to compete with these other groups, which notoriously offered various incentives, the leaders of the milieu had to disparage their attractiveness and increase their own appeal at the same time. The easiest way to succeed was to defame the other parties as "Jewified" or brand the "Old Catholic" press as "Jewish." "If anywhere, antisemitism is most called for in the most significant fields of literature," proclaimed a pamphlet from the Germania Publishing House in 1891. "We want *one*

Christian literature and *one* Christian press, because the Jewish papers are our moral ruin; and we will have a Christian press as soon as we have freed ourselves from the Jewish influence in this area [emphases in original]."[160] Antisemitism, therefore, outwardly supported this rivalry and weakened the centrifugal powers of the milieu. In this way even the Old Catholics and those Catholic papers and politicians that were not completely loyal to the party line were hit.[161] Finally, the antisemitic parties also appeared on the scene as an alternative. How were the Catholics to be prevented from turning their backs on the Center Party? By introducing the concept of "dual antisemitism." They should have their antisemitism—not the racist, un-Christian, and inefficient kind favored by the antisemitic parties—but the good, true, Christian kind promoted by the Center and the Church, which looked to a Catholic society with a Jew "deprived of power."

The approach that examines the function and value of antisemitism covers a wide area. Yet much of it seems too reductionist. The deeply-rooted convictions concealed behind all the manipulation should not be neglected. What is more, the functionalist approach has the disadvantage that functions can often only be identified with hindsight, when their intention is not concealed by sources of evidence and their effect is not empirically proven. Nevertheless the theory of functionalism, which is used fairly frequently, might help explain why ultramontanism and antisemitism entered into such a long and lasting coalition with each other.

In an attempt to answer the question why antisemitism occurs, twelve possible causes and explanatory approaches have been examined. It is evident that the magic variable that explains everything is nowhere to be found. A refined combination of different approaches is what is necessary. The *Realkonfliktthese* is entirely insignificant, even disastrous, insofar as it is bound to antisemitic received ideas. It is, as has been shown, not based on any evidence. Similarly, the economic crisis theories do not take into account the exceedingly religious atmosphere of the "second confessional age." In comparison, the ultramontanism theory is especially productive. It considers Catholicism's dualist and dogmatic style of thinking which was dependent on many friends—i.e. the Pope, the Virgin Mary, saints, priests, pious people—but also on numerous enemies, such as Freemasons, Jews, wicked people, and those who frequented pubs. The amalgam of dualism, dogmatism, and piety in ultramontanism did not immunize against antisemitism, but it did offer an ideal breeding-ground.

There are, however, more factors which encouraged antisemitism to flourish. If we fail to consider the lengthy traditions of Christian antisemitism and local traditions, we may indeed deprive ourselves of an understanding of modern Catholic antisemitism. Yet this also happens if we have no knowledge at all of its traditionalization. The relatively small degree of urbanization in Catholic society is not the cause of the hostile attitude towards Jews among ultramontanes, although antisemitism was more successful in rural areas than in the cities. True, most editors lived and worked in urban environments, and they used some doses of antisemitism to spice up their Catholic newspapers. From a socio-historical point of view, interested people and disseminators, above all priests, as custodians of the press can be identified as a cause, which does not change the fact that they held firm convictions. Women, fathers, teachers, professors, and priests all acted voluntarily as agents of antisemitic socialization. We could certainly not go on to immediately classify Catholics as "authoritarian personalities," but Adorno's approach suggests that we consider massive dogmatism to be a factor effecting inclusion and exclusion. As a minority suffering discrimination in society, Catholicism united in its "ghetto." It was a minority, and this fact made its antisemitism less radical. Antisemitism had a surrogate function for this minority which held the self-perception of being threatened. Antisemitism was frequently instrumentalized for the vague program of counter-modernization, and furthermore it served to maximize internal coherence and to minimize complexity, which was directed outwards. Finally, anti-Jewish stereotypes helped Catholics compensate for failures and threats and also to compete against rival powers.

It is evident, then, that we advance much further when looking to antisemites themselves for the motives for antisemitism, instead of examining the objects at which their prejudice is directed. Not even Reichmann's idea that there was a direct connection between the "number of Jews present in a non-Jewish society and the strength of the reaction against them" is upheld.[162] In view of present right-wing extremism, we also know that xenophobia often becomes particularly uncontrollable in places where there are hardly any foreigners, but that is not to say that the xenophobe first has to invent the foreigner, that the antisemite has to invent the Jew, as Sartre claimed. Around 1890, for example, both Berlin and Vienna had populations with a high proportion of Jews—about 5 percent—and were starting-points for successful antisemitic movements. So why did Frankfurt, which had the highest proportion of Jews of all German cities in relation to population (11 percent in 1871 and 6.3 percent in 1910) not become an antisemitic stronghold? Why was antisemitism often more pronounced in regions, cities, or villages where there were very few or no Jews?

This phenomenon, also very much apparent in France during the Dreyfus Affair, has been known for some time as "antisemitism without Jews."[163] It once again shows that the tension theory is clearly inferior to other approaches. The discovery of "antisemitism without Jews" can be related to the virulence of antisemitism in a specific region; it was not dependent on the absence or presence of Jews. In addition, however, this approach can also, in a metaphorical sense, be applied to antisemitism research as a whole. Groups which are disposed to antisemitism must be closely examined according to their general mentality. The behavior of the Jews need not be inspected.

As far as antisemitism is concerned, the stimulus-object approach seems to be the one with the weakest analytical power. On the other hand, it possesses the strongest apologetic power, the greatest revisionist magic. The causes should, however, be looked for elsewhere, whether in socio-economic areas, cultural-ideological characters, or charismatic leaders. Functional explanations, which maintain that the deployment of antisemitic prejudices promised certain advantages for the in-group, lead much further. The ultramontanism approach itself is especially productive. Being an ultramontane at the time did not only mean being loyal to the Pope but involved the whole spectrum of Catholic ideology as it had developed since the middle of the nineteenth century. Certain modes of behavior were essential, such as constant devoutness, involvement in Catholic associations, allegiance to the Center, a preference for particular professions—all of this was a part of ultramontanism just as much as an attitude of distrust towards the modern state, towards capitalism, socialism, liberalism, and Freemasonry, in short, towards civil (*bürgerliche*) society principles in general.[164] This pattern was evident throughout ultramontanism, from the bishop, to the priest, and right down to the layman. Those who expressed different opinions within the mentality of the milieu often adopted a different stance to antisemitism and to Jews. In the 1870s the Old Catholics, for instance, were not only firmly opposed to the notion of papal infallibility and the suppression of free speech, but also spoke out vehemently against "Jesuit" antisemitism.[165] Antisemitism was therefore not a consequence of a lack of Christian spirit but the direct consequence of increased Christian spirit, in the ultramontane sense. Walter Zwi Bacharach's analysis of Catholic sermons confirms this connection: "As the craving for religious and moral renewal grew in intensity, anti-Jewish attacks increased."[166]

One last point has however not yet been explained. When Catholics accused the Jews of anti-Catholicism, this was regarded as antisemitism. Consequently, if the Jews accused Catholics of antisemitism, then it would count as anti-Catholicism. However, that would only be the case if, firstly, the Catholics were incorrectly accused of antisemitism and secondly, if Jews actually made this accusation. This has been repeatedly disputed. Some scholars claim that Jews expressly praised Catholicism for the fact that it did not take part in any anti-Jewish smear campaigns. This is another aspect of the issue which has not previously been examined in detail.

NOTES

1. Konrad Löw, "Kirche und Antisemitismus im Kaiserreich und im Dritten Reich," *Deutsche Tagespost*, 1 Oct. 1998; idem, *Die Schuld: Christen und Juden im Urteil der Nationalsozialisten und der Gegenwart* (Gräfelfing 2002), 277.

2. Gavin I. Langmuir, "Toward a Definition of Antisemitism," in *The Persisting Question: Sociological Perspectives and Social Contexts of Modern Antisemitism,* ed. Helen Fein (Berlin 1987), 86–127, quote on 103–4.

3. The term antisemitism has, it is claimed, become a platitude. If it is to have any meaning, "it must be demonstrated that Jews have in fact been the object of a kind of hostility different from that which all major groups confront. The theory I have advanced does identify an unusual quality of hostility toward Jews." Langmuir is unable to refute the objection that other groups (such as witches) were also the victims of chimerical assertions. See Langmuir, "Definition of Antisemitism," 126.

4. Ibid., 110.

5. Instead of the wealth of literature dealing with singularity, incomparability, and inexplicablility, see Yehuda Bauer's clear, comprehensible essay, "The Holocaust: The Specific and the Universal," *Vidal Sassoon International Center for the Study of Antisemitism Annual Report* (1998): 2–7 (address to the Bundestag, 27 Jan. 1998). See also the works of Dan Diner.

6. Herbert A. Strauss and Norbert Kampe, "Einleitung," in *Antisemitismus: Von der Judenfeindschaft zum Holocaust,* eds. Herbert A. Strauss and Norbert Kampe (Bonn 1985), 19–20.

7. August Rohling; *Der Talmudjude: Zur Beherzigung für Juden und Christen aller Stände,* 6th ed. (1871; Münster 1877); idem, *Das Judentum nach neurabbinischer Darstellung der Hochfinanz Israels* (Munich 1903). See Joseph Rebbert, *Blicke ins Talmudische Judenthum: Nach den Forschungen von Dr. Konrad Martin, Bischof von Paderborn* (Paderborn 1876); Rainer Erb, ed., *Die Legende vom Ritualmord: Zur Geschichte der Blutbeschuldigung gegen Juden* (Berlin 1993); Stefan Rohrbacher and Michael Schmidt, *Judenbilder: Kulturgeschichte antijüdischer Mythen und antisemitischer Vorurteile* (Hamburg 1991). See also Christoph Nonn, "Ritualmordgerüchte als Form des populären Antisemitismus—eine katholische Spezialität?" in *Katholischer Antisemitismus im 19. Jahrhundert: Ursachen und Traditionen im internationalen Vergleich,* eds. Olaf Blaschke and Aram Mattioli (Zürich 2000), 145–62.

8. Cf. the judicial proceedings between Rohling and Rabbi Bloch in 1883 or the trial in Marburg in 1888 against the antisemite Ferdinand Fenner, about which accusation philosopher Hermann Cohen wrote a report. See also Ulrich Sieg, "'Der Wissenschaft und dem Leben tut dasselbe not: Ehrfurcht vor der Wahrheit': Hermann Cohens Gutachten im Marburger Antisemitismusprozeß," in *Philosophisches Denken—Politisches Wirken: Hermann-Cohen-Kolloquium Marburg 1992,* eds. Reinhard Brandt and Franz Orlik (Hildesheim 1993), 222–48.

9. See Olaf Blaschke, *Katholizismus und Antisemitismus im Deutschen Kaiserreich,* 2d ed. (Göttingen 1999), 104–12.

10. Norman Cohn, *Warrant for Genocide: The Myth of the Jewish World Conspiracy and the Protocols of the Elders of Zion* (New York 1967); E. Piper, "Die jüdische Weltverschwörung," in *Antisemitismus: Vorurteile und Mythen,* eds. Julius H. Schoeps and Johannes Schlör (Munich 1995), 127–35.

11. For the Alliance, see A. Chouraqui, *Cent ans d'histoire: L'Alliance Israélite Universelle et la renaissance juive contemporaine (1860–1960)* (Paris 1965), 188: The AIU fought for human rights for Jews. It granted material and educational help to suffering Jews. But it failed in its promotion campaign. "All of this was in vain: antisemitic propaganda saw in the works of the Alliance Israélite Universelle the diabolical elements of machinations against the Christian people. . . . It was claimed that the Jews were conspiring to seize control of the entire world and that the Alliance . . . was the instrument of this conspiracy," ibid., 132. See also Blaschke, *Katholizismus und Antisemitismus,* esp. 105–7.

12. *Kölnische Volkszeitung,* no. 139 (22 May 1880); See also *Der Mauscheljude,* Bonifacius-Broschüren: Populäre Erörterungen über den Katholizismus und die Einsprüche seiner Gegner, no. 11 (Paderborn 1880), 125–68, esp. 130–31, 136–37.

13. Ludwig Erler, "Historisch-kritische Übersicht der national-ökonomischen und social-politischen Literatur," *Archiv für katholisches Kirchenrecht* 41 (1879): 3–96, esp. 83–84; see also ibid., 42 (1879): 3–80; 43 (1880): 361–408; 44 (1880): 353–416; "Die Judenverfolgungen des Mittelalters," 48 (1882): 3–52; "Die Juden des Mittelalters, " ibid.: 369–416; 50 (1883): 3–64; 53 (1885): 3–70.

14. *Bayerisches Vaterland,* no. 57 (3 Mar. 1872). Sigl's occasional comrade-in-arms, Georg Ratzinger, a priest, did not overlook any antisemitic arguments in 1893. He saw Judaism as the biggest danger for Church and society due to the immorality of the Talmud and "the *secret connections and conspiracies*." The "Alliance Israélite," he declared, was a plotting, political "association of Jews." "Even when it was founded it was already apparent that the Jews were striving for world domination." "*Freemasonry* is . . . merely the stooge of Jewish world domination," since it "came from Jewish secret societies." Georg Ratzinger [here: Robert Waldhausen], *Jüdisches Erwerbsleben: Skizzen aus dem sozialen Leben der Gegenwart,* 3rd ed. (Passau 1893; 1st ed. 1892), 68–69, 93. The *Stimmen aus Maria-*

Laach backed up this opinion in 1887: "The completely Jewish character of the lodge's rituals in particular, as well as the frequent use of Hebrew words in the secret organizations, can only be explained if one assumes that it was the Jews who founded freemasonry," *Stimmen aus Maria-Laach* 33 (1887): 541–42. See also review of the most influential book, *Judaisme et Franc-Maçonnerie: La Franc-Maçonnerie est-elle d'origine juive?* (Bruges 1887); "Allgemeine israelitische Allianz," *Stimmen aus Maria-Laach* 29 (1885): 578–80. Pater Baumgarten proclaimed that "the dirtiest and most cruel Jewish papers were on intimate terms with the lodge, from which they received instructions." See his *Zur Naturgeschichte der Presse: Eine kulturhistorische Skizze,* Frankfurter Zeitgemäße Broschüren, no. 7 (Frankfurt 1886), 73–104, quotes on 80, 85–86. See also *Der Mauscheljude,* 139–40.

15. R. H. Phelps, "Dokumentation: Hitlers 'grundlegende' Rede über den Antisemitismus," *Vierteljahrshefte für Zeitgeschichte* 16 (1968): 390–400 (introduction); 400–20 (document), esp. 415.

16. See Stefan-Ludwig Hoffmann, *Die Politik der Geselligkeit: Freimauerlogen in der deutschen Bürgergesellschaft 1840–1918* (Göttingen 2000).

17. *Israelitische Wochenschrift* 13 (1882): 270–71.

18. Langmuir, "Definition of Antisemitism," 106.

19. *Israelitisches Wochenblatt* 11 (1912): 574. See Shulamit Volkov, "Antisemit ismus als kulturelle Code," in *Jüdisches Leben und Antisemitismus im 19. und 20. Jahrhundert* (Munich 1990), 13–36, first published in *Leo Baeck Institute Year Book* 23 (1978): 24–45.

20. Monika Richarz, "Die soziale Stellung der jüdischen Händler auf dem Lande am Beispiel Südwestdeutschlands," in *Jüdische Unternehmer in Deutschland im 19. und 20. Jahrhundert,* eds. Werner E. Mosse and Heinrich Pohl (Stuttgart 1992), 271–83. "Even in 1917, 25,000 cattle dealers were Jewish, over 60 percent of all those active in the cattle trade in Germany." The proportion was higher in the west and south and slightly lower in the east and north. "In Hesse, Baden, Wurttemberg, Franconia, the Rhineland, and Westphalia the cattle trade remained to a large extent under Jewish control, and this only began to change slowly after the war." See Arthur Prinz, *Juden im deutschen Wirtschaftsleben: Soziale und wirtschaftliche Struktur im Wandel 1850–1914,* ed. Avraham Barkai (Tübingen 1984), 175, 1 respectively.

21. According to Prinz, *Juden im Deutschen Wirtschaftsleben,* 128–29, the farmers suffered from rising costs and, after 1875, from the import of grain from the United States, southern Russia, and Austria-Hungary. In addition, the division of land was a problem, especially in Wurttemberg, Bavaria, and Hesse. Many farmers could hardly feed their families anymore and tried to purchase additional land. They also took out mortgages or loans, although they were usually unaware of the consequences. "The creditor was in many cases a Jew, resident in or near a village and familiar with all the necessary circumstances. Often having moved into the

lending business from the livestock trade or pawn-broking, the Jewish dealer took on a kind of monopoly position, since hardly any other credit facilities existed for farmers. The calculating, skilful, and often Jewish businessman frequently took advantage of the situation, while the farming community had to restrain their powerless fury and hatred." For Jews this situation often had unfortunate consequences, see ibid., 87–88. "The Jew," it is claimed, was often economically superior to the farmers and "just as 'opportunity creates thieves' it also gives rise to exploitation."

22. A. Kulik, *Breslauer Wuchergeschichten* (Breslau 1879); pamphlet offprinted from *Schlesische Volkszeitung,* no. 200 (31 Aug. 1879). See also idem, *Der Schnapsjude* (Breslau 1879), pamphlet offprinted from *Schlesische Volkszeitung,* no. 230 (5 Oct. 1879). *Der Schnapsjude* was written as a novel and claimed that the "brandy-[selling] Jew" demoralized the lower and middle classes.

23. For information on the repeal of the profiteering law in all states on 1st Jan. 1872 see K. Peschke, "Wucher," in *Handbuch der Staatswissenschaften,* 4th ed. (Jena 1928), 1081–1108, esp. 1092. All that remained on the books was a law to protect minors (*Strafgesetzbuch* §§ 301–302). Regarding the profiteering laws (the first law was voted through regardless of the Fortschrittspartei and the Social Democrats) the risk taken by the creditor was significant; setting a maximum interest percentage, which many Catholics called for, was avoided. see "Wucher," in *Politisches Handbuch der Nationalliberalen Partei,* ed. Zentralbüro der Nationalliberalen Partei Deutschlands (Berlin 1907), 1133–35. See also Prinz, *Juden im Deutschen Wirtschaftsleben,* 126–32, esp. 130–31. Banks offering loans found a way around it here, since all measures against profiteering were considered to be "completely inadequate"; see Oswald von Nell-Breuning, "Wucher," in *Staatslexikon,* 5th ed. (Freiburg 1932), 5:1467–78, esp. 1476.

24. Hans Rost, *Beiträge zur Moralstatistik* (Paderborn 1913), 165; V. Guerber, *Der Socialismus als Erzfeind steht vor der Thüre* (Straßburg 1891), 15–20, 52–53.

25. Joseph E. Jörg, "Wie das alte Jahr dem neuen die Judenfrage vermacht," *Historisch-politische Blätter* 87 (1981): 1–18, quotes on 14.

26. Cf. Michael Walzer, "Liberalism and the Jews: Historical Affinities, Contemporary Necessities," in *Values, Interests and Identity: Jews and Politics in a Changing World,* ed. Peter Y. Medding (=*Studies in Contemporary Jewry* 11 [1995]): 3–10.

27. Uwe Mazura, *Zentrumspartei und Judenfrage 1870/71–1933: Verfassungsstaat und Minderheitenschutz,* Veröffentlichungen der Kommission für Zeitgeschichte, Reihe B: Forschungen, vol. 62 (Mainz 1994), 187.

28. Albert S. Lindemann, *Esau's Tears: Modern Anti-Semitism and the Rise of the Jews,* 2d ed. (Cambridge 2000), 123.

29. Massimo Ferrari Zumbini, *Die Wurzeln des Bösen: Gründerjahre des Antisemitismus: Von der Bismarckzeit zu Hitler* (Frankfurt 2003), 131. For a review see Olaf Blaschke, < http://hsozkult.geschichte.hu-berlin.de (20. Sept. 2003)>.

30. *Fränkisches Volksblatt,* 27 Apr. 1871; Rebbert, *Blicke ins Talmudische Judenthum,* 7, 88–89, 95–96. For Lasker und Bamberger see Margaet L. Anderson, *Windthorst: Zentrumspolitiker und Gegenspieler Bismarcks* (Düsseldorf 1988), 168–69.

31. Lindemann, *Esau's Tears,* 122. The latest examination of Jewish positions towards the Jesuit bill is Michael B. Gross, *The War against Catholicism: Liberalism and the Anti-Catholic Imagination in Nineteenth-Century Germany* (Ann Arbor 2004), 127, 258–75; see also idem, "Anti-Catholicism, Liberalism and German National Identity, 1848–1880," Ph.D thesis, Brown University, 1997; James F. Harris, *A Study in the Theory and Practive of German Liberalism: Eduard Lasker, 1829–1884* (Lanham, Md. 1984); Stanley Zucker, *Ludwig Bamberger: German Liberal Politician and Social Critic* (Pittsburgh 1975).

32. *Akten deutscher Bischöfe über die Lage der Kirche 1933–1945*, ed. Bernhard Stasiewski Mainz 1975), 1:54; *Akten Kardinal Michael Faulhaber 1917–1945,* ed. Ludwig Volk (Mainz 1975), 1:705, both quoted in Heinz Hürten, "'Endlösung' für den Katholizismus? Das nationalsozialistische Regime und seine Zukunftspläne gegenüber der Kirche," in idem, *Katholiken, Kirche und Staat als Problem der Historie: Ausgewählte Aufsätze 1963–1992,* ed. H. Gruber (Paderborn 1994), 174–89 (first published: *Stimmen der Zeit* 203 [1985]: 534–46), quotes on 174–78.

33. "Joseph Eberle, Jesuiten und Juden," *Allgemeine Rundschau,* quoted from *Israelitisches Wochenblatt* 11 (1912): 686. See two works by von Eberle: *Großmacht Presse: Enthüllungen für Zeitungsgläubige: Forderungen für Männer* (Munich 1912); *Die Überwindung der Plutokratie: Vierzehn Aufsätze über die Wiederverchristlichung von Volkswirtschaft und Politik* (Vienna 1918).

34. "Die Juden im Culturkampf," *Mitteilungen aus dem Verein zur Abwehr des Antisemitismus* 3 (1893): 58.

35. See Aram Mattioli, "Das letzte Ghetto Alteuropas: Antisemitismus im Kirchenstaat bis 1870," in *Katholischer Antisemitismus*; David I. Kertzer, *Die Päpste gegen die Juden: Der Vatikan und die Entstehung des modernen Antisemitismus* (Berlin 2001).

36. *Rerum Novarum,* para. 22, in *Texte zur katholischen Soziallehre: Die sozialen Rundschreiben der Päpste und andere kirchliche Dokumente,* ed. Bundesverband der Katholischen Arbeitnehmer-Bewegung Deutschlands (Kevelaer 1975), 31–68, quote on 46. See also Victor Cathrein, "Sociale Frage," in *Wetzer und Welte Kirchenlexikon* (Freiburg 1899), 11: 431–65, esp. 464.

37. Emil Siegfried, *Schild gegen feindliche Geschosse alter und neuer Lügen, für's katholische Volk angefertigt* (Werl 1861), 7, 11.

38. Abraham Geiger, *Nachgelassene Schriften,* ed. Ludwig Geiger (Berlin 1878), 5: 225–26. Many thanks to Andreas Gotzmann for bringing it to my attention.

39. Christel Köhle-Hezinger, *Evangelisch-Katholisch. Untersuchungen zu konfessionellem Vorurteil und Konflikt im 19. und 20. Jahrhundert vornehmlich am Beispiel Württembergs* (Tübingen 1976), 98–105; Helmut Walser Smith, ed., *Protestants, Catholics and Jews in Germany 1800–1914* (Oxford 2001); Olaf Blaschke, ed., *Konfessionen im Konflikt: Deutschland zwischen 1800 und 1970: ein zweites konfessionelles Zeitalter* (Göttingen 2002).

40. Gottfried Mayer, *Österreich als "katholische Großmacht": Ein Traum zwischen Revolution und liberaler Ära* (Vienna 1989), 196–98, 214–15. See also Erika Weinzierl-Fischer, *Die österreichischen Konkordate von 1855 und 1933* (Vienna 1960).

41. Shulamit Volkov, "Die Erfindung einer Tradition: Zur Entstehung des modernen Judentums in Deutschland," *Historische Zeitschrift* 253 (1991): 603–28, quote on 613. See Heinrich Graetz, *Geschichte der Juden von den ältesten Zeiten bis auf die Gegenwart,* 11 vols. (Leipzig et al. 1853–1876; rprt. of the later edition with a foreword by Reuven Michael and a biography (1904) by Philipp Bloch: Berlin 1996); idem, *Volkstümliche Geschichte der Juden* (Vienna 1888; rprt. Cologne 2000), 2:1037; English version, *Popular History of the Jews,* tr. A. B. Rhine, 6 vols. (New York 1919), 5:500–02; Shmuel Ettinger, "Graetz, Heinrich," in *Encyclopaedia Judaica* (Jerusalem 1971), 7:845–50. See also Michael A. Meyer, "Heinrich Graetz and Heinrich von Treitschke: A Comparison of Their Historical Images of the Modern Jew," *Modern Judaism* 6 (1986): 1-11; Reuven Michael, "Graetz contra Treitschke," *Bulletin des Leo Baeck Instituts* 4 (1961): 301–22; idem, "The Unknown Heinrich Graetz: From His Diaries and Letters," *Leo Baeck Institute Year Book* 13 (1968): 34–50; Heinrich von Treitschke, "Unsere Aussichten," *Preußische Jahrbücher* 44 (1879): 559–76; Lindemann, *Esau's Tears,* 139–42; Christhard Hoffmann, "Geschichte und Ideologie: Der Berliner Antisemitismusstreit 1879/80," in *Vorurteil und Völkermord: Entwicklungslinien des Antisemitismus,* eds. Wolfgang Benz and Werner Bergmann (Bonn 1997), 219–51.

42. Graetz, *Volkstümliche Geschichte,* 2:170; *Popular History,* 3:295.

43. See Mattioli, "Das letzte Ghetto Alteuropas" (n. 35 above).

44. Graetz, *Volkstümliche Geschichte,* 2: 969–70.

45. Ibid., 2:1022; see also ibid., 2:973 ("ein Stück Mittelalter" refers to the postponing of equal rights laws in Prussia); 974 ("The grinning figure of the Middle Ages rose up once more" at the *Hep-Hep* demonstrations in 1819); 975 ("The Jews were officially slaughtered, as in the Middle Ages"); 976 (the "smear campaigns against the Jews, like those of the Middle Ages" in Bavaria in 1819). The 1844 pilgrimage to the so-called "holy shroud" in Trier is also described as an "an example of excessive belief reminiscent of the Middle Ages" (1036).

46. Ibid., 2:1046; *Popular History,* 5:541.

47. See Manfred Klug, *Rückwendung zum Mittelalter? Geschichtsbilder und hisorische Argumentation im politischen Katholizismus des Vormärz* (Paderborn 1995).

48. Graetz, *Volkstümliche Geschichte,* 2:944; *Popular History,* 5:543.

49. Graetz, *Volkstümliche Geschichte*, 2:920, 1025.

50. Ibid., 2:1048.

51. See Olaf Blaschke, "Der Altkatholizismus 1870 bis 1945: Nationalismus, Antisemitismus und Nationalsozialismus," *Historische Zeitschrift* 261 (1995): 51–99.

52. Joseph Leute, *Der Ultramontanismus in Theorie und Praxis* (Berlin 1911), 350–52, with reference to the articles published by both papers in July 1901 concerning Brother Alfons Rodriguez of the Apostolischen Lehrgesellschaft in Rome. For information on the *Bayerischen Kurier* (from 1857 onwards), which had 9,000 subscribers in 1877 and as many as 12,000 by 1880, see Leo Woerl, *Die Publicistik der Gegenwart: Eine Rundschau über die gesammte Presse der Welt,* 6 vols. (Würzburg 1879–1881), 4:212–13. He classified the *Kurier* as part of the "Catholic" press and suggested that "the *Bayerische Kurier* has the potential of becoming the main organ of the Bavarian Catholics." See also Heinrich Keiter, *Handbuch der katholischen Presse Deutschlands, Österreich-Ungarns, der Schweiz, Luxemburgs und von Nord-Amerika,* 5th ed. (Essen 1913), 34; Klemens Löffler, *Geschichte der katholischen Presse Deutschlands* (München-Gladbach 1924), 63.

53. See Elisabeth Kraus, *Die Familie Mosse: Deutsch-jüdisches Bürgertum im 19. und 20. Jahrhundert* (Munich 1999).

54. Heinz Hürten, "Antisemit, weil Katholik?" *Stimmen der Zeit* 216 (1998): 499.

55. *Jüdisches Volksblatt* 16, no. 34 (26 Aug. 1910): 334–35.

56. "An der Schwelle des zwanzigsten Jahrhunderts," *Frankfurter Zeitung und Handelsblatt, Morgenblatt* no. 362, 2 (31 Dec. 1899). See Olaf Blaschke, "Der Teufel ist ein geflügeltes Krokodil am Klavier: Mit Horrorgeschichten die Gläubigen gefoppt: Vor hundert Jahren erschütterte die Taxil-Affäre Europa," *Süddeutsche Zeitung (SZ am Wochenende),* 19 Apr. 1997.

57. *Frankfurter Zeitung,* no. 270 (26 Sept. 1872). For the background see Blaschke, "Altkatholizismus." See recently Gross, *The War against Catholicism,* 273–74: "The *Frankfurter Zeitung*...opposed from the beginning the exceptional law and the repressive measures of the Kulturkampf." Gross refers to *Geschichte der Frankfurter Zeitung, 1856 bis 1906* (Frankfurt a. M. 1906).

58. "Sonnemann, Leopold," in *Brockhaus' Konversations-Lexikon,* 14th ed. (Leipzig 1898): 15:51–52. See Klaus Gerteis, *Leopold Sonnemann: Ein Beitrag zur Geschichte des demokratischen Nationalstaatsgedenkens in Deutschland* (Frankfurt a. M. 1970).

59. The fact that Sonnemann actually exercised influence over the editors, in the party-political sense, reveals the extent to which liberal, middle class values prevailed over religious ones. See. Jörg Requate, *Journalismus als Beruf: Entstehung und Entwicklung des Journalistenberufs im 19. Jahrhundert: Deutschland im internationalen Vergleich* (Göttingen 1995), 203–5. Concerning Stein, see ibid., 337; Anderson, *Windhorst,* 252. Regarding the Jewish press see Barbara Suchy, "Die jüdische Presse im Kaiserreich und in der Weimarer Republik," in *Juden als Träger bürgerlicher Kultur in Deutschland,* ed. Julius H. Schoeps (Stuttgart 1989), 167–91; Kurt Koszyk, *Deutsche Presse im 19. Jahrhundert, Geschichte der deutschen Presse,* vol. 2, 2nd ed. (Berlin 1986); idem, "Der jüdische Beitrag zum deutschen Presse- und Verlagswesen," in *Jüdische Unternehmer in Deutschland,* 196–217; E. Kahn, "Die *Frankfurter Zeitung,*" *Leo Baeck Institute Year Book* 2 (1957): 228–35. Almut Todorow, *Das Feuilleton der 'Frankfurter Zeitung' in der Weimarer Republik: Zur Grundlegung einer rhetorischen Medienforschung* (Tübingen 1996), examines the numerous Jewish authors who wrote contributions for the *feuilleton,* including Theodor W. Adorno, Walter Benjamin, Günther Anders, and more. For the Catholic press see Michael Schmolke, *Die schlechte Presse: Katholiken und Publizistik zwischen "Katholik" und "Publik" 1821–1968* (Münster 1971).

60. *Frankfurter Zeitung,* no. 141 (21 May 1874).

61. Jörg, "Wie das alte Jahr…," 2–3.

62. "It will have to be noted!" *Jüdisches Volksblatt,* 23 Sept. 1910.

63. Quoted from "Die ultramontanen Hetzereien gegen die Juden," *Israelitische Wochenschrift* 6 (1875): 209–10.

64. Ibid.: 210; Alexander Joskowicz, "Liberal Judaism and Confessional Politics of Difference in the German Kulturkampf," *Leo Baeck Institute Yearbook* 50 (2005): 177–97, 182, seems to have noticed this article but hides it in a footnote about Jewish anti-ultramontanism. He doesn't quote it and doesn't interpret it because it diametrically contradicts his argument. The footnote should bolster his argument that liberal Jewish papers fought against fanaticism. In fact, this article from the *Israelitische Wochenschrift* is all but a good example for "fanatical" anti-ultramontanism among Jews.

65. Ibid. 11 (1912): 639.

66. See Klaus Schreiner, "'Wann kommt der Retter Deutschlands?' Formen und Funktionen von politischem Messianismus in der Weimarer Republik," *Saeculum* 49 (1998): 107–59, esp. 153; see also Klaus Breuning, *Die Vision des Reiches: Deutscher Katholizismus zwischen Demokratie und Diktatur (1929–1934)* (Munich 1969). Heinz Hürten, *Deutsche Katholiken 1918–1945* (Paderborn 1992), 214–30, examines attempts at bridge-building between Catholicism and National Socialism.

67. *Im Deutschen Reich* 6 (1900): 319.

68. *Israelitische Wochenschrift* 13 (1882): 293–94; see also "Oberschlesischer Centrums-Antisemitismus," *Jüdisches Volksblatt* 16 (1910): 333–34.

69. *Israelitisches Wochenblatt* 11 (1912): 85. For the Jewish press see Herbert A. Strauss, "The Jewish Press in Germany, 1918–1933 (1943)," in *The Jewish Press that Was: Accounts, Evaluations and Memories of Jewish Newspapers in Pre-Holocaust Europe* (Tel Aviv 1980), 321–53, quote on 333; Suchy, *Jüdische Presse*; Trude Maurer, *Die Entwicklung der jüdischen Minderheit in Deutschland (1780–1933): Neuere Forschungen und offene Fragen* (Tübingen 1992), 51–54.

70. See "Die Päpstliche Encyclica," *Allgemeine Zeitung des Judenthums* 29 (10 Jan. 1865): 554–55;"Der große Kampf," *Allgemeine Zeitung des Judentums* 37 (15 July 1873): 465–69; "Zur Charakteristik des Fanatismus," *Israelitische Wochenschrift* 7 (21 Dec. 1876): 499–501. Parallel to the work on this study, which was finished in 2002, Alexander Joskowicz studied these two liberal Jewish weeklies for the 1870s and 1880s, led by a similar question but coming to a slightly different result, which was published in 2005 in "Liberal Judaism," 186 (n. 64 above). His notion is that the "liberal Jewish press"—a courageous generalization from the examination of two journals—"embraced the anti-Catholic rhetoric of the *Kulturkampf*," probably meaning anti-ultramontane rhetoric. It is important that he emphasizes (p. 196) the "clear cut dichotomy between 'humanity' versus 'fanaticism' that had been developed in detail at the height of the *Kulturkampf*" in the two liberal journals. It is an exaggeration to assert that they identified the Catholic Church "as a principal enemy." In fact, there were more critical articles about other groups (orthodox Protestants, orthodox Jews, antisemites) than about Catholics.

71. Mazura, *Zentrumspartei,* 80–81.

72. "Die Rückschritte," *Israelitische Wochenschrift* 1 (1870): 141–42, 149–50.

73. L. Koch, "Jesuiten und Juden," *Stimmen der Zeit* 109 (1925): 435–52; Blaschke, *Katholizismus und Antisemitismus,* 243.

74. "Wider den Strom," *Israelitische Wochenschrift* 3 (1872): 107–8. Uriel Tal, *Christians and Jews in Germany: Religions, Politics and Ideology in the Second Reich, 1870–1914* (London 1974), 96–109, shows that the leaders of Jewish communities were in a "dilemma" at the beginning of the Kulturkampf, wavering "between two extremes: identification with the aims of the war in theory, and disassociation from the violent course that the war took in practice; support for the liberal camp which had endorsed Bismarck's policies at the beginning of the struggle and, at the same time, a fear of the growing étatist tendencies within this camp in favor of a strong centralized state." It fact, however, Tal's evidence that "the Jewish communities showed great interest in its [Kulturkampf] progress" proves to be decidedly sparse and dubious: the sources "in our possession" (p. 98, n. 49) refer to Berlin, Breslau, Cologne, etc., but their authenticity is not proven specifically.

75. "Wider den Strom," *Israelitische Wochenschrift* 3 (1872): 116–17. See also "Ein Wendepunkt: Was hat die Religion bei der gegenwärtigen Tendenz des Staates zu tun? " *Allgemeine Zeitung des Judentums* 36 (6 Jan. 1874): 17–18.

76. The following interpretation is somewhat awkward: "Yet the priests want to have complete power, oppress and attribute 'that which God did not decree and would never have dreamed of' to a 'God-given right.' They do not want to simply teach by persuasion, but by force, and think that the state should assist them in this; they do not merely want to refer to the folly of people of different faiths, but also wish to punish them for it. This is not the law of God." See "Der Kampf zwischen Kirche und Staat," *Israelitische Wochenschrift* 3 (1872): 227–28.

77. *Jüdisches Literatur-Blatt* 12 (1883): 13–14, 133–34, 481; *Israelitische Wochenschrift* 5 (1875): 266–67, 275; 13 (1882): 293–94. See also 12 (1881): 60–61.

78. Jacob Toury, *Die politische Orientierung der Juden in Deutschland. Von Jena bis Weimar* (Tübingen 1966), 246–61, esp. 248–49; see also *Allgemeine Zeitung des Judentums* (1875): 643; *Israelitische Wochenschrift* (1875): 316; see also, more recently, Joskowicz, "Liberal Judaism and Confessional Politics."

79. Karl-Heinz West, "'Der Stellvertreter'—Ein Stück und seine Wirkung," *Rottenburger Jahrbuch für Kirchengeschichte* 2 (1983): 203–47, esp. 228–30. Heinz Galinski, in "Der Streit um den Stellvertreter," *Stuttgarter Zeitung,* 13 Mar. 1963.

80. *Stimmen aus Maria-Laach* 42 (1892): 583–85, a review of Sebastian Brunner, *Der Nebeljungen Lied,* 4 ed. (1845; Regensburg 1891). See also Sebastian Brunner, *Zwei Buschmänner—Börne und Heine* (Paderborn 1891); Heinrich Keiter, *Heinrich Heine: Sein Leben, sein Charakter und seine Werke,* Vereinsschrift der Görresgesellschaft, 3 (Cologne 1891). Keiter's book actually falls outside the context of antisemitic writing. He expressly stresses Heine's distancing himself from Judaism ("He has nothing to do with Jews") and suggests that his anti-Catholicism "cannot be traced back to his Jewish origins alone." Nevertheless, he writes that Heine's contact with the Reform Jews of Berlin strengthened his hatred of Catholicism. All in all, Heine is portrayed as a poet, but not, as is usually the case, as a guiding intellectual force behind Judaism; Keiter, *Heine,* 8, 12, 119. By way of comparison see the antisemitic "Enthüllungsschrift" by Brunner, *Zwei Buschmänner,* which summons up all available accusations. Heine is charged with denying the Jewish ritual murders. Brunner writes (p. 178) that "Jewish hatred has remained fermenting in Börne's soul." See also J. Staarstecher, *Heinrich Heine* (Cologne 1893).

81. *Geständnisse,* quoted from Ruth L. Jacobi, *Heinrich Heines jüdisches Erbe* (Bonn 1978), 106.

82. Ibid., 106–7.

83. In a letter to Immanuel Wohlwill in 1823 Heine gives an honest description of his discrimination: "The hope that Christianity could finally collapse becomes more plausible. This lazy idea has been around for long enough. I refer to Christianity as an

idea, but what kind is it? It gives rise to further filthy ideas, which implant themselves in the cracks of this old world, in the abandoned bedsteads of the divine spirit, just as families of bedbugs infest the Polish Jew's bed. If one of these delusions is crushed, it leaves behind a stench which can still be detected for centuries afterwards. One such delusion is Christianity, which was stamped on before the 1800s, and which is still polluting the air which we poor Jews have to breathe." See Christian Höpfner, *Romantik und Religion: Heinrich Heines Suche nach Identität* (Stuttgart 1997), 238.

84. See Paul Peters, *Heinrich Heine "Dichterjude": Die Geschichte einer Schmähung* (Frankfurt 1990); Jacobi, *Heinrich Heines jüdisches Erbe*; Höpfner, *Romantik,* 238–39, 250–55. See also Gert Mattenklott, *Über Juden in Deutschland* (Frankfurt 1993), 76–77.

85. Brunner, *Buschmänner,* 278. Brunner even recommended Theodor Fritsch's *Deutsch soziale Blätter* as an excellent means of properly recognizing "the wheeling and dealing of the Jews" and were therefore "indispensable" (p. 404). See Sebastian Brunner, *Woher? Wohin? Geschichten, Gedanken, Bilder und Leute aus meinem Leben,* 3rd ed. (1855; Regensburg 1891), 2:20; idem, *Unter Lebendigen und Todten: Spaziergänge in Deutschland, Frankreich, England und der Schweiz,* 2d ed. (Vienna 1863), 80; see also H. K. Lenz, *Judenliteratur und Literaturjuden: Aus Sebastian Brunners Werken dargestellt* (Münster 1893), 31–38. "Rezension von Brunner, Buschmänner," *Historisch-politische Blätter* 109 (1892): 74–80, where the author suggests that Brunner is completely right, that Heine and Börne never gave up their Jewish "racial hatred" against the "*Gojim.*" For a counterargument see Don Josaphet, *Bibel und Judentum* (Passau 1893), 77–78, who regards Heine as an "'Antisemite' par excellence, who cannot regret his Jewish descent enough. Neither . . . Singer, nor Heine is regarded as a Jew, just as we do not consider Reinkens to be a Catholic." See also the *Boykottappell* (call to boycott Jews) by Jakob Overmans, S.J., "Die deutsche Literatur und die Juden," *Stimmen aus Maria-Laach* 81 (1911): 535–43, who says that Christian funds should not be used to support "Jewish" literature and theater. For more stereotypes of this kind see Hans-Peter Bayerdörfer, "'Vermauschelt die Presse, die Literatur': Jüdische Schriftsteller in der Literatur zwischen Jahrhundertwende und Erstem Weltkrieg," in *Judentum, Antisemitismus und europäische Kultur,* ed. Hans Otto Horch (Tübingen 1988), 207–32.

86. See Günther Hirschmann, *Kulturkampf im historischen Roman der Gründerzeit 1859–1878* (Munich 1978), 50–51, 193. For the field of Catholic literature see Jutta Osinski, *Katholizismus und deutsche Literatur im 19. Jahrhundert* (Paderborn 1993).

87. B. Duhr, review in *Stimmen aus Maria-Laach* 50 (1896): 578, of Heinrich Keiter, *Konfessionelle Brunnenvergiftung: Die wahre Schmach des 19. Jahrhunderts*

(Regensburg 1896). Gross, *War,* 1; for a detailed discussion of Gross' book and of the second confessional age, see chapter one above.

88. All quoted from Heinrich Keiter, *Brunnenvergiftung,* 2d ed., reworked by Bernhard Stein (Essen 1908), 1–3, 170, 32, 176 dealing with Fanny Lewald, *Benedikt* (Berlin 1874), Jacob Wassermann, *Die Juden von Zirndorf* (Munich 1897) and *Der Moloch* (Berlin 1903).

89. Langmuir is somewhat vague himself. He suggested that those who made realistic judgments were trying to use all available information to confirm the reality of the outgroup. "By realistic hostility I mean that an effort to analyse the outgroup and its members objectively without wishful or fearful thinking has preceded the negative evaluation or advocacy of discrimination" (Langmuir, "Definition of Antisemitism," 104). There is a lot to be said against that. Subjective attitudes can also lead to an excess of information and objective assumptions are hardly possible. How does antisemitism occur otherwise? See two works by Max Weber, "Die 'Objektivität' sozialwissenschaftlicher Erkenntnis" and "Der Sinn der 'Wertfreiheit' der Sozialwissenschaften," both in Max Weber, *Soziologie: Universalgeschichtliche Analysen, Politik* (Stuttgart 1973), 186–310. In Langmuir's case the difference between xenophobic and realistic attitudes lies in two criteria, first in accurately obtaining information, then in making non-negative assumptions. However, what about negative assumptions made by a person who has researched accurately, or objective assumptions made by a person who has not?

90. Arnold Zweig, *Bilanz der deutschen Judenheit: Ein Versuch* (1st ed. Amsterdam 1934; Leipzig 1990), 100.

91. "26. Fraktionssitzung, 26. Nov. 1901," in *Die Protokolle der Landtagsfraktion der Bayerischen Zentrumspartei 1893–1914,* ed. Dieter Albrecht (Munich 1990), 2:105–7.

92. Prinz, *Juden im Deutschen Wirtschaftsleben,* 46. Without exercising any criticism, However, Prinz frequently and conspicuously relies on dubious antisemitic sources such as Werner Sombart, Waltershausen, or Otto von Glagau; see 81.

93. Helmut Berding, *Moderner Antisemitismus in Deutschland* (Frankfurt 1988), 38–39. The fact that two-thirds of the Jews belonged to the middle class (in the narrowest sense of the term) contests conventional assumptions, according to Till van Rahden, *Juden und andere Breslauer: Die Beziehungen zwischen Juden, Protestanten und Katholiken in einer deutschen Großstadt von 1860 bis 1925* (Göttingen 2000).

94. Thomas Nipperdey, *Deutsche Geschichte 1866–1918,* vol. 1: *Arbeitswelt und Bürgergeist* (Munich 1990), 396–413, esp. 399. For Jewish history in the context of German history see Jacob Toury, *Soziale und politische Geschichte der Juden in Deutschland 1847-1871: Zwischen Revolution, Reaktion und Emanzipation* (Düsseldorf 1977); Samuel Moyn, "German Jewry and the Question of Identity:

Historiography and Theory," *Leo Baeck Institute Year Book* 41 (1996): 291–308; for a serious and concise overview of Jewish history, see Arno Herzig, *Jüdische Geschichte in Deutschland: Von den Anfängen bis zur Gegenwart* (Munich 1997). See also Ivar Oxaal, "Die Juden im Wien des jungen Hitler: Historische und soziologische Aspekte," in *Eine zerstörte Kultur: Jüdisches Leben und Antisemitismus im Wien seit dem 19. Jahrhundert,* ed. Gerhard Botz et al. (Buchloe 1990), 29–60, esp. 55–59, which stresses the competitive situation between Jews and non-Jews. John Bunzl, "Zur Geschichte des Antisemitismus in Österreich," in John Bunzl and Bernd Martin, *Antisemitismus in Österreich: Sozialhistorische und soziologische Studien* (Innsbruck 1983), 13–88, also examines this seriously, however just as a cause, as a "welcome misinterpretation" (referring to Eva Reichmann); more precise in comparison is Albert Lichtblau, *Antisemitismus und soziale Spannung in Berlin und Wien 1867–1914* (Berlin 1994). On the "presence" of Jews in Vienna in the modern age see Steven Beller, "Soziale Schicht, Kultur und die Wiener Juden um die Jahrhundertwende," in *Eine zerstörte Kultur,* 61–82, esp. 66–67. On "Jewish dominance" in Hungary and particularly Budapest (60 percent of industrialists and 50 percent of doctors were Jewish) see V. Karady, "Jüdische Unternehmer und Prozesse der Verbürgerlichung in der Habsburger-Monarchie (19.–20. Jahrhundert)," in *Jüdische Unternehmer in Deutschland im 19. und 20. Jahrhundert,* eds. W. E. Mosse and H. Pohl (Stuttgart 1992), 36–53, esp. 37, 53. Nevertheless, Austria-Hungary is said to have been the only country in the world in which the proportion of Jewish military officers (8 percent) was greater than the proportion of Jews in the population as a whole (4.5 percent); see George E. Berkley, *Vienna and its Jews: The Tragedy of Success, 1880–1980* (Lanham, Md. 1988), 37, 40. For general information on the subject see Maurer, *Entwicklung*; Werner E. Mosse, *Jews in the German Economy: The German-Jewish Economic Élite 1820–1935* (Oxford 1987); idem, "Integration and Identity in Imperial Germany: Towards a Typology," *Leo Baeck Institute Year Book* 37 (1992): 83–93; and the volume of essays *Jüdische Unternehmer.* For the Weimar Republic see Moshe Zimmermann, *Die deutschen Juden 1914–1945* (Munich 1997).

95. Cf. Christopher M. Clark, *The Politics of Conversion: Missionary Protestantism and the Jews in Prussia 1728–1941* (Oxford 1995), 262–63.

96. Wassermann, quoted in Bruce Pauley, *Eine Geschichte des österreichischen Antisemitismus: Von der Ausgrenzung zur Auslöschung* (Vienna 1993), 80; first published as *From Prejudice to Persecution: A History of Austrian Anti-Semitism* (Chapel Hill, N.C. 1992).

97. Prinz, *Juden,* 63. For "Catholic inferiority" see Martin Baumeister, *Parität und katholische Inferiorität: Untersuchungen zur Stellung des Katholizismus im Deutschen Kaiserreich* (Paderborn 1987).

98. "The extraordinary industrious activity of the Semitic race" must be recognized as an explanation for the Jews' advantage, "but one must, however, refer to the fact that the favorable financial circumstances which they enjoyed, mainly due to trading, put Jewish parents in a position to be able to provide their children with a higher education." See Georg von Hertling, "Katholicismus und Wissenschaft," *Historisch-politische Blätter für das katholische Deutschland* 119 (1897): 897–917; 120 (1897): 131–49; 220–37, quotes on 140, 228, 133–34 respectively.

99. Gangolf Hübinger, "Die Intellektuellen im wilhelminischen Deutschland: Zum Forschungsstand," in *Intellektuelle im Deutschen Kaiserreich,* eds. Gangolf Hübinger and Wolfgang J. Mommsen (Frankfurt 1993), 198–210, esp. 209, 207. For Jewish attitudes towards education see Andrea Hopp, *Jüdisches Bürgertum in Frankfurt am Main im 19. Jahrhundert* (Stuttgart 1997), 253–81; Till van Rahden, "Weder Milieu noch Konfession: Die situative Ethnizität der deutschen Juden im Kaiserreich in vergleichender Perspektive," in *Religion im Kaiserreich: Milieus, Mentalitäten, Krisen,* eds. Olaf Blaschke and Frank-Michael Kuhlemann (Gütersloh 1995), 409–34, esp. 418; George L. Mosse, "Das deutsch-jüdische Bildungsbürgertum," in *Bildungsbürgertum im 19. Jahrhundert,* vol. 2: *Bildungsgüter und Bildungswissen,* ed. Reinhart Koselleck (Stuttgart 1990), 168–80.

100. Harry Graf Kessler, *Gesichter und Zeiten: Erinnerungen* (1935; Berlin 1962), 145–46.

101. "Jülich—eine Festung des Katholizismus: Der 'Deutsche Verein für die Rheinprovinz,'" in *Jülich im Jahre 1875: Dokumentation einer Pressepolemik zwischen Katholiken und Liberalen während des "Kulturkampfes,"* ed. Günter Bers (Cologne 1996), 16, 29. The "educated" and "intellectuals" were, however, viewed just as negatively by conservatives and later by right-wing extremists; see Dietz Bering, *Die Intellektuellen: Geschichte eines Schimpfwortes* (Berlin 1982).

102. Rudolf Vierhaus, "Bildung," in *Geschichtliche Grundbegriffe* (Stuttgart 1980), 1:508–51, quote on 508.

103. Theodor Mönnichs, S.J., *Die Weltanschauung des Katholiken: Für weitere Kreise ältern und neuern Irrtümern gegenübergestellt* (Cologne 1911), 9, 143, 146.

104. Hermann Cardauns, *Aus dem Leben eines deutschen Redakteurs* (Cologne 1912), 156–57. See also Hans-Ulrich Wehler, *Deutsche Gesellschaftsgeschichte,* vol. 3: *Von der "Deutschen Doppelrevolution" bis zum Beginn des Ersten Weltkrieges 1849–1914* (Munich 1995), 3:732, for education ("Bildung") as "Ersatzreligion"; for nationalism as "political religion" see 3:942–45. For anti-clericalism and anti-ultramontanism see Norbert Schloßmacher, "Antiultramontanismus im Wilhelminischen Deutschland: Ein Versuch," in *Deutscher Katholizismus im Umbruch zur Moderne,* ed. Wilfried Loth (Stuttgart 1991), 164–98; Gross, "Anti-Catholicism" and idem, *War*; idem, "Kulturkampf and Unification: German Liberalism and the War against the Jesuits," *Central European History* 30 (2001): 545–66.

105. "Religionsbekenntniß und Bildungstrieb in Preußen," *Stimmen aus Maria-Laach* 39 (1890): 108–12, esp. 109.

106. Joseph Pohle, "Der Friede unter den Konfessionen in Deutschland," in *Deutschland und der Katholizismus,* eds. Max Meinertz and Hermann Sacher (Freiburg 1918), 175–96, esp. 186; for a more detailed discussion see Olaf Blaschke, "Die Kolonialisierung der Laienwelt: Priester als Milieumanager und die Kanäle klerikaler Kuratel," in *Religion im Kaiserreich: Milieus, Mentalitäten, Krisen,* eds. Olaf Blaschke and Frank-Michael Kuhlemann (Gütersloh 1995), 125–26; Dieter Langewiesche, "'Volksbildung' und 'Leserlenkung' in Deutschland von der wilhelminischen Ära bis zur nationalsozialistischen Diktatur," *Internationales Archiv für Sozialgeschichte der deutschen Literatur* 14 (1989): 108–25.

107. Shulamit Volkov, "Die Verbürgerlichung der Juden in Deutschland als Paradigma," in *Jüdisches Leben und Antisemitismus im 19. und 20. Jahrhundert* (Munich 1990), 111–30; Simone Lässig, "Juden und Mäzenatentum in Deutschland: Religiöses Ethos, kompensierendes Minderheitsverhalten oder genuine Bürgerlichkeit?" *Zeitschrift für Geschichtswissenschaft* 46 (1998): 211–36.

108. Zweig, *Bilanz.*

109. Nipperdey, *Deutsche Geschichte 1866–1918,* 402–3. See also Michael Brenner, Stefi Jersch-Wenzel, and Michael M. Meyer, *Emanzipation und Akkulturation 1780–1871*, Deutsch-jüdische Geschichte in der Neuzeit, eds. Michael A. Meyer and Michael Brenner, vol. 2 (Munich 2000); Steven M. Lowenstein, *Umstrittene Integration, 1871–1918,* ibid., vol. 3 (Munich 2000).

110. Jean-Paul Sartre, *Anti-Semite and Jew,* tr. George J. Becker (New York 1948), 16.

111. Even if religion is accepted as a criterion for competition, it was frequently fictitious or exaggerated. Though antisemitism was certainly especially noticeable among craftsmen, there nevertheless was no conflict of interest between them and Jews; see Volkov, "Antisemitismus als kulturelle Code," 24. However, where colleagues and competitors of various faiths were represented in a profession, the relationship was often good, such as in free professions, among doctors and lawyers, for instance. See also John Weiss, *Der Lange Weg zum Holocaust: Die Geschichte der Judenfeindschaft in Deutschland und Österreich* (Hamburg 1997), 205.

112. Jacob Borut, "Vereine für Jüdische Geschichte und Literatur at the End of the Nineteenth Century," *Leo Baeck Institute Yearbook* 41 (1996): 89–114; Shulamit Volkov, "Die Dynamik der Dissimilation: Deutsche Juden und die ostjüdischen Einwanderer," in *Jüdisches Leben und Antisemitismus im 19. und 20. Jahrhundert* (Munich 1990), 166–80; Michael Brenner, *The Renaissance of Jewish Culture in Weimar Germany* (New Haven 1996). An excellent comparison between the forming of the Catholic milieu and Jewish openness is offered by van Rahden, "Milieu," who

is critical of the term "subculture" as used by David Sorkin, *The Transformation of German Jewry, 1780–1840* (New York 1987).

113. See Lässig, "Juden und Mäzenatentum"; idem, *Jüdische Wege ins Bürgertum: Kulturelles Kapital und sozialer Aufstieg im 19. Jahrhundert* (Göttingen 2004). See also Erika Bucholtz, *Henri Hinrichsen und der Musikverlag CF Peters: Deutsch-jüdisches Bürgertum in Leipzig von 1891 bis 1938* (Tübingen 2001).

114. Schmolke, *Die schlechte Presse,* is still the standard work on the Catholic press.

115. Koszyk, "Jüdische Beitrag," 202–03.

116. "Juden und Katholiken," *Israelitisches Wochenblatt* 11 (1912): 540.

117. For the student associations Bund Jüdischer Akademiker (religious) and Bund Jüdischer Corporationen (nationalist) see Keith H. Pickus, "Images of God and Country: Jewish National and Religious Identities in Wilhelmine Germany," *Aschkenas: Zeitschrift für Geschichte und Kultur der Juden* 8 (1998): 425–38.

118. "Assimilation into the middle class and the modern age happened so quickly [among the Jews] that they actually exceeded the normality for which they were striving and therefore remained distanced from non-Jews," Nipperdey, *Deutsche Geschichte 1866–1918*, 407. See Leon Botstein, *Judentum und Modernität: Essays zur Rolle der Juden in der deutschen und österreichischen Kultur, 1848–1938* (Vienna 1991). See three works by Michael A. Meyer; *Response to Modernity: A History of the Reform Movement in Judaism* (New York 1988); "Recent Historiography on the Jewish Religion," *Leo Baeck Institute Yearbook* 35 (1990): 3–16; *Jüdische Identität in der Moderne* (Frankfurt 1992). See also Peter Gay, "Begegnung mit der Moderne: Die deutschen Juden in der wilhelminischen Kultur," in *Freud, Juden und andere Deutsche: Herren und Opfer in der modernen Kultur* (Hamburg 1986), 115–88; Shulamit Volkov, "Verbürgerlichung."

119. Sartre, *Anti-Semite and Jew,* 17.

120. Julius H. Schoeps and Johannes Schlör, "Einleitung," in *Antisemitismus: Vorurteile und Mythen,* 10–12.

121. Mönnichs, *Weltanschauung.* Max H. Meyer, *Die Weltanschauung des Zentrums in ihren Grundlinien* (Munich 1919), examined the ideology of Catholicism: its position towards socialism, capitalism, nationalism, and antisemitism. For France, see Bernhard Groethuysen, *Die Entstehung der bürgerlichen Welt- und Lebensanschauung in Frankreich,* vol. 1: *Das Bürgertum und die katholische Weltanschauung*; vol. 2: *Die Soziallehren der katholischen Kirche und das Bürgertum* (1927; Frankfurt 1978). For the conception of ideology which replaced the outdated and offensive tern "world-view" see Theodor Geiger, *Ideologie und Wahrheit* (Vienna 1953); Kurt Lenk, "Zum Strukturwandel politischer Ideologien im 19. und 20. Jahrhundert: Begriff und Phänomen des ideologischen Bewußtseins," in *Ideologien im Bezugsfeld von Geschichte und Gesellschaft,* ed. A.

Pelinka (Innsbruck 1981), 97–107; Hans-Joachim Lieber, *Ideologie: Eine historisch-systematische Einführung* (Paderborn 1985).

122. Few works critically compare several approaches. See Helen Fein, "Explanations of the Origin and Evolution of Antisemitism," in *Persisting Question,* 3–22; Robert Wuthnow, "Antisemitism and Stereotyping," in ibid., 128–63. The following discussion partly corresponds to my approach in "Wie wird aus einem guten Katholiken ein 'guter' Judenfeind? Zwölf Ursachen des katholischen Antisemitismus auf dem Prüfstand," in *Katholischer Antisemitismus,* 77–110.

123. Konrad Algermissen, "Los-von-Rom-Bewegung," in *Lexikon für Theologie und Kirche* (Freiburg 1961), 6:1153–56.

124. Gordon W. Allport, *Die Natur des Vorurteils* (Cologne 1971; first published as *The Nature of Prejudice* [Reading 1954]). See also Bernhard Estel, *Soziale Vorurteile und soziale Urteile* (Opladen 1983). A fascinating introduction into the field has recently been written by Jens Förster, *Kleine Einführung in das Schubladendenken.. Über Nutzen und Nachteil des Vorurteils* (Munich 2007).

125. Lindemann, *Esau's Tears,* 547.

126. Ibid., 537.

127. Ibid. See for example Lindemann's line of argument concerning Italy: Why was there less antisemitism? "The [small] size of the Jewish community is an element of the explanation, but hardly sufficient, since France, too, had a small Jewish community. More important was the nature of the Italian Jewish community," since Jews were more dispersed and mixed freely in non-Jewish society (ibid., 472).

128. Ibid., 100, 532.

129. Daniel J. Goldhagen, *Die katholische Kirche und der Holocaust: Eine Untersuchung über Schuld und Sühne* (Berlin 2002); first published as *A Moral Reckoning: The Role of the Catholic Church in the Holocaust and its Unfulfilled Duty of Repair* (New York 2002). For a critical review see *Menora: Jahrbuch für deutsch-jüdische Geschichte* 14 (2003) [=*Goldhagen, der Vatikan und die Judenfeindschaft,* eds. Julius H. Schoeps, a.o. (Berlin and Vienna 2003)].

130. See, for example, *Der ewige Judenhaß: Christlicher Antijudaismus, deutschnationale Judenfeindlichkeit, rassistischer Antisemitismus,* eds. Christina von Braun and Ludger Heid, 2d ed. (Berlin 2000).

131. Gerhard Czermak, *Christen gegen Juden: Geschichte einer Verfolgung* (Nördlingen 1989), 16–17. See Rudolf Krämer-Badoni, *Judenmord, Frauenmord, Heilige Kirche* (Frankfurt 1992), 94–95; Friedrich Heer, *Gottes erste Liebe: 2000 Jahre Judentum und Christentum* (Frankfurt 1986), 3.

132. See Eric Hobsbawm and Terence Ranger, eds., *The Invention of Tradition* (Cambridge 1983).

133. Lindemann, *Esau's Tears,* 537.

134. See Hans Gruber, "Vom Agrarantisemitismus zum katholischen Antisemitismus in Vorarlberg des 19. Jahrhunderts," in *Katholischer Antisemitismus,* 317–36.

135. James F. Harris, *The People Speak! Antisemitism and Emancipation in Nineteenth-Century Bavaria* (Ann Arbor 1994); Ronald Byrnes, *Antisemitism in Modern France: The Prologue of the Dreyfus Affair* (New York 1969), 252–61; Blaschke, *Katholizismus und Antisemitismus,* 177, 183–84.

136 Lindemann, *Esau's Tears,* xiii: "Anti-Jewish feelings were not the creation of a few 'bad leaders' but rather emerged from the experience and deeply ingrained mind-sets of millions of Germans." Lindemann does not say that this "experience" involved Jews, but what else can he mean? He chooses his words carefully, to avoid being sued, but they still remain suggestive enough: "Modern antisemitism satisfied emotional needs for some Germans, but those needs meshed in intricate ways with real experiences [with Jews!?]" (145).

137. For regional differences in antisemitic intensity and their political consequences see Stefan Scheil, *Die Entwicklung des politischen Antisemitismus in Deutschland zwischen 1881 und 1912: Eine wahlgeschichtliche Untersuchung* (Berlin 1999). For information on places in which cult worship was practiced see Rohrbacher and Schmidt, *Judenbilder,* 286–95.

138. See Olaf Blaschke, "Schlesiens Katholizismus: Sonderfall oder Spielart der katholischen Subkultur? Eine vergleichende Probe anhand des Antisemitismus," *Archiv für Schlesische Kirchengeschichte* 57 (1999): 161–94.

139. See James F. Harris, "Public Opinion and the Proposed Emancipation of the Jews in Bavaria in 1849–1850," *Leo Baeck Institute Yearbook* 34 (1989): 67–79; Hans-Jürgen Puhle, *Agrarische Interessenpolitik und preußischer Konservatismus im Wilhelminischen Reich 1893–1914,* 2d ed. (Bonn 1975).

140. Helmut von Gerlach, *Von Rechts nach Links* (Zurich 1937), 170–71, quoted from Paul W. Massing, *Vorgeschichte des politischen Antisemitismus* (Frankfurt 1986), 84.

141. Georg Friedrich Dasbach, in *Trierische Landeszeitung,* 23 Feb. 1893. See Walter Zwi Bacharach, *Anti-Jewish Prejudices in German-Catholic Sermons* (Lewiston, N.Y. 1993); Michael Langer, *Zwischen Vorurteil und Aggression: Zum Judenbild in der deutschsprachigen katholischen Volksbildung des 19. Jahrhunderts* (Freiburg 1994); Blaschke, *Katholizismus und Antisemitismus,* 229–83.

142. See Till van Rahden, "Ideologie und Gewalt: Neuerscheinungen über den Antisemitismus in der deutschen Geschichte des 19. und frühen 20. Jahrhunderts," *Neue politische Literatur* 41 (1996): 22–23.

143. See Johannes Heil, "Antisemitismus, Kulturkampf und Konfession: Die antisemitischen 'Kulturen' Frankreichs und Deutschlands im Vergleich," in *Katholischer Antisemitismus,* 195–228.

144. Hans Rosenberg, *Große Depression und Bismarckzeit* (Berlin 1967), 88–117, esp. 95–96; Rohrbacher and Schmidt, *Judenbilder,* 323–31.

145. Wuthnow, "Antisemitism and Stereotyping," 143–44.

146. For the comment by the mother in 1847 see Eleonore O. Sterling, *Er ist wie du: Aus der Frühgeschichte des Antisemitismus in Deutschland (1815–1850)* (Munich 1956), 63; for the other quotes see "Die Idee des Katholizismus im Alten Testament," *Der Katholik* 57 (1877): 23–26, quote on 23; Franz Kayser, *Die Ausbeutung des Bauernstandes durch die Juden* (Münster 1894), 17, 40. See Jürgen Kocka, "Bildung und Bürgerlichkeit," in *Bürgertum im 19. Jahrhundert: Deutschland im europäischen Vergleich,* ed. Margaret Kraul (Munich 1988), 3:45–73, esp. 72–73.

147. Theodor W. Adorno et al., *The Authoritarian Personality* (New York 1950). See also Wolfgang Stroebe et al., eds., *Sozialpsychologie: Eine Einführung,* 2d ed., (Berlin 1992), 404–6; Wuthnow, "Antisemitism and Stereotyping," 153–55.

148. Christoph Weber, "Ultramontanismus als katholischer Fundamentalismus," in *Deutscher Katholizismus im Umbruch zur Moderne,* ed. Wilfried Loth (Stuttgart 1991), 20–45.

149. Wuthnow, "Antisemitism and Stereotyping," 149–50.

150. See Blaschke, *Katholizismus und Antisemitismus*; Josef Lang, "Ultramontanismus und Antisemitismus in der Urschweiz—oder: der Kampf gegen die Säkularisierung von Staat und Gesellschaft (1858–1878)," in *Katholischer Antisemitismus,* 337–72; see also Viktoria Pollmann, "'Ungebetene Gäste im christlichen Haus': Die Kirche und die Juden im Polen des 19. und frühen 20. Jahrhunderts," in *Katholischer Antisemitismus im 19. Jahrhundert,* 259–86; idem, *Untermieter im christlichen Haus: Die Kirche und die 'jüdische Frage' in Polen anhand der Bistumspresse der Metropolie Krakau 1926–1939* (Wiesbaden 2001). For Spain see Manfred Böcker, *Antisemitismus ohne Juden: Die zweite Republik, die antirepublikanische Rechte und die Juden, Spanien 1931 bis 1936* (Frankfurt 2000).

151. "Der Abgeordnete Dr. Bachem und die Juden," *Gladbacher Merkur* 6 (20 Mar. 1894), followed on the front page by "Kann ein Katholik Antisemit sein?" See *Stenographische Berichte des Deutschen Reichstags 1893/94,* 3:1737–51. Bachem is also mentioned by Mazura, *Zentrumspartei,* 94–96.

152. Christhard Hoffmann, "Das Judentum als Antithese: Zur Tradition eines kulturellen Wertungsmusters," in *Antisemitismus in Deutschland: Zur Aktualität eines Vorurteils,* ed. Wolfgang Benz (München 1995), 25–46. For ultramontanism as dualism see Weber, "Ultramontanismus."

153. Hans Rost, Gedanken und Wahrheiten zur Judenfrage: Eine soziale und politische Studie (Trier 1907), 66, 83. Philippikus, Die jüdische Invasion und das katholische Deutschland: Eine Rede an die deutsche Nation (Leipzig 1893), 4–5, 42.

154. For a more detailed examination see Blaschke, *Katholizismus und Antisemitismus,* 131–43.

155. Albert Stöckl, *Christenthum und die modernen Irrthümer: Apologetisch-philosophische Meditationen* (Mainz 1886), 321; *Augsburger Postzeitung,* no. 10 (13 Jan. 1881); Volkov, "Antisemitismus als kulturelle Code."

156. Philippikus, *Die jüdische Invasion,* 37–40; "Das Resultat der Judendebatte im preußischen Abgeordnetenhause," *Christlich-soziale Blätter* 13 (1880): 769–74, quote on 773.

157. See Blaschke, "Kolonialisierung."

158. "Die Judenfrage, Part VII," *Deutscher Volksfreund,* 13 Feb. 1880.

159. Hans Rost, *Die wirtschaftliche und kulturelle Lage der deutschen Katholiken* (Cologne 1911), 8, 184, 187–88; Georg Ratzinger, *Die Volkswirtschaft in ihren sittlichen Grundlagen,* 2d ed. (Freiburg 1895), 435.

160. Athanus Wolf, *Der ewige Preßjude oder: Die Mauschelperiode der deutschen Literatur,* Katholische Flugschriften zur Lehr und Wehr 32 (Berlin 1891), 5, 64.

161. On 17 April 1871 the *Fränkische Volksblatt* declared: "The agitation in the Döllinger affair is intensifying continuously. The best thing about it is that far fewer Catholics are taking part in it than Jews or Protestants." See Blaschke, "Altkatholizismus."

162. Eva G. Reichmann, *Flucht in den Haß: Die Ursachen der deutschen Judenkatastrophe,* 6th ed. (Frankfurt 1969), 34. For a critical view see Lichtblau, *Antisemitismus.*

163. See *Im Deutschen Reich* 5 (1899): 71: "Antisemitism is mostly widely spread in areas where the people are not familiar with Jews, where there are no opportunities to observe them, and where people therefore form a picture of them which corresponds with the customary distorted image from the antisemitic pamphlets."

164. See Olaf Blaschke, "Bürgertum und Bürgerlichkeit im Spannungsfeld des neuen Konfessionalismus 1830 bis 1930," in *Juden, Bürger, Deutsche: Zur Geschichte von Vielfalt und Differenz 1800–1933,* eds. Andreas Gotzmann, Rainer Liedtke, and Till van Rahden (Tübingen 2001), 33–66; idem, *Katholizismus und Antisemitismus*; Karl Gabriel, *Christentum zwischen Tradition und Postmoderne,* 2d ed. (Freiburg 1998); Gerhard Besier, *Kirche, Politik und Gesellschaft im 19. Jahrhundert* (Munich 1998).

165. Blaschke, "Altkatholizismus."

166. Bacharach, *Anti-Jewish Prejudices*, 18.

CHAPTER 3

Jewish Views of Catholic Antisemitism

While few researchers have empirically examined the complex issue of Jewish attitudes towards Catholicism, there are various general works on the Jewish perception of antisemitism in general.[1] Some scholars have devoted parts of their study to a specific analysis of the Jewish position on Catholic antisemitism. Once again, we cannot rule out the possibility that certain investigations concerning Catholicism are motivated by an interest in proving that Jews testified to the absence of antisemitism in Catholicism. The chapter by Walter Zwi Bacharach on this issue simply does not do justice to the expectations raised when he declared that "the Catholic attitude towards the Jews can also be ascertained from Jewish sources." However, the five-page-long chapter of insubstantial information does not refer to any new sources but is primarily based on the memoirs of Jews which Monika Richarz had already collected and interpreted. Bacharach concludes that "most Jewish testimonies emphasize the element of latent antisemitism in society. On the one hand, they believed that it stemmed from the economic friction between the Christian day-laborers in villages and their Jewish employers. But on the other hand, it is evident that the breeding-ground of this hostility was religious hatred."[2]

The relevant chapters in the books by Walter Hannot and Uwe Mazura are seminal in comparison. Hannot's work on the years 1923 to 1933 criticizes the thesis of Catholic antisemitism as being too indiscriminate. He claims that comments about Jews in the Catholic press were seldom negative and seldom positive, rather "tending towards neutrality." In order to support this argument, Hannot analyzed two Jewish newspapers to see how they expressed their views on Catholicism. The Zionist *Jüdische Rundschau* only commented on it from 1930 onwards. It censored a few anti-Jewish remarks from the Catholic side maintaining that they did not correspond to the official line of the Center Party. In general, the Zionist paper maintained a distanced stance to political Catholicism, as it did to the non-socialist parties in general. In comparison, the *CV-Zeitung* gave more consideration to this issue. It was the main organ of the Centralverein deutscher Staatsbürger jüdischen Glaubens, which had been devoted to Jewish integration on a fundamentally liberal consensus. The name indicated that its adherents did not feel like German Jews or Jewish Germans from an ethnic or racist perspective but rather identified themselves as "German citizens of Jewish faith," which focused on difference of religion. The paper represented one of the most important driving forces of Jewish resistance to antisemitism. It attracted liberal-minded and nationally minded Jews who from 1891 onwards no longer had faith in the non-Jewish Verein zur Abwehr des Antisemitismus—neither in its efforts nor in its belief in assimilation. According to Hannot, the Centralverein had repeatedly confirmed that Catholicism in the Weimar Republic had demonstrated prudence with regard to the "Jewish question." In November 1924 the CV's official organ emphasized that the Center Party, the Democratic Party, and the Social Democratic Party were "above all antisemitism nowadays." Nevertheless, it did not conceal its disappointment at anti-Jewish remarks in Catholic newspapers, which it always defined as "isolated cases." The more the National Socialist danger increased, the more this Jewish faction tried to present the Center as a party worthy of the Jewish vote. In the CV's paper, the "image of German political Catholicism," Hannot summarized, was "described positively in general." He found the *Jüdische Rundschau,* on the other hand, to be more critical. By and large, from 1930 onwards political Catholicism was regarded by Jewish circles as worthy of their vote.[3]

Mazura examines a somewhat longer period of time, but when questioning Jewish opinions of Catholic antisemitism he likewise deliberately restricts himself to the early twentieth century and omits the Kaiserreich from his account. After a small amount of evidence which includes complaints about the anti-Jewish voices heard in Catholicism, Mazura presents quotations from Jewish newspapers which praise Catholicism's opposition to National Socialism. "In general it can be said that the Center in the Weimar Republic was neither anti-Jewish nor antisemitic in the eyes of the Jews." In his opinion, the recommendations to vote for the Center alone already suggest that Jews did not regard this party and its press as being anti-Jewish.[4]

Did the Center Party receive the best certificate from the Jews? Did they not perceive Catholics as being antisemitic? Where does this positive image come from? The main problem of both interpretations is that Hannot and Mazura rely largely on testimonies dating from about 1930 onwards. For Jews who wanted to support a politically influential party, there was hardly any other alternative at that time but to vote for the Center or the Social Democrats. There is no doubt that both parties opposed National Socialism. Yet at the same time this result should not be projected on the Republic as a whole, nor should we overlook the possibility that the Jews may have joined the party for tactical reasons at the time—in order to find allies in the face of the threat of totalitarianism and antisemitism.

It is important to present the Jewish perception of antisemitic patterns of interpretation in Catholicism as being more complex. Further investigations are necessary. For the time being, as a minority which had only just been emancipated, Jews in the nineteenth century were very careful to restrain themselves from any reaction to the antisemitism of their environment, this in order to avoid any further attacks. When violent anti-Jewish acts took place in 1848 in the wake of the revolution, Jews did not comment on them.[5] This cautious behavior remained characteristic until the 1890s. It was only then that the Centralverein and Jewish journalists became more self-confident in criticizing antisemitism, which was becoming increasingly rampant. Yet this criticism concentrates above all on the phenomenon of brutal street antisemitism, Conservative-Protestant antisemitism, and its extreme party-political form. The Jews remained cautious when dealing with minority groups whom they regarded as potential allies, such as the Catholics.

Were Jews as positive towards Catholicism in regard to its antisemitism as has been suggested? Was the Center "neither anti-Jewish nor antisemitic" in the eyes of the Jews? How can we observe antisemitism among Catholics and within the Center Party, if even Jewish contemporaries did not see that? Jewish judgments seem to have been very limited, casual, and sympathetic.

One result can already be anticipated: Jewish opinions were in no way uniform. Three main positions can be identified: in the first, political Catholicism is described as tolerant; corresponding to this, reports of anti-Jewish attitudes from the Catholics side are styled "exceptions." Third, however, there are also a number of testimonies which attest to a degree of antisemitism present in Catholicism that was reason for concern.

Emphasizing Good Relations between Jews and Catholics

The first thing that should be borne in mind is that Jews definitely took note of antisemitism in its general form. Mentioning it in public was unthinkable for many, but Jewish diaries and personal communications testify to the feelings of anxiety they harbored in an environment which was becoming increasingly hostile. In his unpublished memoirs, Frankfurt industrialist Jacob H. Epstein (1838–1919) chronicled his disappointment with developments which had been taking place since 1848:

> Germany has become great and powerful—and terrible. It is ruled by the Holy Joes and the Junkers. Russian antisemitism, which has been revealed by pogroms, is not as despicable as the form that is reflected

> here in the government and administration, in scholarly life, and in the boards of directors of the large companies. Everywhere are groveling and whining people and it stinks.[6]

It is understandable if Epstein's talk of Holy Joes and Junkers be interpreted as being anti-Christian. But he did not publish these comments, though his observations were plausible. Although Protestant ministers were among the most active of all antisemites, some Catholic clergy had also taken the lead in anti-Jewish aggression. Two out of every three antisemitic books and pamphlets in the Catholic milieu were written by priests. Between one in five and one in nine Center MPs were priests, so their political influence should not be underestimated.[7]

Nevertheless, Jews did not think that Catholicism posed the greatest threat. Even a very quick glance through the "genuinely" Jewish newspapers confirms that they paid far more attention to the radical antisemitic parties, the German Conservatives and later the National Socialist German Workers' Party (NSDAP), than to anti-Jewish comments coming from liberal or Catholic parties like the Center or the Bayerische Volkspartei. There were often Protestants concealed behind the radical antisemites. Jewish papers reported about them and about genuine Protestant antisemitism, yet they reported only a little less frequently about antisemitic Catholics. If we wanted to acquit Catholicism of antisemitism with the help of Jewish documentary evidence, an analysis of Protestantism would be a good model for comparison.[8]

At the same time, the Jewish newspapers searched meticulously for evidence of Protestant and Catholic tolerance. The same handful of Catholic heroes crops up again and again, primarily Windthorst, his successor Ernst Lieber, Friedrich Frank (who had written books attacking both the ritual murder legend and Rohling), and cardinals Georg Kopp and Antonius Fischer.[9] When a Catholic circular distanced itself from antisemitism, the Jewish papers seized upon it straight away. When a dignitary condemned the ritual murder hate campaign and referred to every irenic encounter between Catholics and Jews, this was sure to receive coverage in their pages. A typical example is the report from Neisse which was reprinted in *Im Deutschen Reich*. On 22 October 1893 the local authority in Neisse held a banquet in honor of Cardinal Kopp, Prince-Bishop of Breslau. It was reported that the local teacher of religion in the Jewish school, Max Ellguther, had sat with him. "The cardinal told Herrn Ellguther that he considered his presence at the celebration proof of the unity among the confessors of different religions, a unity which prevailed in the town." The bishop hoped with all his heart that this unity would endure.[10] In 1896, the *Zentralorgan* reported from

Nordstetten in Wurttemberg, where Jewish author Berthold Auerbach was born, that "pleasant relations between the Catholic priest and the Israelite community" prevailed there. According to the paper Father Ginter had given a donation to deprived Jews in the area in celebration of his fiftieth year in office. In return the Jewish community had donated a trophy to the altruistic priest on the occasion of his anniversary as a district school inspector.[11]

Jewish newspapers sometimes gave Catholic authors the opportunity to declare their opposition to antisemitism, especially in the Weimar Republic. From the beginning of the Kaiserreich until the end of the Republic, there is a steady increase in the number of examples which testify to the Catholics' positive relationship to the Jewish people. But what is their value as evidence? It is rather limited. We should not overlook the fact that they also had the function of an appeal, in that they were supposed to remind Catholics that antisemitism was un-Christian and warn them of the aporia in which the believer could become entangled if he were to go against the authority of high clerics and succumb to racial hatred.[12]

When the opportunity arose, Jewish newspapers defended the Catholics against accusations of antisemitism. In 1908 the followers of the radical antisemite Liebermann von Sonnenberg put together a list of Jews, which went as far back as the twelfth century, trying to shock readers by suggesting that certain Catholic and Protestant priests were actually Jewish. The *Israelitische Familienblatt* did its best to prove these claims nonsensical. It was, it admitted, unable to check all of the names, but was certain that Dr. Friedrich Frank, who wrote several works against antisemitism—the only Catholic priest in the Kaiserreich to do this—did not have any Jewish ancestors.[13] The arbitrary manner in which antisemites labeled unpopular individuals "Jewish" is particularly reminiscent of the procedure of branding non-ultramontane newspapers as "Jewish papers."

Presenting Catholic Antisemites as Exceptions

Anti-Jewish remarks by Catholics are very often trivialized as isolated cases or exceptions. This leads us to the second perspective which was widespread among Jews. Not only did they exercise caution towards Catholic individuals such as August Rohling, but also applied it to antisemitic remarks in the ultramontane press, which were played down as slips or errors. Jewish authors were not at all mistaken when they claimed that there were fanatically anti-Jewish Catholics, for Rohling and those who followed his example were prime examples. Yet how was the Jewish press to deal with him? Instead of presenting his behavior as an indication of the Catholic mentality, instead of concluding that this was simply what Catholicism was like, all Jewish newspapers constantly endeavored to dissociate him from Catholicism, trying to portray him as an unfortunate outsider. In turn they expected similar treatment from the Catholic side. In 1910, when Nathan, the Jewish mayor of Rome, gave an injurious speech on the fortieth anniversary of the Italian national movement's taking of the city, Catholic newspapers were furious with the whole of Jewry. The *Jüdische Volksblatt* explained that this "method of generalization is of purest antisemitic spirit and reason, so much so that we are stunned to have encountered the Center on this road to antisemitism. . . . We Germans have absolutely nothing to do with Mayor Nathan's speech."[14]

Jews themselves avoided employing this strategy of generalization. They did not pretend that obscene comments by individual Catholics were typically Catholic—except for remarks made by the Pope, of course. They certainly recognized the danger inherent in such comments, but often, and against their better judgment, made out that they were simply errors by certain individuals. With this technique Jewish newspapers indirectly proved the ultramontane method—judging the whole of Jewry according to isolated cases—to be corrupt. Jews did not reconstruct such cases themselves; Catholics continually cited examples of Jewish transgressions in their daily papers and suggested that they were characteristic of Jewry. In the 1880s, the *St Paulinusblatt* of Trier even established a column called "Das Wucherunkraut" (The weeds of usury) in which only Jews starred. In comparison, Jewish papers did indeed refer to instances of fanatical antisemitism, but always made it clear that they were to be ascribed to the individuals concerned and were subject to the principle of individualism.

Following this logic, "Jewry" as a whole would therefore be just as little to blame for Jewish mistakes as Catholicism was to blame for the mistakes of Catholics. Without being anti-ultramontane, Jews defended themselves. The fact that they feared re-Catholicization and a clerical counter-emancipation movement, which had declared war on secular, civil society and the class-capitalist world, should not be confused with an anti-Church stance or anti-Catholicism. Neither should their outrage at obviously anti-Jewish behavior, their skepticism regarding the *Syllabus,* or their resistance against Catholic antisemitism. They strove for enlightenment in the face of superstition and a rejection of the antisemitic method of generalization.

This interpretation contests the theory that marking antisemitic attacks in Catholicism as exceptions reflects reality and that antisemitic behavior really was the exception. The Jewish interpretation often distorted and enhanced the true facts. Shortly after the death of August Rohling in 1912 the *Israelitische*

Wochenblatt reported that it had kept quiet about this "apostle of hatred" for years. The Catholic high clergy, claimed the paper, had "recognized that Rohling's accusations against the Jews were hollow and made sure that this demagogue in priest's clothing did not continue to compromise the Catholic Church." The paper did not mention the fact that Rohling was not disciplined by the Church because of his hostile *Talmudjude,* but due to theological differences over his apocalyptic theory. Nevertheless Rohling, whose anti-Talmudism first became influential in Catholicism and later in broader circles, was not portrayed as an archetype of Catholicism or identified with the Church, while among Catholics every Jew was quickly depicted as representative of all Jews.[15]

The Reform *Israelitische Wochenblatt* repeatedly complained about Catholic antisemitism, but was careful to renounce every anti-ultramontane polemic and show great prudence at all times. It declared: "We are liberal, because our attitude is modern." In spite of its ideological distance from anti-modern ultramontanism it refrained from publishing any propaganda against the Center Party or in support of any specific liberal party, even in the context of the *Judenwahlen* (the 1912 Reichstag elections, which were soon dubbed the "Jewish elections"). After 1911 the parties of the "black-blue bloc" (aristocratic conservatives and clericals) attempted to gloss over their increasing differences with the antisemitic tide—a scheme which also penetrated political Catholicism. Like its partner, however, it forfeited votes: the German conservatives decreased in number and the Antisemites suffered a disaster which cost them thirteen of their sixteen seats. The winner was the SPD, now twice as strong as in 1907. Twice as many MPs of Jewish descent represented them in parliament and there were now a total of eighteen Jews present where there had previously been eight. These results prompted the losers of January 1912 to stir up the antisemitic election climate even beyond the *Judenwahlen.*[16]

The *Israelitische Wochenblatt* was not blind to the Catholics' antisemitic strategy. Nevertheless it remained diplomatic in the run-up to the elections, not wanting to give a political directive to anybody. All that was certain, the paper said, was that the concept of equal rights for all was being rejected from various sides. "Reaction is our enemy, and we can only be sure that our rights will be respected when fair, liberal beliefs exist." The paper did not reveal whether it considered the Center as "an enemy." Two articles later it expressed itself more clearly: "We are not pursuing any party politics here and do not wish to fight against the Center Party as such." But it was "sad" to observe how much "reaction is increasing here and there in the Center and obscuring its great past." The Center used to support equal rights for all citizens. "Today, however, it seems to know no greater enemy than liberalism. In the struggle against liberalism it now joins in with the Conservatives' repulsive behavior and even curses Jews and Judaism from time to time." The *Wochenblatt* cited the *Koblenzer Volksfreund* as an example, a paper which had allegedly written that Christian businesses could avoid ruin by always observing the following rule: "Whether Moses, Abraham, Mayer, or Stern, you should always stay away from the Jews" ("Ob Moses, Abraham, Mayer oder Stern, Von Juden halte mich immer fern"). This was not just "spiteful and tasteless, but extremely regrettable," commented the *Wochenblatt*. "The Center has often tried to attract Jewish votes." Even after Windthorst and Lieber, the party did not lack honest men. "But if these leaders made sure that such things were never printed, they would be doing their party a big favor, for nothing can lower a party as much as the bestial instincts of antisemitism."[17]

Two weeks later the *Israelitische Wochenblatt* complained that one could "hardly read an editorial in the conservative papers and in the Center papers—let alone in the antisemitic press—without finding jibes or abuse aimed at the Jews." It added that "referring to a politician's religious background in a campaign is cheap and pathetic."[18] This diagnosis was depressing. Nevertheless, Jewish papers endeavored to appeal to the Catholics' sense of reason. They tried to marginalize their antisemitic tendencies, to stylize them as exceptions, and to appear willing to build up trust.

This policy is clearly reflected in the commentary about the chairman of the Heidelberg Center Party, Judge Dietz, who launched an antisemitic attack in 1912. At the local party assembly he called upon the German people not to attack ultramontanism, as was so popular in the second confessional age, but to "make a stand once and for all against the advance of the Semitic spirit, which is hanging over the country like a miasma, poisoning the young." Nevertheless, the *Israelitische Wochenblatt* was "convinced that an outburst of this kind will provoke huge indignation." The *Wochenblatt* could certainly not prove the existence of such indignation, yet this episode indicates the great extent to which Jews were intent on avoiding polemics and sweeping judgments, invoking the goodwill of the Catholics and making well-balanced judgments.[19]

Jews pointed to pro-Jewish Catholics and claimed that anti-Jewish Catholics were exceptions. Anyone quoting this as evidence for a non-antisemitic attitude of Catholics should be very careful. These "observations" were part of a certain policy; they are in no way convincing enough to prove Catholic philosemitism or their detachment from xenophobia, as some historians have tried to do. Quotations such as this too easily could lead us to "conclude" that Catholicism was not antisemitic if they are quoted in an isolated fashion. This, of course, assumes that we view them as a serious reflection of reality and refrain from interpreting them as tactically motivated. Yet just as frequent—and far more significant than previously claimed—is the documentary evidence in which Jews testify to the very opposite, expressing extreme vigilance towards a real, latent Catholic antisemitism.

Referring to Antisemitism Directly

When Catholic antisemitism came to a head in the Kulturkampf, when the same opinions could be heard everywhere, even outside Germany, the *Israelitische Wochenschrift für die socialen Interessen des Judenthums,* of Magdeburg, felt impelled to comment:

> For a few months now, smear articles aimed at the Jewish population have been appearing in the ultramontane papers, in the so-called *Kaplanspresse* (curate's press) almost daily, and, possibly with ever-increasing relentlessness. This in itself is neither new, nor remarkable. Some newspapers of this particular kind have always done this . . . but until now it had not been a characteristic of the Catholic press. . . .

"Until now we have not mentioned the smear articles in these papers," declared the *Wochenschrift,* stressing its restraint once again. "It would be foolish to make refutations here." Yet the

> anti-Jewish articles have recently been published in official, ultramontane newspapers abroad as well, as unanimous and uniform as if they had all been drafted in one place and then colored according to local taste and tone. They appear in the same way in "atheist" France, in "sanctimonious" Belgium, in Switzerland, where everyone is supposedly "equal," in Tyrol, with its standard beliefs, in sarcastic Berlin, in "*gemütlich*" Vienna, in North America, and in Romania. Does the "black pope" give orders for certain rumors to be spread everywhere? Possibly. . .possibly not. Has the situation now become dangerous? It would be an extremely cold comfort if, as concerns our life, our possessions, our blood, we had to rely on the doubtful assurances from articles that they only know love, prayer, and patience, only want to warn us and safeguard us.

The paper's warning appealed more to its own religious community than to the Catholics (who didn't read Jewish papers anyway). A few Jews, most of whom were allegedly no longer Jews by name, had already spoken out scornfully and offensively in the press against religion and Christianity, it said.[20]

Thus, during the Kulturkampf ultramontanism and its dual antisemitism, which were both internationally uniform, were already subject to strict observation. This criticism did not subside decades later. The *Israelitische Wochenblatt,* for example, did indeed mainly report on Theodor Fritsch's anti-Jewish stance and on similar attitudes in student associations, among the Conservatives, and in other countries, especially Austria and Russia. Yet it did not overlook ultramontane agitation. The paper had the highest admiration for the modern age, for its culture and education. Great progress had been achieved everywhere, it mocked in 1912, even in the area of clericalism:

> If you were to now pick up the clerical, antisemitic political smear-sheets, you would be inclined to believe that you were no longer living in the enlightened, culture-friendly, dazzling twentieth century, the era of electricity, railways, airships, and wireless telegraphy, but rather in the dark, cruel Middle Ages. The confessors of Judaism, whose holy book, the Torah, absolutely forbids every act of misanthropy, every lust for revenge and persecution, and an excessively generalized love of mankind, . . . are preached to day after day in these papers, by, of all people, those gentlemen who wear the consecrated priest's dress. . . .

"They are attacked with real medieval weapons, fought against, vilified in the most obscene way, besmirched and stained," the journal continued, so that they become victims of contempt and persecution. Conditions at the beginning of the nineteenth century had been different, confirmed the *Israelitische Wochenblatt,* when the priest Philipp Joseph Brunner had published a *Prayer-book for Enlightened Catholic Christians* in 1804 which included a prayer for Jewish people. Today that could never happen; such a priest would be denounced and persecuted. "This is the enormous progress achieved by modern clericalism."[21] What is significant is that the *Wochenblatt* quotes such an early text in order to refer to positive or non-antisemitic remarks by Catholics. Obviously it did not find another one. In fact the paper sensed that with increasing clericalism and ultramontanism, anti-modernism was growing and with it clerical resentment towards Jews. The tone of the author, who signed "Amitai," was extremely accusatory and forthright.

Catholic antisemitism, then, did not escape the notice of Jewish observers. In a similarly frank way, some enlightened representatives of Judaism referred to it by name and almost lost the composure which, as far as ultramontanism was concerned, most distinguished their religious group. The *Allgemeine Zeitung des Judenthums* frequently complained during the Kulturkampf about the "furor of ultramontanes" (not: "Catholics" [!]) against the Jews. In April 1873 the journal became agitated when the Pope and his press complained about Jews. Encouraged by his example, "Jew-baiting" increased in the ultramontane press. "During the past few days the clerical press has been flinging about some strange and extreme ideas," commented the *Allgemeine,* referring to a report by the liberal *Kölnische Zeitung* about the Jesuit *Voce della Verità*. The latter paper had demanded that Jews in Italy leave the political arena and that the Papal States—in which the Jews did not have equal rights—be reestablished. The *Allgemeine Zeitung des Judenthums* frankly responded to this, displaying a degree of rage which was rare for the paper:

> So the Pope's main newspaper, the *Voce della Verità*—a name which is hardly appropriate—has followed at his heels. This blunt language, this unconcealed hostility means that we need not, indeed, should not, make any more allowances from our side. Let us therefore speak—not with the same spitefulness, but with the same openness. The Church as such was always the arch enemy of Judaism and the Jewish people, and among various Churches the Roman Catholic one has always fulfilled this role to the greatest extent.

In this way the *Allgemeine Zeitung* took a look back through history and attempted to interpret ecclesiastical antisemitism at the same time. This Church had regarded Jewry as the opposition, the paper claimed, as a "restriction of its monopoly of power," since "during the time when it enjoyed absolute rule, after all sects had been eradicated, it was the Jews alone who did not share its principles but still steadfastly persisted in believing in the one God and one God only." The entire history of the Church does not offer evidence of any kind of attack by the Jews, only of their loyalty to their own confession. "Even the polemics," which the *Allgemeine* admits did exist, "were always provoked by the Church. The reason for the Church's hatred can therefore only lie in the simple existence of their religion, which contradicts Catholic doctrine."

After having brought up the era of Constantine and the persecution of the Jews in the Middle Ages the paper expresses surprise that "the Jews did not die out completely" in Catholic countries. This can be put down to the fact that the Jewish people were so widely dispersed. The paper then returns to the present: "After the spirit of justice and humanity had wrested the bloody weapons from the Church and put an end to practices such as burning people at the stake, the Church always insisted on at least keeping the Jews excluded from all civil rights and confined to ghettos. The Protestant Church shared this desire with the Roman Catholics." This may seem an extremely harsh judgment on the part of the Jewish contemporaries but we must remember that Jews were restricted to the ghetto in Rome and other Papal cities until 1870. We should also recall the Catholics' attempts at re-Catholicization, which were carried out both verbally and physically from the beginning of the nineteenth century onwards. A high point of this movement was the *Syllabus,* to which the *Allgemeine* also referred: "We only need to remember how the *Syllabus* condemned the equal rights of all faiths in the state." Yet "luckily there is a significant difference between the teachings of the Church and the Catholics' sense of right and wrong."[22]

In this the *Allgemeine* was mistaken. It is correct that the *Syllabus* confirmed the conviction *extra ecclesiam nulla salus,* because, as was stated in clause 21, "the religion of the Catholic Church is exclusively and absolutely the true religion." Number 18 of a total of 80 errors of judgment reads: "Protestantism is nothing other than a different form of one and the same true Christian religion, in which mankind can receive God's mercy, just as he can in the Catholic Church." Catholic believers were convinced of the superiority of their Church. In an article in Wetzer and Welte's *Kirchenlexicon* of 1891, which was based on the *Syllabus,* maintained that, "no matter how commendable their way of life may be, those who are separated from this Catholic Church will, just by being divorced from the Church, not enjoy eternal life, but will be subjected to God's rage."[23]

Anton Westermayer also openly defended the *Syllabus* against anarchic liberalism, which, he claimed, hated the Church and the Pope, declaring: "In truth . . . the Pope is not aiming for anarchy, but for the harmonization of minds, for the unification rather than separation of souls." Consequently the Pope wanted "the separation to stop," hoping "that Jews and unbelieving Christians [and] Protestants convert to Catholicism . . . every genuine Catholic should and must share this wish." Monopolization of the "truth" in this way would obviously have pleased neither Protestants nor Jews.[24]

The Jews' rejection of Catholicism should not, therefore, be interpreted as anti-Catholicism. It is much more a reaction to the ultramontane doctrine, its monopolization of the notion of salvation, and demand that non-Catholics become Catholics. It was possible to simply ignore those doctrines and leave the Church alone with them. But the Church did much more; it strove for a revision of the social, civic, and legal conditions that had developed since 1789. The *Allgemeine Zeitung des Judenthums* was well aware of this. Its harsh criticism surely stemmed from fear of counteremancipation. The newspaper separated the believers' sense of right and wrong from that of their Church. Even in primarily Catholic states the Church could not prevent the equal rights of cults and freedom of conscience "becoming a fundamental principle of modern society. But there can be no doubt," the *Allgemeine* remarked pointedly, "that as soon as the Church recovered its rule over the State, the ruthless exclusion of the Jews would happen once more, if not something worse. The *Syllabus* has dogmatized this, the Pope and the ultramontane newspapers declare it every day." This was a typically liberal denunciation of the *Syllabus,* in which the terms "Jew" or "Jewish" did not actually occur at all. Yet the *Allgemeine*'s prognosis most definitely corresponded to the long-term aims of ultramontanism, as is evident from the Church laws at the time, or, for example, from the behavior of Pius IX. As dictator of the Papal States, as some historians term him, he once again imprisoned the Jews in the Roman ghetto. Hadn't the Catholic press and literature formulated the vision of a "Christian," or better still, "Catholic" society, in which Jews were not allowed to hold any official positions or teaching jobs? In the face of this, civil society principles, which were called into question by the Catholic side, needed to be defended.

Jews were justified, therefore, in fearing that Catholic complaints about their emancipation were linked to far-reaching hopes of counter-emancipation. "The world would firstly have to be reduced to the Middle Ages, then the Jews would run in freely too," affirmed the *Allgemeine* towards the end of the article, with scrupulous rhetoric. However, this was immediately qualified by the concluding sentence, which once more sounded an optimistic tone:

> Nevertheless we believe that all these efforts by the ultramontanes will arouse renewed hatred of Jews in the hearts of many faithful Catholics, and we regret this deeply. But they will change nothing regarding the development and the course of things. Let us, therefore, rather than be moved by it, just be strong, just strive forwards with integrity and splendor and seek to rectify our mistakes!

Surely, Jewish opposition to the reinstallment of the medievals, to reactionary Catholicism, and to antisemitism also served to stabilize a fragile Jewish identity, but it should not be reduced to this function.

When this text was completed, its author received an editorial from the Viennese *Vaterland.* That Catholic paper described the "German scholars" who professed their faith in Old Catholicism as being "under the control of the Jews." In fact the whole dissident movement was discredited as being "Jewish." The article in the *Allgemeine* replied to this provocation: "Such lies and absurdities are only calculated to even more make the movement look like rubbish to the blind followers of this party, and in addition to spread antisemitism. We would not have mentioned them at all, had not the author . . . been so bold as to give *false* information." What had happened? *Vaterland* referred to a resolution made by the "first Israelite synod of Leipzig" in 1869, according to which the congress strove for a reconciliation of Judaism and modern society, as well as rule of law and denominational tolerance. "The synod recognizes the development and realization of these principles as the best way to a safer society for Judaism and its followers in the present and in the future, the best conditions for its continued existence and the highest development of Judaism." *Vaterland* had manipulated this sentence, in order to "prove" that the Jews were really striving for world domination: "The congress recognizes that expansion and the realization of modern principles is the most secure way of protecting Judaism at present and in the future. They are the best conditions for extending and developing the power of Jewry." Embittered that the Jews were permanently coming under fire from the ultramontanes, the *Allgemeine* strongly denounced this "twisting" of the language. *Vaterland* insinuated that the Jews were "intent on expanding Jewry and were striving for external power, whereas we actually only spoke of surviving and of developing internally through working through and clarifying things. This is the way ultramontanism works; it accuses the Jews of the most despicable things."[25]

A few days later the Jewish paper was able to report that the *Vaterland* had gone on to print a corrected version on 17 April 1873. The *Allgemeine* commented that this was all they had wanted. "We assume that even from the correct version an ultramontane paper will find a way of twisting things, of squeezing out its poisonous intentions and standing by its claims. This has since happened, with an article in the *Vaterland* called 'Confessions of Jewry,' in its edition of the 18th [of April]." This was, according to the *Allgemeine,* full of "stupidity." But the Jewish newspaper maintained that it only wished to quote certain points from it, such as the claim that all Freemason lodges were puppets controlled by the Jews. For the *Vaterland,* as it defended itself, the text of the synod may well have been somewhat different to the one they quoted, but "the wording and sense is exactly the same."[26]

Considering the abundance of antisemitic Catholic voices, especially during the Kulturkampf, it is on the one hand surprising that Jewish newspapers did not refer to this more often. Instead they simply ignored many of the "absurdities." On the other hand, it is really no wonder that the *Allgemeine Zeitung des Judentums* reacted to the ultramontane impositions in an extremely forceful manner.

Reacting to ultramontane antisemitism was not restricted to the 1870s. Jews were aware of hostility all the time. In the early twentieth century, for example, we find some very harsh criticism of Catholicism, which was not just blamed for being antisemitic but even held responsible for triggering modern antisemitic propaganda: In 1910, Martin Philippson wrote in the second volume of his *Neusten Geschichte des jüdischen Volkes* (1907-1911) that the Kulturkampf represented the trigger, and Catholicism the driving force, behind anti-Jewish agitation, modern antisemitism. He went even further:

> Then the religious leaders of the Center formulated a plan, as clever as it was treacherous, to portray the Kulturkampf as a war of Judaism and Jewish influences versus Christianity, of the "foreign" Jewish element set against the essential Germanic spirit. Therefore they aimed their battery with full force at Judaism and the Jewish people and it was the highest authority of Catholic Christendom, Pope Pius IX, who gave the signal of attack. This marked the hour of birth of modern antisemitism.

Thus the Catholics in question, he says, tried to blow up the ranks of their enemy and draw the Conservatives over to their side.[27]

Philippson was not alone in this interpretation. In 1918, on the twenty-fifth anniversary of the Centralverein deutscher Staatsbürger jüdischen Glaubens, Paul Rieger published a corresponding paper. It is a very remarkable jubilee issue, due to the sheer analytical quality of its retrospective account of half a century of anti-Jewish attitudes. At the time, however, it still expressed a sense of concern similar to that of the *Allgemeine* half a century earlier. Rieger put forward an even more detailed interpretation than Philippson's. The founding of the Centralverein in March 1893, a triumphant year for the antisemitic parties, had followed the notorious Xanten ritual murder case in 1891 and the German Conservatives' "Tivoli Program" in 1892, when antisemitic demands were included in the agenda of a leading state party for the first time. With regard to the assessment of Catholic antisemitism, the official newspaper of the Centralverein, which was called *Im Deutschen Reich* at the time, adopted a less reserved attitude than other papers. At the same time, however, it made just as great an effort to achieve a balance.

In comparison, after twenty-five years of working for the society, the opinion of the leading Rabbi Rieger was much fiercer. He dedicates his opening sentences to Catholicism, going into even greater detail than does Philippson's work. Rieger recalls the time when equal rights were granted to all citizens in 1869. "Then the Kulturkampf awoke slumbering passions. In the *Voce della Verità,* clerical circles launched a campaign against Judaism as the alleged stronghold of anti-papal liberalism. The French and German Catholic press took up their refrain. The Old Catholic movement had a reputation for being the work of the Jews" and the "hatred towards Jews harbored by ultramontane circles flared up violently" when the school law (*Schulaufsichtsgesetz*) was introduced in 1872. This law banned priests from working as school inspectors and put the state in charge of all public and private educational establishments.

> It was none other than Pope Pius IX who declared in December 1872 that the Kulturkampf was a Jewish attack against Christianity and thus transformed the general hostility against Jews into hatred. Soon the European Catholic press had gone over into the anti-Jewish camp. Hand in hand with it, Catholic theologians began a smear campaign against the Talmud. . . . Keywords were created, which have since remained tools of the anti-Jewish movement. While naming the Jewish press and Jewish politics, all newspapers and governmental measures which were not acceptable to the clerical circles were denounced. Treacherous tactics were employed to project the mistakes and transgressions of individual Jews onto the Jewish population as a whole.

Rieger, then, did not doubt that the first antisemitic initiative originated in Catholicism and that its topoi remained influential. "The Protestant circles steered clear of this hate campaign against the Jews until the government planned legal decrees, by which the Protestant-pietistic circles felt threatened themselves, and in June 1875 ultramontane and Protestant zealots cunited against the Jews." He refers here to the common campaign against Judaism by the Conservative-Protestant *Kreuzzeitung* and the ultramontane *Germania.* This periodization corresponds to the outcome which is described by historians today. With the decline of political liberalism and the growth of "positive *Kirchlichkeit*" (loyalty to the Church) and of nationalism, anti-Jewish sentiments had grown stronger. Finally, Raphael Löwenfeld established the Centralverein in 1893. In the end, Rieger's review focused on the fatal contribution of Catholicism to antisemitism. Yet the Centralverein resolved to always let both sides make themselves heard—anti-Jewish Catholics and those who were pro-Jewish.[28]

Jewish publications were, quite rightly, uneasy about the fact that, "most of the South German Center papers, particularly the [ultramontane] *Augsburger Postzeitung,* are extremely hostile when discussing anything Jewish and often injure our most sacred feelings with their extremely callous, antisemitic tone. It is completely understandable that this provokes embitterment in Jewish circles," reaffirmed the *Israelitische Wochenblatt.*[29]

Jewish organs cannot, therefore, be blamed for the fact that they reacted critically to the ultramontane attempts to turn the principles of civil society upside down. These principles hung in the balance in particular where the freedom of art and culture was concerned. In May 1900 the German Reichstag wanted to reach a decision on an issue which had already been causing feelings to run high in public and in parliament for years. It involved the amendment to paragraph 184 of the penal code, known as "Lex Heinze." Together with the Conservatives, the Center supported censorship of art and more severe punishments, in order to be able to take action against obscene texts, pictures, and theater performances which, they claimed, "are an insult to all sense of shame and morality." Rhineland lawyer Hermann Roeren, as a Center MP, tirelessly took up the battle in support of the amendment. To the amusement of some MPs, he even brought a personal collection of "indecent" pictures with him, including such illustratons as variations on Leda with the swan, declaring them to be deterrent evidence. Roeren demanded that such filth finally be attacked in order to combat the "abyss of moral depravity," as he called it, and to halt "the moral contamination of further social classes, brought about through the spreading of indecency."

The liberal MPs appeared to be less culturally pessimistic. For them the freedom of art and science was at stake. They could not comprehend the "crisis" which was being dramatically discussed. "I want to resolutely deny" that "we are in a period of moral decline," was the reaction of Liberal MP Johannes Gaulke. He thought that the question of whether some passages of text by Goethe, an author spurned by Catholics, should be described as immoral depended entirely on subjective opinion. In spite of this, the Center had entered into a reactionary coalition with Stoecker's Conservatives and the Antisemites in March 1899.

Now divergent groups within Catholicism and its educational elite found themselves united in their mentality of crisis, including all the prominent figures of the Center Party, whether Conservative-integrationist or more modernly disposed: the "chaplain of slander" Georg Friedrich Dasbach, judge Adolf Gröber, who introduced the Volkverein für das katholische Deutschland into Wuerttemberg, the lawyers Trimborn and von Hertling, and Ernst Lieber. The counter-alliance consisted of Liberals and Social Democrats who feared an end to freedom of opinion, art, culture, and literature. Attitudes among the infuriated public mirrored those of the parties. The Liberal press, enlightened Jews, and *Kulturprotestanten* turned to committed resistance. The sarcastic journal *Kladderadatsch* enjoyed presenting anti-clerical malice.

As usual, the Catholic press adopted even harsher tones than its MPs. "Now, with the Lex Heinze, we have once again had to experience," complained *Im deutschen Reich* in 1900, the "rage" of the Center press aimed "almost entirely against Jews and Judaism, because a few Jews also played a role in the enormous protest movement. As though the Jewish citizen, who is threatened the most by the spirit of darkness, did not have the right to think in modern terms and to become enthusiastic about noble and beautiful things. And yet we would be logically and ethically justified to expect tolerance and understanding for Judaism from the Catholics of all people. After all, they are also a minority group in Germany and they also suffered a lot" under the power of prejudice. "How can they continually struggle for parity and revile Jews at the same time? Only psychology, with its ability to penetrate the complexities of the human heart, can explain this inner contradiction." Incidentally, public resistance to stricter censorship was so great that the amendment was rejected in May 1900.[30]

In the long term, the weight shifted. In the Weimar Republic positive remarks dominated the official newspaper of the Centralverein, called the *CV-Zeitung* as of 1922. Jewish criticism of Catholic antisemitism always appeared tiny compared to the energy with which Jews battled against religious antisemitism. When they wrote of Catholic antisemitism, they mainly concentrated on the rabble-rousers, on various ritual murder cases, and on the "Center press."[31] Moreover, opinions oscillated according to the waves of antisemitism. Criticism was harsher during the Kulturkampf and during the "*Judenwahlen*" of 1912. In comparison, the Jewish papers bestowed unlimited praise upon Windthorst's commitment in the "antisemite debate" of 1880.[32]

Sometimes Jews turned to Catholic papers, whether in order to induce a good relationship between Catholics and Jews or to complain. In a reader's letter to the *Kölnische Volkszeitung* in October 1906, a Cologne Jew corrected an article published in that paper, saying that there were no "Jewish papers." His impression was "that antisemitism is also gaining ground among Catholics and it appears that the Catholics no longer oppose antisemitism on principle, but merely for practical or tactical reasons." The *Volkszeitung* immediately published a reply. It once again bemoaned the anti-clericalism of many Jews and appealed to the harmless ones among them to please be critical and peaceful.[33]

The Jews' hopes were dashed. The Catholic minority did not fulfill Jewish expectations by rejecting the hate campaign against Jewry. The theory that the Jews showed great enthusiasm about Catholic philosemitism and that they put their trust in the rhetoric about the protection of the minority is therefore untenable. Actually, Jewish opinion remained tainted by anxiety and skepticism. Even positive remarks about Catholics should not be seen as proof that it was good-natured. These remarks require careful consideration. They were often nothing more than an indication of the Jewish strategy of searching desperately for positive models demonstrating that it was possible to be Catholic without necessarily being anti-Jewish.

This was a desperate attempt to clear the Catholics of their antisemitic reputation by singing their praises.[34] The *Israelitische Wochenblatt,* for instance, ignoring the antisemitic attacks, announced in 1882: "The fact that, with rare exceptions, they have closed their eyes and ears to every smear pamphlet and every furious tirade only serves to elevate the Catholic population of Germany. This is sufficient proof that Catholicism goes hand in hand with tolerance and humanity."[35] This assessment was far removed from the depressing reality. It is a dramatic document of how overly positive Jews tried to see Catholicism, in spite of better knowledge.

Jewish papers often warned Catholics that they should resist having anything to do with the radical antisemites, in order to avoid damage to the Church, in their own interests. In 1896, *Germania* commented on the fact that the court preacher Stoecker had been forced to leave the Conservative Party. The Catholic paper claimed that "the Jewish-liberal press burst into shouts of joy about it." Stoecker and *Germania* were unanimous in their views on the treatment of the "Jewish question," but differed in belonging to different denominations. *Im deutschen Reich,* in referring to this harmony, expressed surprise about talk of "shouts of joy" and stressed once again that Jewish party members had not been pleased with the Kulturkampf. It then warned *Germania* that antisemites could turn out to be very dangerous for Catholicism. Catholics should realize that antisemites view them as their enemy. They only had to look at the *Badische Volksblatt* which on 6 February 1896 advised: "Let us not be caught by the Center press's occasional antisemitic moods. The Center is fundamentally and irrevocably our enemy. Its leaders know all too well that we will never succumb to the power of the priests, no matter how hard they try to make it happen." The Jewish side portrayed the antisemites' goals as pernicious—for Catholicism as well.[36]

Considering how restrained were the leaders of the Center and that the ultramontane press contained antisemitic articles, it was difficult for the Jews to judge what was analytically correct and politically astute at the same time. In addition, constantly insisting that one was not antisemitic when one definitely *was,* irritated the external observer. "The Center Party's most influential newspapers appear to reject antisemitism for the most part, for religious and ethical reasons, even if they do make remarks from time to time which do not seem to be in accordance with this position," cautiously commented *Im deutschen Reich* in 1896. The *Kölnische Volkszeitung*'s article about Jewish criminality statistics is cited as an example. The Centralverein's paper correctly recognized that "the smaller ultramontane papers, especially individual Polish papers, encourage antisemitism as always, even when they condemn it for religious reasons." A reader's letter to *Lech,* published in Gnesen, is quoted, which certainly protested against antisemitism but did not object to self-defense against Jews (dual antisemitism). The reader demanded: "Don't work for Jews. . .don't buy from Jews" and "don't subscribe to and don't read Jewish newspapers." *Im deutschen Reich*'s reaction was that the reader of *Lech* had actually proven himself to be "of the same mind" as those whom he was rejecting. This tone "belongs to the variety of our adversaries, who do things in practice which they reject in theory."[37]

Antisemitism was "openly supported by individual ultramontane papers, but combated against by others with great decisiveness," reported the CV organ resignedly in 1899.[38] Even informed Jews were astounded by the antisemitic "tactic of the Center press" since they believed it was logical that, as a minority group, Catholics, of all people, would be tolerant towards Judaism. In actual fact the Catholics' minority position both constrained and triggered their antisemitism.[39]

The Center Party itself was judged far more leniently than its press. Sometimes the judgments were so jubilant that for anyone familiar with the Catholic mentality and media landscape, they appeared almost as unrealistic as Catholic antisemitism under inverse conditions. In this case it is clear that Jews tried to sweet-talk the Catholics, whom they hoped to win over as allies. The *Israelitische Wochenschrift* stated in 1882: "While Protestant orthodoxy built stakes at which to burn the followers of Judaism, Catholicism raised itself into the sphere of pure humanity and, through outstanding representatives, expressed its abhorrence of the race-hate campaign which was gaining ground." (However, the paper could only produce foreign witnesses to support this claim, namely Archbishop Cöllestin Gangelbauer in Vienna and Cardinal Manning in England.) This had had an effect on the Center party, the paper maintained: "Even the ultramontane press, which had earlier pronounced a crusade against the Jews. . .is now displaying more positive behavior." "We can no longer read opinions on the harmfulness of the Jewish mob, yet they appeared in every issue of the Center's official paper [*Germania*] up until less than a year ago. Only now and again does the bell of antisemitism still sound in a letter sent from abroad." The Jewish paper was almost shamefully intent on playing down the potential threat to its people: "On the whole the leaders of the ultramontane press have been enlightened." Seemingly, the Catholic press had finally given up the delusion that the Jews had instigated the Kulturkampf. "We therefore believe," concluded the *Israelitische Wochenschrift,* that it is time "for the ultramontane press to adopt the same attitude to the Jewish question as Herr Reichensperger, when he was fighting for the emancipation of the Jews," just like Windthorst.

What are we to make of Jewish statements such as these? There is some danger that we may not recognize the rather obvious pleas inherent in such articles and hastily interpret them as precise observations of the ultramontane press, despite the authors' intentions, and ignore the fact that Catholic antisemitism had definitely not died down by 1882.[40]

A further way of playing down obviously anti-Jewish attitudes was to differentiate between the Center, its press, and its mentality. A prominent example is *Im deutschen Reich,* which made an effort to enlighten the Catholic elite and voters by highlighting the differences between the Center's political objectives and the Catholic press. In 1895 it acknowledged that "antisemitism, by beating the Jews, curbs progress"—and this is its function. The paper appealed to all "state supporting" parties to break off all contact with the antisemites, since associating with them was likely to ruin their reputations. It found it "strange" that *Germania,* as "a Center paper, promotes antisemitism, while the leaders of the Center, loyal to Windthorst's principles, always. . .defend. . .the freedom of religious convictions."[41]

There were actually some Jews who felt politically connected to this party. In the first years of the Kaiserreich, those who did so were quite few and far between. However the numbers grew; around 1900 about five percent of Jews holding the franchise chose to vote for the Center. Mazura observes that the "number of Jewish Center voters [was] continually increasing since 1867." At first, he informs us, the figure was around one to two percent, rising to four percent in 1879. "The 1880s were characterized by development of closer contact with each other," claims Mazura. Since then the Center represented a "political alternative" for Jews; indeed, by 1914 the Center had become "increasingly attractive," especially for Zionists and Orthodox Jews. The data, however, present a different result.[42]

According to the graph (p. 175), the Center was the least favored party among the Jews, for quite a long time even less popular than the Conservatives. Not until after the Conservatives adopted their antisemitic Tivoli Program in 1892 did the Catholic party outstrip them, but still remained far behind all the other large parties in Jewish support. The

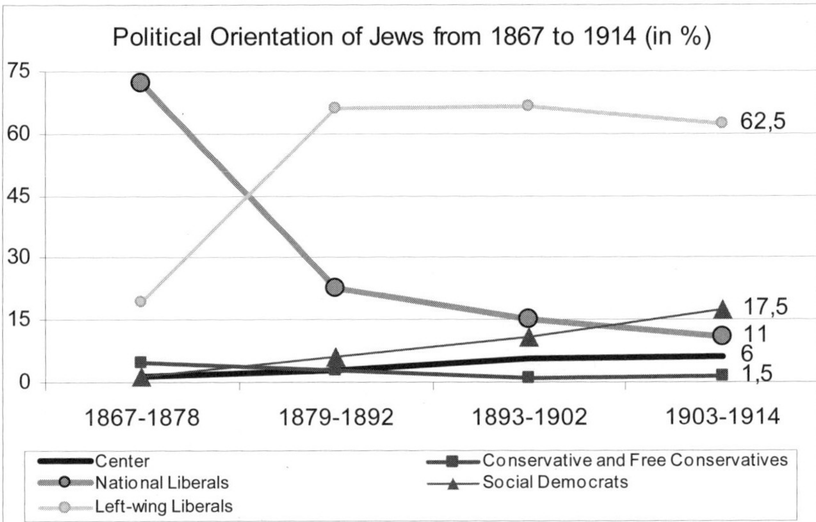

Source: Jacob Toury, *Die politische Orientierung der Juden in Deutschland: Von Jena bis Weimar* (Tübingen 1966), 275 (figures have been rounded off to the nearest one-half percent)

National Liberals received far more votes than did the Center Party. In 1878 they were replaced by the left-wing Liberals, while the Social Democrats visibly won more Jewish votes. In other words, of all parties that did not officially subscribe to antisemitism, i.e., excluding the Antisemites and the Conservatives, the Center was the least popular. Mazura does not make this relationship transparent at all. In truth, his figures are not very impressive.

What alternative was left for a Jew who did not hold liberal political views and did not feel like voting for liberal parties? Since the conservative parties were not open to him, if he was conservative he could only vote for the Center Party. The *Allgemeine Zeitung des Judetums* openly admitted that it was acceptable to vote for a Center MP if need be, as he was "the lesser evil." It is extremely distorting to use figures from the late Weimar Republic in order to suggest that the Center welcomed Jews and was worthy of their votes. For a long time there had not been any other haven other than the SPD or the Center to which people could turn to halt the National Socialist threat.[43] Jews who voted for the Center did not do so because it was an attractive alternative, but because there were no other alternatives for non-liberal Jews. "The Orthodox or Conservative Jew," observed the *Israelitische Familienblatt* in 1922, had "no other party which he could join."[44] The Center's flock of Jewish voters was very small indeed, while the number of its Jewish MPs was even less. During the era of the Kaiserreich no Jews represented this party in parliament.[45] Thus, even the Conservatives had more

Jewish MPs than the Center, not to mention the relatively high number of MPs who were Jewish or of Jewish heritage among the Social Democrats, the left-wing Liberals, and the National Liberals. The order of precedence only changed in the late Weimar Republic, although the Center tried extremely hard from the very beginning to attract votes from groups other than the ultramontanes. During the Kulturkampf it had already appealed to "faithful" Protestants and "sensible" Jews. However, this election practice is not proof of the interdenominational nature or the "primarily political character" of the Center by any means.[46]

Actually the Center's concept was doomed to failure. The hidden motive behind this attempt at recruitment was too transparent. In 1921, when the *Bayerische Kurier* tried to persuade "positive" Jews to become followers of the Center, the *Israelitische Wochenblatt* reacted: "Those familiar with the antisemitic tendencies of this paper" [*Bayerische Kurier*] would see through this "hypocrisy" which was nothing more than blatant vote-catching. "Even in the Center" there was no lack of "reactionaries par excellence, and in Bavaria in particular the Center has strongly antisemitic leanings. In any case, there is no place for Jews in the Center Party," for it was "decidedly Catholic," tolerant in a religious respect but unreliable in a political respect.[47]

The Catholic press and party were not the only phenomena to which *Im deutschen Reich* gave its attention. It also regularly reported on everyday occurrences, acts of violence, disturbances, acts of vandalism, or anti-Jewish lectures. In this matter it was also essential to report much more frequently on events in which German Conservative perpetrators were involved than on those in which Church-affiliated Catholics played a role. Nevertheless, there were a few damaging examples involving Catholics. The ritual murder legend, for example, repeatedly caused large-scale unrest, as did the rumor about poisoned meat. In 1896, for instance, a pamphlet which claimed that Jewish butchers were purposefully contaminating meat intended for Christians caused a scare in Catholic Papenburg and East Friesland. *Im deutschen Reich* reported:

> The reappearance of ritual murder tales, lies about the Jewish custom of drawing blood, alleged instances of food contamination, and similar evil products of antisemitic insanity is surely a bad sign of the times, just like the. . .strange and bizarre accusations made against the Freemasons in the past, which have also been re-established.

The fact "that superstition of the stupidest kind is spreading alongside materialistic unbelief at the end of the nineteenth century" even seemed to have worried a few Center papers.

One particular individual who largely contributed to the spread of the contamination myth was the editor of the antisemitic *Generalanzeiger,* Karl Sedlatzek, who played the "loyal Catholic" in court. Charges of slander and public nuisance brought against him were dismissed. In comparison, a Jewish butcher named Bonn, who came from Burgwaldniel in the Lower Rhine Valley, had been sentenced to imprisonment for four months by a court in Kleve in 1892. "The witnesses and the accused live in a region which has been deeply unsettled due to antisemitic agitation," pronounced the Jewish newspaper in 1896. The priest Dr. Danneil was trying his hand at antisemitic demagoguery and gave lectures on the "ritual murder" myth in Burgwaldniel and in nearby Xanten. In the end, however, the priest, suspended from his office due to alcoholism, had to be committed to the Bethel institution for insane people, near Bielefeld.

Another priest, Dr. Laakmann, when asked for information by a third party, confirmed the deliberate contamination of meat with excrement. According to a report by the CV paper, he replied by letter in June 1892 and revealed that once a Jew had been caught in the act and forced "to lick the faeces from the carcass. I have also heard of other instances of contamination. If I had thought that Jews from the Waldniel did this to meat, then I would certainly have never bought anything from them, admittedly, I have . . . almost always stuck with Christians." It could not always be proven whether the Jews did what was written in the Talmud, conceded Laakmann, but "the Jewish press and its activities are discernible and provoke hostility."

Obviously, Laakmann immediately seized upon the public mood and channeled it towards ultramontanism by transforming the idea of contamination from the concrete notion of poisoning food into a metaphor for the poisoning of society. "There is still a callous, impudent, ungodly hate campaign targeted at everything. . .Catholic. We do not intend to stand there and say nothing while the Semites, the intruders, abuse us. We must defend ourselves. It is the most sensible and reasonable thing to do." Skillfully, the cleric combined three elements: anti-Talmudic superstitions, already well established, the more earthly fears of rural consumers, and the ultramontane ideology, which was what he wanted to support. He managed to fit the population's naïve beliefs into the coordinates of ultramontanism.

The secret of ultramontanism's success lay in this method of unification. Copies of Laakmann's letter were made and circulated. "Witnesses," with their indisputable authority, definitely unsettled the population even more, and antisemitic slogans began to appear in the streets. *Im deutschen Reich* was alarmed. It described how this letter had a direct effect on Catholics' beliefs—they became more certain than ever that the Jews really were carrying out such repulsive deeds. In many respects, the paper complained, this case was "typical."[48]

Often, Jewish papers reported on anti-Jewish riots. Catholics were rarely involved; this was not their way of being antisemitic. On 6 March 1900 the paper reported that an event held by the Demokratischer Verein which had taken place the other evening in the Krugbräu restaurant in Munich was also attended by Jews. Large numbers of antisemites and members of Catholic organizations, cozily united in their common interests, turned up to disrupt the event. After the police superintendent had been forced to terminate the meeting there was an "almost indescribable commotion." Wengg, the leader of the Antisemites, continuously proposed cheers for Lueger, the landlord Kern played the Lueger-March, and "many Jews were beaten or attacked with beer tankards and glasses. Eggs, apples, bread rolls, and beer-mats flew across the room." The Democrats hurriedly left. "'Out with the Jews, knock them all down!' and similar cries rose above the ferocious noise." Finally Wengg explained that they wanted to celebrate the "pleasant victory" which the city—"Bavarian, Catholic, antisemitic Munich"—had "won today."[49]

The Jews, who were unable and did not wish to dissociate themselves from German society, were well aware that pious Catholics were only permitted close contact with their fellow believers. This applied to all areas, including clubs and organizations, the press and the economy. Some Catholic profit-seekers purposefully operated with the ideals of an economically independent milieu and antisemitism in mind, as the *Israelitische Wochenblatt* complained in 1912. The Gutenberg catalogue, from Koblenz, was an index of firms that appealed exclusively to clerics and monasteries, who were supposed to conduct all their business with these companies. "But this list is particularly valuable since Jewish firms have been completely excluded," proclaimed the catalogue. "There are no Jewish advertisements in our listings . . . priests and monasteries should quite rightly avoid Jewish shops. . . . [T]hey should only consider Christian firms. We definitely think that . . . our lists" will disappoint nobody, though "a few of the most reverend gentlemen might suggest that we could disturb religious peace by excluding Jewish businesses." The catalogue affirmed that the intention of those who prepared it was not to cause religious upheaval, but that the "only way" by which to ensure that a Christian businessman could achieve "salvation" was to help him to compete financially with the Jews. The *Israelitische Wochenblatt* commentated ironically on this advertisement and said it hoped that the priests with whom the catalogue was trying to curry favor would give this "economic antisemitism" the consideration it deserved.[50]

After assessing Jewish opinions on Catholicism, it can no longer be claimed that Jews regarded it as being philosemitic or neutral. Jewish contemporaries recognized and acknowledged the existence of Catholic antisemitism—albeit with great caution. Until 1933 they continued to maintain the hope that they would be able to gain the support of Catholics and their politicians, but with little success.

Notes

1. General information: Arnold Paucker, "Die Abwehr des Antisemitismus in den Jahren 1893–1933," in *Antisemitismus: Von der Judenfeindschaft zum Holocaust*, eds. Herbert A. Strauss and Norbert Kampe (Bonn 1985), 143–71; idem, "The Jewish Defense against Antisemitism in Germany, 1893–1933," in *Living with Antisemitism. Modern Jewish Responses,* ed. Jehuda Reinharz (Hanover, N.H. 1987), 104–32; Sanford Ragins, *Jewish Responses to Antisemitism in Germany 1870–1914: A Study in the History of Ideas* (Cincinnati 1980).

2. Walter Zwi Bacharach, *Anti-Jewish Prejudices in German-Catholic Sermons* (Lewiston, N.Y. 1993), 89–93, quotes on p. 93. See Monika Richarz, ed., *Jüdisches Leben in Deutschland,* 3 vols. (Stuttgart 1976–1982); for a selection see idem, *Bürger auf Widerruf: Lebensszeugnisse deutscher Juden 1780–1945* (Munich 1989).

3. *C.V.-Zeitung,* 7 Nov. 1924, quoted in *Die Judenfrage in der katholischen Tagespresse Deutschlands und Österreichs 1923–1933,* by Walter Hannot (Mainz 1990), 256; for his entire discussion, see 255–80.

4. Uwe Mazura, *Zentrumspartei und Judenfrage 1870/71–1933: Verfassungsstaat und Minderheitenschutz,* Veröffentlichungen der Kommission für Zeitgeschichte Reihe B: Forschungen, vol. 62 (Mainz 1994), 184–90, quote on 190.

5. See Trude Maurer, *Die Entwicklung der jüdischen Minderheit in Deutschland (1780–1933): Neuere Forschungen und offene Fragen* (Tübingen 1992), 103.

6. Jacob. H. Epstein, "Erinnerungen" in 7 parts (Frankfurt 1908–1919), part 1, 90, in the private possession of R. Heibrunn, quoted from Andrea Hopp, *Jüdisches Bürgertum in Frankfurt am Main im 19. Jahrhundert* (Stuttgart 1997), 289.

7. See Olaf Blaschke, *Katholizismus und Antisemitismus im Deutschen Kaiserreich,* 2d ed. (Göttingen 1999), 229–45; idem, "Die Kolonialisierung der Laienwelt: Priester als Milieumanager und die Kanäle klerikaler Kuratel," in *Religion im Kaiserreich: Milieus, Mentalitäten, Krisen,* eds. Olaf Blaschke and Frank-Michael Kuhlemann (Gütersloh 1995), 93–135.

8. See Wolfgang E. Heinrichs, *Das Judenbild im Protestantismus des Deutschen Kaiserreichs: Ein Beitrag zur Mentalitätsgeschichte des deutschen Bürgertums in der Krise der Moderne* (Cologne 2000).

9. *Israelitisches Wochenblatt* 11 (1912): 574; Fischer: 512, similarly 496; see "Ein edler Priester,": 317; see also 117.

10. *Im Deutschen Reich* 1 (1895): 263.

11.*Im Deutschen Reich* 2 (1896): 113.

12. Mazura, *Zentrumspartei,* 184–88, provides sufficient evidence; see also *Im Deutschen Reich* 1 (1895): 263; 2 (1896): 113, 402, 435–36; 3 (1897): 159–60, 431; 6 (1900): 107, 476; 3 (1897): 159–60; *Jüdisches Volksblatt* 12 (1906): 274; 13 (1907): 480–81; 16 (1910): 304; *Israelitische Wochenschrift* 13 (1882): 293–94.

13. *Israelitisches Familienblatt,* 21 May 1908.

14. *Jüdisches Volksblatt* 16 (11 Nov. 1910): 439–40; see also "Excommunication im Judenthum und im Katholicismus," *Israelitische Wochenschrift,* 19 Aug. 1875: 266–67; 26 Aug. 1875: 275.

15. *Israelitisches Wochenblatt* 11 (1912): 338, 236–37, respectively. See in comparison Mazura, *Zentrumspartei,* 171–220.

16. *Israelitisches Wochenblatt* 11 (1912): 113–14. Figures according to Werner Angress, "The Impact of the 'Judenwahlen' of 1912 on the Jewish Question," *Leo Baeck Institute Yearbook* 28 (1983): 367–410, esp. 372–73, 384.

17. "Zentrum und Juden," *Israelitisches Wochenblatt* 11 (1912): 22.

18. *Israelitisches Wochenblatt* 11 (1912): 54.

19. See "Antisemitismus im Zentrum," *Israelitisches Wochenblatt* 11 (1912): 58 (Dietz is quoted in this article from *Pfälzer Bote*); see also: 639–40.

20."Die ultramontanen Hetzereien gegen die Juden," *Israelitische Wochenschrift für die socialen Interessen des Judenthums* (Magdeburg), 1 July 1875: 1–2.

21. "Ein Edler Priester," *Israelitisches Wochenblatt* 11 (1912): 21. See "Der parlamentarische Antisemitismus," *Israelitisches Wochenblatt* 11 (1912): 85; *Israelit* 53, n. 3 (1912): 2; *Im Deutschen Reich* 17 (1911): 77–78, 678–79; R. Lerchenthal, "Die Juden und die Parteien des Reichstags: Skizze zu den kommenden Wahlen," *Kartell Convent Blätter*, 1 Jan. 1912; see also Angress, "Impact": 374, 386–87.

22. "Der Judenhaß des Ultramontanismus," *Allgemeine Zeitung des Judentums* 37, no. 17 (22 Apr. 1873): 271–74; no. 18 (29 Apr. 1873): 305–7, quotes on 273, 307; see also ibid., 37, no. 15 (15 Apr. 1873). See, in addition, "Die Verfolgungswut der Ultramontanen gegen die Juden," ibid. 39 (5 Sept. 1875): 658–60; "Die ultramontanen Hetzereien gegen die Juden," ibid. 39 (1 July 1875): 209–10; ibid., 295, 311; ibid. 39 (1875): 295, 311; "Ultramontanismus im Niedergang," ibid. 40 (1876): 149; "Ultramontane Weltliga," ibid. 41 (1877): 533; "Katholiken und Antisemiten," ibid. 54 (1890): 623–25; "Für die Germania," ibid. 57 (1893): 169–70. Alexander Joskowicz confirms the observation that Jews tried to protect their civil liberties against Cathlic antisemitism, though Joskowicz also shows that the two journals he examined sometimes went further. Typical for the times, they fell victim to the contemporary misunderstandings of the declaration on papal infallibility

(1870), believing the pope was claiming "omnipotence." Alexander Joskowicz, "Liberal Judaism and Confessional Politics in the German Kulturkampf," *Leo Baeck Institute Yearbook* 50 (2005): 177–97, 182–86.

23. Paul Schanz, "Kirche," in *Wetzer und Weltes Kirchenlexikon* (Freiburg 1891), 7: 477–513, quote on 491.

24. Anton Westermayer, *Der Papst im Kampfe gegen den Fortschritt, den Liberalismus und die moderne Civilisation: Predigt am Lichtmessfeste über den 80sten Satz des Syllabus* (Regensburg 1865), 18.

25. "Der Judenhaß des Ultramontanismus," I, *Allgemeine Zeitung des Judentums* 37, no. 17 (22 Apr. 1873): 271–74.

26. "Der Judenhaß des Ultramontanismus," II, ibid. (29. Apr. 1873): 305–7.

27. Martin Philippson, *Neueste Geschichte des jüdischen Volkes,* 3 vols. (Leipzig 1907–1911), 2:2–3. I am indebted to Johannes Heil for this quotation.

28.Paul Rieger, *Ein Vierteljahrhundert im Kampf um das Recht und die Zukunft der deutschen Juden: Ein Rückblick auf die Geschichte des Centralvereins deutscher Staatsbürger jüdischen Glaubens in den Jahren 1893–1918* (Berlin 1918), 5–6, 15, 18–19. For the Centralverein see Paucker, "Abwehr," esp. 143–52 and the literature listed there); Ragins, *Jewish Responses.*

29. *Israelitisches Wochenblatt* 11 (1912): 640.

30. *Stenographische Berichte über die Verhandlungen des Reichstags, 10. Legislaturperiode, 1. Session*, vol. 2: 9 Mar. 1899, 1405–12; ibid., vol. 5: 7 Feb. 1900, 3927–53, 3939; *Im Deutschen Reich* 6 (1900): 817. For background see Robin Lenman, *Die Kunst, die Macht und das Geld: Zur Kulturgeschichte des kaiserlichen Deutschland 1871–1918* (Frankfurt 1994), 36–58; idem, "Control of the Visual Image in Germany," in *Zensur und Kultur: Zwischen Weimarer Klassik und Weimarer Republik: Mit einem Ausblick bis heute,* ed. by John A. McCarthy and Werner von der Ohe (Tübingen 1995), 111–22.

31. See *Im Deutschen Reich* 1 (1895): 256–57, which examines Ratzinger as a spokesman for antisemitism; in addition see ibid. 3 (1897): 342–43, 376, 395–96; for Bavaria, see ibid. 3 (1897): 401–7, 504; for a balanced view: ibid. 5 (1899): 70–71. A Catholic teacher of religion from Wiesbaden defends the joke-baptism of a Jew, claiming that it is justified and permissible, ibid. 5 (1899): 159; a serious disturbance in Munich: ibid. 6 (1900): 153–54; on the Konitz incidents: ibid. 6 (1900): 214–16; on antisemitism in the Center press: ibid. 2 (1895):106–7, 6 (1900): 403, 421–22. Hannot, *Die Judenfrage,* 256–80, provides some evidence from the Weimar Republic which is pro-Center; about the case of the Konitz ritual murder, cf. Christoph Nonn, *Eine Stadt sucht einen Mörder. Gerücht, Gewalt und Antisemitismus im Kaiserreich* (Göttingen 2002). Helmut Walser Smith, *The Butcher's Tale: Murder and Anti-Semitism in a German Town* (New York 2002); in German: *Die Geschichte des*

Schlachters. Mord und Antisemitismus in einer deutschen Kleinstadt (Göttingen 2002).

32. See "Der parlamentarische Antisemitismus," *Israelitisches Wochenblatt* 11 (1912): 85; *Israelit* 53, no. 3 (1912): 2; *Im Deutschen Reich* 17 (1911): 77–78, 678–79; see also Angress, "Impact": 374, 386–87.

33. *Kölnische Volkszeitung,* no. 912 (25 Oct. 1906). The author referred to the *Volkszeitung*'s issue no. 891. For further material see *Jüdisches Volksblatt,* 21 Nov. 1902, 449–50 (Strack vs Rohling); a Jewish girl is forced to enter a convent, ibid. 15 (1909): 245 (referring to a case in Galicia). On the ambivalent dealings with Jews in local Center politics see ibid. 13 (1907): 459 (in Trier); 15 (1909): 146 (in Lippstadt). The *Jüdische Volksblatt* criticized the Christian "morals of the Center Party's demagogues," which the Social Democrats regarded as hypocritical and "Jewified" "Das Zentrum und der Antisemitismus," *Jüdisches Volksblatt* 17 (1911): 119. See also on antisemitism in the Center Party: *Israelitisches Wochenblatt* 11 (1912): 21–22, 58, 85, 270; on the Catholic press: ibid.: 54, 182; see also: 236–37, 338; the desecration of a cemetery in Tunxdorf bei Papenburg: 275; opposing Hans Rost: 450; see also: 467, 686, 718, 755, 786; on the clerical boycotting of Jewish firms: 117–18.

34. See *Jüdisches Volksblatt* 8 (18 Apr. 1902): 147.

35. *Israelitische Wochenschrift* 13 (1882): 293–94. See *Im Deutschen Reich* 1 (1895): 263, claiming that Kopp had held a banquet with Jews; see also ibid. 2 (1896): 113; "Die katholische Wahlagitation mit Juden in Freiburg," ibid.: 402; "Zentrumspresse gegen den Antisemitismus," ibid.: 435; see also ibid.: 436; 3 (1897): 431; 6 (1900): 476. "Katholiken erkennen Antisemitismus als Gefahr," ibid. 3 (1897): 159–60; 6 (1900): 107. See *Jüdisches Volksblatt* 12 (1906): 274 telling how the "splendid Father Mommert…received a good shaking" from Cardinal Kopp; see also ibid. 16 (1910): 304; for an account of the good-natured characters of the popes see "Papst und Jude," ibid. 13 (1907): 480–81. Mazura, *Zentrumspartei,* 184–88 provides further documentary evidence.

36. *Im Deutschen Reich* 2 (1896): 105–6; see also ibid., 329, a report about how the antisemitic Volksfreund in Koblenz attacked the *Koblenzer Volkszeitung.*

37. *Im Deutschen Reich* 2 (1896): 435–37.

38. *Im Deutschen Reich* 5 (1899): 150.

39. *Im Deutschen Reich* 6 (1900): 817–18; see also ibid. 2 (1896): 435–37.

40. "Der Ultramontanismus und die Judenhatz," *Israelitische Wochenschrift* 13 (1882): 118.

41. *Im Deutschen Reich* 1 (1895): 282; ibid. 6 (1900): 403.

42. Mazura, *Zentrumspartei,* 188–89.

43. *Allgemeine Zeitung des Judentums,* 1907: 1, quoted from Toury, *Politische Orientierung,* 256. See Ernst Hamburger and Peter Pulzer, "Jews as Voters in the Weimar Republic," *Leo Baeck Institute Yearbook* 30 (1985): 3–66, esp. 55; idem,

"Die jüdische Beteiligung an der Politik," in *Die Juden im Wilhelminischen Deutschland 1890–1914,* ed. W. E. Mosse (Tübingen 1976), 143–240; Maurer, *Die Entwicklung,* 101–42. The theories of Hannot and Mazura, *Zentrumspartei,* 184–86, mainly rely on Jews who voted for the Center from 1930 onwards. Mazura refrains from comparing figures.

44. *Israelitisches Familienblatt,* 2 Mar. 1922, quoted by Mazura, *Zentrumspartei,* 189.

45. Fritz Victor, a baptised Jew and owner of a mining company, is an exception. He represented the Center in the upper chamber at the end of the nineteenth century; see Toury, *Politische Orientierung,* 254, 353.

46. Mazura, *Zentrumspartei,* 190.

47. *Israelitisches Wochenblatt* 11 (1912): 270.

48. *Im Deutschen Reich* 2 (1896): 465–90; 559–60, quote on 476. See also *Israelitisches Wochenblatt* 11 (1912): 467. In and around the Catholic town of Konitz, the population's uneasiness increased after the murder of Ernst Winter on 11 Mar. 1900, encouraged by teachers and priests; see Stefan Rohrbacher and Michael Schmidt, *Judenbilder: Kulturgeschichte antijüdischer Mythen und antisemitischer Vorurteile* (Hamburg 1991), 348–55. Krösel, a priest of unknown denomination from Kloxin, was particularly industrious, giving lectures in schools on ritual murder. His sermons, which were read out on Sundays by his sexton, give us some idea of the nature of Krösel's private studies of the Konitz case and how absorbed he was by Rohling's defamatory pamphlets. Though Krösel did indeed warn against violent acts, yet, as *Im deutschen Reich* ascertained, the violence which broke out proved what "dangerous effects the good priest's 'scientific' remarks actually had on a credulous audience. Quietly tolerating such a restoration of medieval superstition from such an authoritative source," it maintained, could wreak havoc. A few weeks previously in Konitz, the synagogue and shop windows had been damaged; see *Im Deutschen Reich* 6 (1900): 214–16, 635–36.

49. *Im Deutschen Reich* 6 (1900): 153–54. There are frequent reports of shop windows being smashed and of rioting; see, e.g., ibid.: 215–16. Violence between members of other camps hardly occurred in the Empire, even contacts were meticulously avoided; only the antisemites were more prone to violence. Cf. Armin Owzar, *"Reden is Silber, Schweigen ist Gold." Konfiktmanagement im Alltag des wilhelminischen Obrigkeitsstaates* (Konstanz 2006), 352.

50. "Konfessioneller Boykott oder antisemitische Spekulation," *Israelitisches Wochenblatt* 11 (1912): 117–18.

CONCLUSION

Explaining Antisemitism without Reference to the Jews

Three central conclusions can be drawn from this study. First, the evidence of Catholic antisemitism remains strong, notwithstanding ongoing campaigns by Catholic historians to distort the facts. Second, revisionist and apologetic efforts made by historians to prove the Jews partly responsible for Catholic antisemitism turn out to be untenable. Their "evidence" has to be examined meticulously. Antisemitic rumors as source materials are no basis for alleged Jewish behavior. The notion that antisemitism is "understandable" stands on shaky ground.

Third, the argument that Jews would not have been able to recognize any antisemitic trends in Catholicism also proves to be a fallacy. "The" Jewish opinion was neither as homogenous as antisemites imagined, nor as tangible as some researchers of Catholicism claim. In fact, the various Jewish attitudes towards Catholicism were characterized neither by excessive trustfulness nor by anti-ultramontanism; they were ambivalent. This holds true for both liberal and orthodox papers. There are numerous reports of Jews viewing the Center Party and particularly the Catholic mentality with skepticism. On the other hand, many Jewish newspapers tried their best to make Catholicism appear in a good light, especially in comparison with conservative and racial antisemitism, whose manifestations they carefully observed and fervently criticized. This approach concealed a certain set of tactics—the Catholics were to be distanced from antisemitism.

In order to explain antisemitism, the *Realkonfliktthese* is insufficient, if not downright incorrect. Thus Sartre's view that the problem of antisemitism lies with the non-Jews would be confirmed. Karl Lueger's proclamation, "*I* determine who is a Jew" would support it. As leader of the antisemitic Christian Socialist party in Austria from 1891 and then mayor of Vienna in 1895, where antisemitism was deliberately used as a "lightning rod," Lueger revealed just how arbitrary is what antisemitism refers to.[1] Although

Catholics repeatedly found a base in reality to which they could refer—the liberalism of most Jews, and ultimately the very existence of Jews—Catholic antisemitism, as with any antisemitism, was the problem of its agents. It was an expression of compensation, particularly for those Catholics who refused to accept that they no longer occupied a significant position and were unable to see that they could not reestablish the High Middle Ages in an age of intense industrialization. The triumphant progress of ultramontanism in the Catholic Church is a far more adequate explanation for antisemitism within Catholicism than alternative patterns of interpretation.

Was it true, then, that there was no grain of truth, that there was (antisemitic) smoke even though there was no fire? As far as the principal Catholic complaints are concerned, i.e., that the Jews took part in the Kulturkampf and that the supposedly "Jewish" press and the actual Jewish press were anti-Catholic, there is no sign of a blaze in the areas which have been carefully examined in this study. If, however, there were flames deriving from other circumstantial evidence, in the area of socio-economic competition, for instance, then the fire had been rekindled by antisemites themselves and by Christians in the pre-emancipation era. What had happened was that the ingroup looked at the outgroup's positive values, which posed a threat to them, and turned them into negative values. Antisemitism is based on the attribution of certain characteristics to another group. If prejudices describe the normal case—as research into prejudice, the psychology of perception, and social psychology all stress—then it hardly seems plausible to assume that Catholics were free from Jew-related prejudices. To be consistent, this would also have to apply inversely. In fact we cannot rule out the possibility that Jewish writers or journalists also harbored prejudices against Catholics, whether priests or Jesuits. Ultimately, Jews could not be expected to share the ultramontane world view. Anti-Catholic stereotypes were widespread in society. In the nineteenth century ultramontanism, with its nostalgic utopianism, did not attract great sympathy.

However, there are two marked differences between the two perspectives. First, the key notions of rigid and destructive anti-Catholicism in the Jewish press and among Jewish authors, as well as the topos of the Kulturkampf being initiated by Jews are, as has been shown, impossible to prove. Second, and more importantly, when Jewish authors did discuss the Church and criticized ultramontane demands, they mostly communicated not as Jews, but primarily as Germans, Democrats, Liberals, Socialists, or philosophers of the enlightenment, just like other Democrats, Liberals, and so forth. In comparison, the ultramontane Catholics—the only Catholic group examined in this study—did indeed act and speak as Germans and as ultramontanes at one and the same time, chiefly as followers of their Church and its holistic ideology. That was the motivational starting point of their remarks. Their goal was to support this organization and ideology. Primarily they wanted to strengthen Catholicism, while Jews who criticized Catholics primarily remained bound to humanity and civil society as a whole.

While anti-Catholicism served as a negative foil for utterly fragmented Protestantism and for National-Liberalism, and while anisemitism helped to stabilize group cohesion among Catholics in the second age of confessionalism, Jews did not become involved in this anti-Catholic campaign, though it would have been so easy.

It follows logically that the causes of Catholic antisemitism did not lie in the behavior of the Jews, but rather in the behavior and disposition of the Catholics themselves. With similar empirical evidence, this result can be applied to other large groups and other countries. In the end it would prove—contrary to the theory of a real conflict and a real Jewish threat—that antisemitism has nothing to do with Jewry, but only with the antisemites themselves.

NOTES

1. John Bunzl, "Zur Geschichte des Antisemitismus in Österreich," in *Antisemitismus in Österreich: Sozialhistorische und soziologische Studien,* by John Bunzl and Bernd Martin (Innsbruck 1983), 19, 21–22, 30–34; Isak A. Hellwing, *Der konfessionelle Antisemitismus im 19. Jahrhundert in Österreich* (Vienna 1972), 111; Bruce Pauley, *From Prejudice to Persecution: A History of Austrian Antisemitism* (Chapel Hill, N.C. 1992), 77.

Sources and Literature

Journals and Newspapers

Most articles used from primary journals and newspapers are not listed again.

Allgemeine Zeitung des Judenthums. Ein unparteiisches Organ für alles jüdische Interesse 29–57 (1865–1893).

Bayerisches Vaterland (1872–1874).

Der Israelit: Ein Zentralorgan für das orthodoxe Judentum 12–22 (1871–1881).

Frankfurter Zeitung (1870–1900).

Fränkisches Volksblatt (1871–1873).

Gladbacher Merkur: Organ für die christlichen Handwerker, Arbeiter und Landleute (1894).

Im deutschen Reich 1–5 (1895–1899).

Israelitische Wochenschrift für die religiösen und sozialen Belange des Judentums 1–13 (1870–1883).

Israelitisches Wochenblatt: Zentralorgan für die gesamten Interessen des Judentums 11 (1912).

Israelitisches Familienblatt 1908.

Jüdisches Literatur-Blatt 8–19 (1879–1890).

Jüdisches Volksblatt: Unabhängiges Organ für die Interessen von Gemeinde, Schule und Haus 8–17 (1902–1911).

Kölnische Volkszeitung (1871–1881).

Mitteilungen aus dem Verein zur Abwehr des Antisemitismus 1–5 (1891–1895).

Neue Mosel-Zeitung (1875).

St. Paulinusblatt (1877–1883).

Sources

Albrecht, Dieter, ed. *Protokolle der Landtagsfraktion der Bayerischen Zentrumspartei 1893–1914*. Munich 1990.

Anonymous. *Der Mauscheljude, Bonifacius-Broschüren: Populäre Erörterungen über den Katholizismus und die Einsprüche seiner Gegner,* no. 11. Paderborn 1880.

Bachem, Karl. *Vorgeschichte, Geschichte und Politik der Deutschen Zentrumspartei.* Vols. 1–9. Cologne 1927–1932.

Baumgarten, P. *Zur Naturgeschichte der Presse: Eine kulturhistorische Skizze.* Frankfurter Zeitgemäße Broschüren, no. 7, 73–104. rankfurt 1886.

Bodewig, Hartmann. *Geistliche Wahlbeeinflussungen in ihrer Theorie und Praxis dargestellt.* Munich 1909.

Brunner, Sebastian. *Unter Lebendigen und Todten: Spaziergänge in Deutschland, Frankreich, England und der Schweiz.* 2d ed. Vienna 1863.

———. *Woher? Wohin? Geschichten, Gedanken, Bilder und Leute aus meinem Leben.* 3rd ed. 1855; Regensburg 1891.

———. *Zwei Buschmänner—Börne und Heine.* Paderborn 1891.

Burger, C. *Antisemitenspiegel: Die Antisemiten im Lichte des Christentums, des Rechts und der Wissenschaft.* 2d ed. Danzig: Verein zur Abwehr des Antisemitismus, 1900.

———. *Antisemitenspiegel: Die Antisemiten im Lichte des Christentums, des Rechts und der Wissenschaft.* 3d ed. Berlin: Verein zur Abwehr des Antisemitismus, 1911.

Cardauns, Hermann. *Aus dem Leben eines deutschen Redakteurs* (Cologne 1912).

Cathrein, Victor. "Sociale Frage." In *Wetzer und Welte Kirchenlexikon* 11: 431–65. Freiburg 1899.

Eberle, Joseph. *Großmacht Presse: Enthüllungen für Zeitungsgläubige: Forderungen für Männer.* Munich 1912.

———. *Die Überwindung der Plutokratie: Vierzehn Aufsätze über die Wiederverchristlichung von Volkswirtschaft und Politik.* Vienna 1918.

Erler, Ludwig. "Historisch-kritische Übersicht der national-ökonomischen und social-politischen Literatur." *Archiv für katholisches Kirchenrecht* 41 (1879): 3–96, esp. 83–84; ibid., 42 (1879): 3–80; ibid., 43 (1880): 361–408; ibid., 44 (1880): 353–416.

———. "Die Judenverfolgungen des Mittelalters." *Archiv für katholisches Kirchenrecht* 48 (1882): 3–52.

———. "Die Juden des Mittelalters." *Archiv für katholisches Kirchenrecht* 48 (1882): 369–416; 50 (1883): 3–64; ibid., 53 (1885): 3–70.

Freudl, Joseph. *Geistliche Blumensträußlein gepflücket aus dem großen Baum- und Myrrhengarticleen des ehrw. P. Marticlein von Hochheim und aus anderen schönen Büchern*. 3d ed. Hilbetten 1865.

Geiger, Abraham. *Nachgelassene Schriften*. Ed. Ludwig Geiger, 5:225–26. Berlin 1878.

Göpfert, Friedrich Adam. *Moraltheologie*. Paderborn 1897.

Guerber, V. *Der Socialismus als Erzfeind steht vor der Thüre*. Straßburg 1891.

Hertling, Georg von. "Katholicismus und Wissenschaft." *Historisch-politische Blätter für das katholische Deutschland* 119 (1897): 897–917; 120 (1897): 131–49; 220–37.

Hilgenreiner, Karl. "Antisemitismus." In *Kirchliches Handlexikon: Ein Nachschlagebuch über das Gesamtgebiet der Theologie und ihrer Hilfswissenschaften*. Ed. Michael Buchberger. 2 vols., 1:257–58. Freiburg 1907–1912.

Hitler, Adolf. *Mein Kampf*. 170th ed. Munich 1936.

Hunt-Radowsky. *Hartmut von. Judenspiegel: Ein Schand- und Sittengemaelde alter und neuer Zeit*. Würzburg 1819.

Jörg, Joseph E. "Wie das alte Jahr dem neuen die Judenfrage vermacht." *Historisch-politische Blätter* 87 (1981): 1–18.

Josaphet, Don. *Bibel und Judentum*. Passau 1893.

Justus, Dr. [=Aron Briman]. *Judenspiegel, oder 100 neuenthüllte, heutzutage noch geltende, den Verkehr der Juden mit den Christen betreffende Gesetze der Juden*. Bonifacius Broschuren: Populaere Erörterungen über den Katholizismus und die Einsprüche seiner Gegner, nos. 3–5. Paderborn 1883; reprint Paderborn 1921.

Kayser, Franz. *Die Ausbeutung des Bauernstandes durch die Juden* Münster 1894.

Keiter, Heinrich. *Heinrich Heine: Sein Leben, sein Charakter und seine Werke*. Vereinsschrift der Görresgesellschaft, 3. Cologne 1891.

Kessler, Harrry Graf. *Gesichter und Zeiten: Erinnerungen*. 1935; Berlin 1962.

Koch, L. "Jesuiten und Juden." *Stimmen der Zeit* 109 (1925): 435–52.

Kulik, A. *Breslauer Wuchergeschichten*. Breslau 1879; pamphlet offprinted from *Schlesische Volkszeitung*, no. 200 (31 Aug. 1879).

———. *Der Schnapsjude*. Breslau 1879; pamphlet offprinted from *Schlesische Volkszeitung*, no. 230 (5 Oct. 1879).

Lenz, H. K. Judenliteratur und Literaturjuden: Aus Sebastian Brunners Werken dargestellt Münster 1893.

Leo XIII. *Rerum Novarum* (1891). In *Texte zur katholischen Soziallehre: Die sozialen Rundschreiben der Päpste und andere kirchliche Dokumente.* Ed. Bundesverband der Katholischen Arbeitnehmer-Bewegung Deutschlands, 31–68. Kevelaer 1975.

Leute, Joseph. *Der Ultramontanismus in Theorie und Praxis*. Berlin 1911.

Martin, Konrad. *Lehrbuch der katholischen Religion für höhere Lehranstalten*. 13th ed., 2 vols. Mainz 1869.

Meyer, Max H. *Die Weltanschauung des Zentrums in ihren Grundlinien.* Munich 1919.

Mönnichs, Theodor S.J. *Die Weltanschauung des Katholiken: Für weitere Kreise ältern und neuern Irrtümern gegenübergestellt*. Cologne 1911.

Murawski, Friedrich. *Die Juden bei den Kirchenvätern und Scholastikern: Eine kirchengeschichtliche Skizze als Beitrag zum Kampf gegen den Antisemitismus*. Berlin 1925.

Overbeck, Franz. *Werke und Nachlaß*. Vol. 4: *Kirchenlexicon Texte.* Ed. Barbara von Reibnitz. Stuttgart 1995.

Overmans, Jakob S.J. "Die deutsche Literatur und die Juden." *Stimmen aus Maria-Laach* 81 (1911).

Peschke, K. "Wucher." In *Handbuch der Staatswissenschaften*. 4th ed., 1081–1108. Jena 1928.

Philippikus. *Die jüdische Invasion und das katholische Deutschland: Eine Rede an die deutsche Nation*. Leipzig 1893.

Philippson, Martin. *Neueste Geschichte des jüdischen Volkes.* 3 vols. Leipzig 1907–1911.

Pohle, Joseph. "Der Friede unter den Konfessionen in Deutschland." In *Deutschland und der Katholizismus.* Eds. Max Meinertz and Hermann Sacher, 175–96. Freiburg 1918.

Ratzinger, Georg [here: Robert Waldhausen]. *Jüdisches Erwerbsleben: Skizzen aus dem sozialen Leben der Gegenwart.* 3rd ed. 1892; Passau 1893.

———. *Die Volkswirtschaft in ihren sittlichen Grundlagen*. 2d ed. Freiburg 1895.

Rebbert, Joseph. *Blicke ins Talmudische Judenthum: Nach den Forschungen von Dr. Konrad Martin, Bischof von Paderborn*. Paderborn 1876.

Rieger, Paul. *Ein Vierteljahrhundert im Kampf um das Recht und die Zukunft der deutschen Juden: Ein Rückblick auf die Geschichte des Central-*

vereins deutscher Staatsbürger jüdischen Glaubens in den Jahren 1893–1918. Berlin 1918.

Rohling; August. *Der Talmudjude: Zur Beherzigung für Juden und Christen aller Stände*. 6th ed. 1871; Münster 1877.

———. *Das Judentum nach neurabbinischer Darstellung der Hochfinanz Israels*. Munich 1903.

Rost, Hans. *Gedanken und Wahrheiten zur Judenfrage: Eine soziale und politische Studie*. 66, 83. Trier 1907.

———. *Die wirtschaftliche und kulturelle Lage der deutschen Katholiken*. Cologne 1911.

———. *Beiträge zur Moralstatistik*. Paderborn 1913.

Siegfried, Emil. *Schild gegen feindliche Geschosse alter und neuer Lügen, für's katholische Volk angefertigt*. Werl 1861.

Stimmen aus Maria-Laach. "Allgemeine israelitische Allianz," 29 (1885): 578–80.

Stöckl, Albert. *Christenthum und die modernen Irrthümer: Apologetisch-philosophische Meditationen*. Mainz 1886.

Treitschke, Heinrich von. "Unsere Aussichten," *Preußische Jahrbücher* 44 (1879): 559–76.

Westermayer, Anton. *Der Papst im Kampfe gegen den Fortschritt, den Liberalismus und die moderne Civilisation: Predigt am Lichtmessfeste über den 80sten Satz des Syllabus*. Regensburg 1865.

Wiesinger, Albert. *Literarische Bildergalerie von "Antisemitischen Dummköpfen, Narren und Verbrechern": Erstes Christenwort zur Judenfrage*. Münster 1894.

Wilmers, Wilhelm, S.J., *Lehrbuch der Religio: Ein Handbuch zu Deharbe's katholischem Katechismus*. 4th ed., 4 vols. Münster 1884–86.

"Wir erinnern: Eine Reflexion über die Shoa: Erklärung der päpstlichen Kommission für die religiösen Beziehungen zu den Juden vom 12. März 1998." *Blätter für deutsche und internationale Politik* 43 (1998): 755–61 In English: Commission for Religious Relations with the Jews, *We Remember: A Reflection on the Shoa*: http://www.vatican.va/roman_curia/pontifical_councils/chrstuni/documents/rc_pc_chrstuni_doc_16031998_shoah_en.html.

Wolf, Athanus. *Der ewige Preßjude oder: Die Mauschelperiode der deutschen Literatur*. Katholische Flugschriften zur Lehr und Wehr 32 (Berlin 1891).

Zentralbüro der Nationalliberalen Partei Deutschlands, ed. *Politisches Handbuch der Nationalliberalen Partei. 1133–35.* Berlin 1907.

Zweig, Arnold. *Bilanz der deutschen Judenheit: Ein Versuch.* Amsterdam 1934; Leipzig 1990.

Literature

Adorno, Theodor W. et al., *The Authoritarian Personality.* New York 1950.

Albrecht, Ansgar. "Konfessionalismus." in *Sacramentum Mundi: Theologisches Lexikon für die Praxis.* 3:1 Freiburg 1969.

Algermissen, Konrad. "Los-von-Rom-Bewegung." In *Lexikon für Theologie und Kirche.* 6:1153–56. Freiburg 1961.

Allport, Gordon W. *Die Natur des Vorurteils.* Cologne 1971; first published as *The Nature of Prejudice.* Reading 1954.

Altermatt, Urs. *Katholizismus und Moderne: Zur Sozial- und Mentalitätsgeschichte der Schweizer Katholiken im 19. und 20. Jahrhundert.* Zürich 1989.

———. "Das Koordinatensystem des katholischen Antisemitismus in der Schweiz 1918–1945." In *Antisemitismus in der Schweiz 1848–1960.* Ed. Aram Mattioli, 465–500. Zürich 1998.

———. *Katholizismus und Antisemitismus: Mentalitäten, Kontinuitäten, Ambivalenze: Zur Kulturgeschichte der Schweiz 1918–1945.* Frauenfeld 1999.

Altgeld, Wolfgang. *Katholizismus, Protestantismus, Judentum: Über religiös begründete Gegensätze und nationalreligiöse Ideen in der Geschichte des deutschen Nationalismus.* Veröffentlichungen der Kommission für Zeitgeschichte, Reihe B: Forschungen, vol. 59. Mainz 1992.

———. "Katholizismus und Antisemitismus. Kommentar." In *Zeitgeschichtliche Katholizismusforschung: Tatsachen—Deutungen—Fragen: Eine Zwischenbilanz.* Veröffentlichungen der Kommission für Zeitgeschichte. Reihe B, vol. 100. Ed. Karl-Josef Hummel, 49–56. Paderborn 2003.

Anderson, Margaret L. *Windthorst: Zentrumspolitiker und Gegenspieler Bismarcks.* Düsseldorf 1988.

———. "Piety and Politics: Recent Work on German Catholicism." *Journal of Modern History* 63 (1991): 681–716.

———. "Living Apart and Together in Germany." In *Protestants, Catholics, and Jews in Imperial Germany.* Ed. Helmut W. Smith, 317–32. Oxford 2001.

Angress, Werner. "The Impact of the 'Judenwahlen' of 1912 on the Jewish Question." *Leo Baeck Institute Yearbook* 28 (1983): 367–410.

Aschheim, Steven A. "German History and German Jewry: Boundaries, Junctions and Interdependence." *Leo Baeck Institute Year Book* 43 (1998): 315–22.

Bacharach, Walter Zwi. *Anti-Jewish Prejudices in German-Catholic Sermons*. Lewiston, N.Y. 1993.

Bailer-Galanda, Brigitte, Wolfgang Benz, and Wolfgang Neugebauer, eds. *Die Auschwitzleugner: "Revisionistische" Geschichtslüge und historische Wahrheit.* Berlin 1996.

Baumeister, Martin. *Parität und katholische Inferiorität: Untersuchungen zur Stellung des Katholizismus im Deutschen Kaiserreich.* Paderborn 1987.

Bayerdörfer, Hans-Peter. "'Vermauschelt die Presse, die Literatur': Jüdische Schriftsteller in der Literatur zwischen Jahrhundertwende und Erstem Weltkrieg." In *Judentum, Antisemitismus und europäische Kultur*. Ed. Hans Otto Horch, 207–32. Tübingen 1988.

Benz, Wolfgang and Werner Bergmann, eds.. *Vorurteil und Völkermord: Entwicklungslinien des Antisemitismus*. Freiburg 1997.

Berding, Helmut. *Moderner Antisemitismus in Deutschland.* Frankfurt 1988.

Berger, Stefan. *The Search for Normality: National Identity and Historical Consciousness in Germany since 1800*. Oxford 1997.

Bergmann, Werner. "Antisemitismus in öffentlichen Konflikten 1949–1994," in *Antisemitismus in Deutschland: Zur Aktualität eines Vorurteils*. Ed. Wolfgang Benz, 64–88. Munich 1995.

Bering, Dietz. *Die Intellektuellen: Geschichte eines Schimpfwortes*. Berlin 1982.

Berkley, George E. *Vienna and its Jews: The Tragedy of Success, 1880–1980*. Lanham, Md. 1988.

Bernstein, Fritz. *Der Antisemitismus als Gruppenerscheinung: Versuch einer Soziologie des Judenhasses*. Berlin 1926.

Bers. Günter, ed. "Jülich—eine Festung des Katholizismus: Der 'Deutsche Verein für die Rheinprovinz.'" In *Jülich im Jahre 1875: Dokumentation einer Pressepolemik zwischen Katholiken und Liberalen während des "Kulturkampfes."* Cologne 1996.

Besier, Gerhard. *Kirche, Politik und Gesellschaft im 19. Jahrhundert.* Munich 1998.

Beyreuther, Erich. "Die Vorgeschichte des Kirchenkampfes zwischen 1918 und 1933." In *Frömmigkeit und Theologie: Gesammelte Aufsätze zu*

Pietismus und zur Erweckungsbewegung. 327–48. Hildesheim 1980; first published in *Tutzinger Hefte*. Munich 1969.

Blackbourn, David. "Roman Catholics, the Centre Party and Anti-Semitism in Imperial Germany." In *Nationalist and Racialist Movements in Britain and Germany before 1914.* Eds. Paul Kennedy and Anthony Nicholls, 106–29. London 1981.

Blaschke, Olaf. "Der Altkatholizismus 1870 bis 1945: Nationalismus, Antisemitismus und Nationalsozialismus." *Historische Zeitschrift* 261 (1995): 51–99.

———. "Kontraste in der Katholizismusforschung: Das antisemitischen Erbe des 19. Jahrhunderts und die Verantwortung der Katholiken." *Neue politische Literatur* 40 (1995): 411–20.

——— and Frank-Michael Kuhlemann. "Religion in Geschichte und Gesellschaft: Sozial-historische Perspektiven für die vergleichende Erforschung religiöser Mentalitäten und Milieus." In *Religion im Kaiserreich: Milieus, Mentalitäten, Krisen.* Eds. Olaf Blaschke and Frank-Michael Kuhlemann, 7–58. Gütersloh 1996.

———. "Die Kolonialisierung der Laienwelt: Priester als Milieumanager und die Kanäle klerikaler Kuratel." In *Religion im Kaiserreich: Milieus, Mentalitäten, Krisen.* Eds. Olaf Blaschke and Frank-Michael Kuhlemann, 125–26. Gütersloh 1996.

———. "Die Elimination wissenschaftlicher Unterscheidungsfähigkeit: Goldhagens Begriff des 'Eliminatorischen Antisemitismus'—eine Überprüfung." In *Geschichtswissenschaft und Öffentlichkeit: Der Streit um Daniel J. Goldhagen.* Eds. Rainer Erb and Johannes Heil, 63–91. Frankfurt 1998.

———. "Nicht die Kirche als solche? Anfragen eines Historikers an die vatikanische 'Reflexion über die Shoa.'" *Blätter für deutsche und internationale Politik* 43 (1998): 862–74.

———. "Schlesiens Katholizismus: Sonderfall oder Spielart der katholischen Subkultur? Eine vergleichende Probe anhand des Antisemitismus." *Archiv für Schlesische Kirchengeschichte* 57 (1999): 161–94.

———. "Der Teufel ist ein geflügeltes Krokodil am Klavier: Mit Horrorgeschichten die Gläubigen gefoppt: Vor hundert Jahren erschütterte die Taxil-Affäre Europa." *Süddeutsche Zeitung (SZ am Wochenende),* 19 Apr. 1999.

———. *Katholizismus und Antisemitismus im Deutschen Kaiserreich.* 2nd ed. (1st ed. 1997) Göttingen 1999.

———. "Das 19. Jahrhundert: Ein Zweites Konfessionelles Zeitalter?" *Geschichte und Gesellschaft* 26 (2000): 38–75.

———. "Wie wird aus einem guten Katholiken ein 'guter' Judenfeind? Zwölf Ursachen des katholischen Antisemitismus auf dem Prüfstand." In *Katholischer Antisemitismus im 19. Jahrhundert: Ursachen und Traditionen im internationalen Vergleich.* Eds. Olaf Blaschke and Aram Mattioli, 77–110. Zürich 2000.

———. "Einleitung: Die Anatomie des katholischen Antisemitismus: Eine Einladung zum internationalen Vergleich." In *Katholischer Antisemitismus im 19. Jahrhundert: Ursachen und Traditionen im internationalen Vergleich.* Eds. Olaf Blaschke and Aram Mattioli, 3–56. Zürich 2000.

——— and Urs Altermatt, "'Katholizismus und Antisemitismus': Eine Kontroverse." *Schweizerische Zeitschrift für Geschichte* 50 (2000): 204–36.

———. "Das Zweite Konfessionelle Zeitalter: Ein Deutungsangebot für Katholizismus- und Sozialhistoriker." In *Konfession, Milieu, Moderne: Konzeptionelle Positionen und Kontroversen zur Geschichte von Katholizismus und Kirche im 19. und 20. Jahrhundert.* Eds. Johannes Horstmann and Antonius Liedhegener, 27–78. Schwerte 2001.

———. "Bürgertum und Bürgerlichkeit im Spannungsfeld des neuen Konfessionalismus 1830 bis 1930." In *Juden, Bürger, Deutsche: Zur Geschichte von Vielfalt und Differenz 1800–1933.* Eds. Andreas Gotzmann, Rainer Liedtke, and Till van Rahden, 33–66. Tübingen 2001.

———. "'Non comprare dagli ebrei': Il Vaticano, l'ultramontanismo e l'antisemitismo: Proposte per una comparazione europea." *Ricerche di storia politica,* n.s. 4 (2001): 147–64.

———, ed. *Konfessionen im Konflikt: Deutschland zwischen 1800 und 1970: ein zweites konfessionelles Zeitalter.* Göttingen 2002.

———. "Hitlers willige Katholiken? Goldhagens Moralpredigt gegen die katholische Kirche aus der Sicht eines anderen Kritikers ihres Antisemitismus." *Zeitschrift für Geschichtswissenschaft* 50 (2002): 1099–1115.

———. "Goldhagen und Hitlers willige Katholiken zwischen Sensationshascherei und Wirklichkeit: Ein ernstes Themenfeld droht zu verbrennen." *Menora: Jahrbuch für deutsch-jüdische Geschichte* 14 (2003) [=*Goldhagen, der Vatikan und die Judenfeindschaft.* Eds. Julius H. Schoeps, a.o. (Berlin and Vienna 2003): 163–93].

———. "Die Inkubationszeit konfessioneller Intoleranz im frühen 19. Jahrhundert." In *Intoleranz im Zeitalter der Revolutionen. Europa 1770–1848*. Eds. Aram Mattioli, et al., 189–209. Zürich 2004.

———. Das zweite konfessionelle Zeitalter als Parabel zwischen 1800 und 1970. zeitenblicke, 2006 http://www.zeitenblicke.de/2006/1/Blaschke/index_html/fedoradocument_view.

Böcker, Manfred. *Antisemitismus ohne Juden: Die zweite Republik, die antirepublikanische Rechte und die Juden, Spanien 1931 bis 1936*. Frankfurt 2000.

Borut, Jacob. "Vereine für Jüdische Geschichte und Literatur at the End of the Nineteenth Century." *Leo Baeck Institute Yearbook* 41 (1996): 89–114.

Botstein, Leon. *Judentum und Modernität: Essays zur Rolle der Juden in der deutschen und österreichischen Kultur, 1848–1938*. Vienna 1991.

Brakelmann, Günter et al, eds. *Protestantismus und Politik: Werk und Wirkung Adolf Stoeckers*. Hamburg 1982.

Braun, Christina von and Ludger Heid, eds. *Der ewige Judenhaß: Christlicher Antijudaismus, deutschnationale Judenfeindlichkeit, rassistischer Antisemitismus*. 2nd ed. Berlin 2000.

Brenner, Michael. *The Renaissance of Jewish Culture in Weimar Germany*. New Haven 1996.

——— and Stefi Jersch-Wenzel and Michael Meyer. *Emanzipation und Akkulturation 1780–1871*. Deutsch-jüdische Geschichte in der Neuzeit. Eds. Michael A. Meyer and Michael Brenner. vol. 2. Munich 2000.

Breuning, Klaus. *Die Vision des Reiches: Deutscher Katholizismus zwischen Demokratie und Diktatur (1929–1934)*. Munich 1969.

Buchanan, Tom and Martin Conway, eds. *Political Catholicism in Europe 1918–1965*. Oxford 1996.

Bucholtz, Erika. *Henri Hinrichsen und der Musikverlag CF Peters: Deutsch-jüdisches Bürgertum in Leipzig von 1891 bis 1938*. Tübingen 2001.

Bunzl, John. "Zur Geschichte des Antisemitismus in Österreich." In *Antisemitismus in Österreich: Sozialhistorische und soziologische Studien,* by John Bunzl and Bernd Martin, 13–88. Innsbruck 1983.

Byrnes, Ronald. *Antisemitism in Modern France: The Prologue of the Dreyfus Affair*. New York 1969.

Chouraqui, A. *Cent ans d'histoire: L'Alliance Israélite Universelle et la renaissance juive contemporaine (1860–1960)*. Paris 1965.

Clark, Christopher. *The Politics of Conversion: Missionary Protestantism and the Jews in Prussia 1728–1941*. Oxford 1995.

———. “Doctrine or Death?” *Times Literary Supplement,* 1 Nov. 2002, 14.

——— and Wolfram Kaiser, eds. *Culture Wars. Secular-Catholic Conflict in Nineteenth-Century Europe*. Cambridge 2003.

Cobet, Christoph. *Der Wortschatz des Antisemitismus in der Bismarckzeit* Munich 1973.

Cohen, Susan Sarah. *Antisemitism: An Annotated Bibliography.* Vols. 4–6 (1988–1990). Munich 1997.

Cohn, Norman. *Warrant for Genocide: The Myth of the Jewish World-conspiracy and the* Protocols of the Elders of Zion. New York 1967.

Czermak, Gerhard. *Christen gegen Juden: Geschichte einer Verfolgung.* Nördlingen 1989.

Damberg, Wilhelm.“Katholizismus und Antisemitismus in Westfalen: Ein Desiderat.” In *Verdrängung und Vernichtung der Juden in Westfalen.* Eds. Arno Herzig, a.o., 44–61. Münster 1995.

Dowe, Christoph and Stephan Fuchs, “Katholische Studenten und Antisemitismus im Wilhelminischen Deutschland.” *Geschichte und Gesellschaft* 30 (2004): 571–93.

Epstein, Simcha. “The ‘Highest Wave of Antisemitism since 1945’—Is It So?” *Vidal Sassoon International Center for the Study of Antisemitism, Annual Report 2001*. (2001): 7–8.

Erb, Rainer, ed. *Die Legende vom Ritualmord: Zur Geschichte der Blutbeschuldigung gegen Juden.* Berlin 1993.

Estel, Bernhard. *Soziale Vorurteile und soziale Urteile*. Opladen 1983.

Ettinger, Shmuel. “Graetz, Heinrich.” In *Encyclopaedia Judaica* [English] 7:845–50. Jerusalem 1971.

Fahlbusch, Erwin. “Konfessionalismus.” In *Evangelisches Kirchenlexikon.* 3d ed. 2:1360–65. Göttingen 1990.

Fein, Helen, ed. *The Persisting Question: Sociological Perspectives and Social Contexts of Modern Antisemitism*. Berlin 1987.

———. “Explanations of the Origin and Evolution of Antisemitism.” In *The Persisting Question: Sociological Perspectives and Social Contexts of Modern Antisemitism.* Ed. Helen Fein, 3–22. Berlin 1987.

Finkelstein, Norman. *The Holocaust Industry.* London 2000.

Flanzbaum, Hilene. “The Americanization of the Holocaust.” *Journal of Genocide Research* 1 (1999): 91–104.

Fleckenstein, Heinz. "Konfessionalismus." In *Staatslexikon.* 6th ed. 4: 1206–1208. Freiburg 1959.

Förster, Jens. *Kleine Einführung in das Schubladendenken. Über Nutzen und Nacteil des Vorurteils*. Munich 2007.

Fritsch, W. "Verein zur Abwehr des Antisemitismus (Abwehrverein) 1890–1933." In *Die bürgerlichen Parteien in Deutschland: Handbuch der Geschichte der bürgerlichen Parteien und anderer bürgerlicher Interessenorganisationen vom Vormärz bis zum Jahre 1945*. Ed. Dieter Fricke 4:375–78. Leipzig 1974.

Gabriel, Karl. *Christentum zwischen Tradition und Postmoderne*. 2d ed. Freiburg 1998.

Gay, Peter. "Begegnung mit der Moderne: Die deutschen Juden in der wilhelminischen Kultur." In *Freud, Juden und andere Deutsche: Herren und Opfer in der modernen Kultur.* 115–88. Hamburg 1986.

Geiger, Theodor. *Ideologie und Wahrheit.* Vienna 1953.

Gerteis, Klaus. *Leopold Sonnemann: Ein Beitrag zur Geschichte des demokratischen Nationalstaatsgedenkens in Deutschland.* Frankfurt a. M. 1970.

Goldhagen, Daniel J. *Hitler's Willing Executioners.* New York 1996.

———. *Die katholische Kirche und der Holocaust: Eine Untersuchung über Schuld und Sühne*. Berlin 2002. First published as *A Moral Reckoning: The Role of the Catholic Church in the Holocaust and its Unfulfilled Duty of Repair*. New York 2002.

Grab, Walter. "Kritische Bemerkungen zur nationalen Apologetik Joachim Fests, Ernst Noltes und Andreas Hillgrubers." *1999* [*Sozialgeschichte des 20. und 21. Jahrhunderts*] 2 (1987): 151–57.

Graetz, Heinrich. *Geschichte der Juden von den ältesten Zeiten bis auf die Gegenwart.* 11 vols. Leipzig et al. 1853–1876; reprint of the later edition with a foreword by Reuven Michael and a biography (1904) by Philipp Bloch. Berlin 1996.

———. *Volkstümliche Geschichte der Juden*. 2 vols. Vienna 1888; reprint Cologne 2000.

Greive, Hermann. "Between Christian Anti-Judaism and National-Socialist Antisemitism: The Case of German Catholicism." In *Judaism and Christianity under the Impact of National Socialism*. Eds. Otto Dov Kulka and Paul R. Mendes-Flohr, 169–79. Jerusalem 1987.

———. *Theologie und Ideologie: Katholizismus und Judentum in Deutschland und Österreich 1918–1933*. Heidelberg 1969.

———. *Geschichte des modernen Antisemitismus in Deutschland.* Darmstadt 1988.

Groethuysen, Bernhard. *Die Entstehung der bürgerlichen Welt- und Lebensanschauung in Frankreich.* Vol. 1, *Das Bürgertum und die katholische Weltanschauung*; vol. 2, *Die Soziallehren der katholischen Kirche und das Bürgertum.* First. ed. 1927; Frankfurt 1978.

Gross, Michael B. "Anti-Catholicism, Liberalism and German National Identity, 1848–1880." Ph.D. diss., Brown University, 1997. Published as *The War against Catholicism: Liberalism and the Anti-Catholic Imagination in Nineteenth-Century Germany.* Ann Arbor, Mich. 2004.

———. "Kulturkampf and Unification: German Liberalism and the War against the Jesuits." *Central European History* 30 (2001): 545–66.

Gruber, Hans. "Vom Agrarantisemitismus zum katholischen Antisemitismus in Voralrlberg des 19. Jahrhunderts." In *Katholischer Antisemitismus im 19. Jahrhundert: Ursachen und Traditionen im internationalen Vergleich.* Eds. Olaf Blaschke and Aram Mattioli, 317–36. Zürich 2000.

Haase, Amine. *Katholische Presse und die Judenfrage: Inhaltsanalyse katholischer Periodika am Ende des 19. Jahrhunderts.* Munich 1975.

Hamburger, Ernst and Peter Pulzer. "Die jüdische Beteiligung an der Politik." In *Die Juden im Wilhelminischen Deutschland 1890–1914.* Ed. W. E. Mosse, 143–240. Tübingen 1976.

——— and Peter Pulzer. "Jews as Voters in the Weimar Republic." *Leo Baeck Institute Yearbook* 30 (1985): 3–66.

Hannot, Walter. *Die Judenfrage in der katholischen Tagespresse Deutschlands und Österreichs 1923–1933.* Mainz 1990.

Harris, James F. *A Study in the Theory and Practive of German Liberalism: Eduard Lasker, 1829–1884.* Lanham, Md. 1984.

———. "Public Opinion and the Proposed Emancipation of the Jews in Bavaria in 1849–1850." *Leo Baeck Institute Yearbook* 34 (1989): 67–79.

———. *The People Speak! Antisemitism and Emancipation in Nineteenth-Century Bavaria.* Ann Arbor 1994.

Healy, Róisin. "Anti-Jesuitism in Imperial Germany: The Jesuit as Androgyne." In *Protestants, Catholics and Jews in Germany 1800–1914.* Ed. Helmut Walser Smith, 153–84. Oxford 2001.

Hecht, Cornelia. *Deutsche Juden und Antisemitismus in der Weimarer Republik.* Bonn 2001.

Heer, Friedrich. *Gottes erste Liebe: 2000 Jahre Judentum und Christentum.* Frankfurt 1986.

Hehl, Ulrich von and Christoph Kösters, eds. *Priester unter Hitlers Terror. Eine biographische und statistische Erhebung*. 2 vols. Paderborn 1996.

Heil, Johannes. "Antisemitismus, Kulturkampf und Konfession: Die antisemitischen 'Kulturen' Frankreichs und Deutschlands im Vergleich." In *Katholischer Antisemitismus im 19. Jahrhundert. Ursachen und Traditionen im internationalen Vergleich.* Eds. Olaf Blaschke and Aram Mattioli, 195–228. Zürich 2000.

Heinen, Ernst. "Antisemitische Strömungen im politischen Katholizismus während des Kulturkampfes," In *Geschichte in der Gegenwart: Festschrift Kurt Kluxen.* Eds. Ernst Heinen. and Hans J. Schoeps, 286–301. Paderborn 1972.

Heinrichs, Wolfgang E. *Das Judenbild im Protestantismus des Deutschen Kaiserreichs: Ein Beitrag zur Mentalitätsgeschichte des deutschen Bürgertums in der Krise der Moderne*. Cologne 2000.

Hellwing, Isak A. *Der konfessionelle Antisemitismus im 19. Jahrhundert in Österreich*. Vienna 1972.

Herzig, Arno. *Jüdische Geschichte in Deutschland: Von den Anfängen bis zur Gegenwart*. Munich 1997.

Hirschmann, Günther. *Kulturkampf im historischen Roman der Gründerzeit 1859–1878*. 50–51, 193. Munich 1978.

"Historikerstreit": Die Dokumentation der Kontroverse um die Einzigartigkeit der nationalsozialistischen Judenvernichtung. Munich 1987.

Hobsbawm, Eric and Terence Ranger, eds. *The Invention of Tradition.* Cambridge 1983.

Hochgeschwender, Michael. "Katholizismus und Antisemitismus." In *Zeitgeschichtliche Katholizismusforschung: Tatsachen—Deutungen—Fragen: Eine Zwischenbilanz.* Veröffentlichungen der Kommission für Zeitgeschichte, Reihe B, vol. 100. Ed. Karl-Josef Hummel, 31–48. Paderborn 2003.

Hoffmann, Christhard. "Geschichte und Ideologie: Der Berliner Antisemitismusstreit 1879/80." In *Vorurteil und Völkermord: Entwicklungslinien des Antisemitismus.* Eds. Wolfgang Benz and Werner Bergmann, 219–51. Bonn 1997.

Hoffmann, Stefan L. *Die Politik der Geselligkeit: Freimauerlogen in der deutschen Bürgergesellschaft 1840–1918*. Göttingen 2000.

Hoffmann, Christhard. "Das Judentum als Antithese: Zur Tradition eines kulturellen Wertungsmusters." In *Antisemitismus in Deutschland: Zur Aktualität eines Vorurteils*. Ed. Wolfgang Benz, 25–46. Munich 1995.

Hogg, Robert F. "Fighting the Religious War of 1866. Silesian Clerics and the Anti-Catholic Smear Campaign in Prussia." In *Religion und Nation. Nation und Religion. Beiträge zu einer unbewältigten Geschichte*. Eds. Michael Geyer and Hartmut Lehmann, 49–75. Göttingen 2004.

Hölscher, Lucian. "Konfessionspolitik in Deutschland zwischen Glaubensstreit und Koexistenz." In *Baupläne der sichtbaren Kirche. Sprachliche Konzepte religiöser Vergemeinschaftung in Europa*. Ed. Lucian Hölscher, 11–52. Göttingen 2007.

Höpfner, Christian. *Romantik und Religion: Heinrich Heines Suche nach Identität*. Stuttgart 1997.

Hopp, Andrea. *Jüdisches Bürgertum in Frankfurt am Main im 19. Jahrhundert*. Stuttgart 1997.

Hübinger, Gangolf. "Die Intellektuellen im wilhelminischen Deutschland: Zum Forschungsstand." In *Intellektuelle im Deutschen Kaiserreich*. Eds. Gangolf Hübinger and Wolfgang J. Mommsen, 198–210. Frankfurt 1993.

Hummel, Karl-Josef, ed. *Zeitgeschichtliche Katholizismusforschung: Tatsachen—Deutungen—Fragen: Eine Zwischenbilanz*. Veröffentlichungen der Kommission für Zeitgeschichte, Reihe B, vol. 100. Paderborn 2003.

Hürten, Klaus. *Deutsche Katholiken 1918–1945*. Paderborn 1992.

———. *Katholiken, Kirche und Staat als Problem der Historie: Ausgewählte Aufsätze 1963–1992*. Paderborn 1994.

———. "Antisemit, weil Katholik?" *Stimmen der Zeit* 216 (1998): 497–500.

Jacobi, Ruth L. *Heinrich Heines jüdisches Erbe*. Bonn 1978.

Jedin, Hubert, ed. *History of the Church*. Vol. 8, *The Church in the Age of Liberalism*. London 1980.

Jochmann, Werner. "Struktur und Funktion des deutschen Antisemitismus 1878–1914." In *Antisemitismus: Von der Judenfindschaft zum Holocaust*. Eds. Herbert A. Strauss and Norbert Kampe, 95–142. Bonn 1985.

Joskowicz, Alexander. "Liberal Judaism and Confessional Politics of Difference in the German Kulturkampf." *Leo Baeck Institute Yearbook* 50 (2005): 177–97.

Kahn, E. "Die Frankfurter Zeitung." *Leo Baeck Institute Year Book* 2 (1957): 228–35.

Karady, Victor. "Jüdische Unternehmer und Prozesse der Verbürgerlichung in der Habsburger-Monarchie (19.–20. Jahrhundert)." In *Jüdische Unternehmer in Deutschland im 19. und 20. Jahrhundert*. Eds. W. E. Mosse and H. Pohl, 36–53. Stuttgart 1992.

Katz, Jacob. *Die Hep-Hep-Verfolgungen des Jahres 1819*. Berlin 1994. Hebrew version in *Zion* 38 (1973): 62–115.

———. "Anti-Semitism through the Ages." In *The Persisting Question: Sociological Perspectives and Social Contexts of Modern Antisemitism*. Ed. Helen Fein, 45–57. Berlin 1987. Also in idem, *From Prejudice to Destruction: Anti-Semitism 1700–1933*. Cambridge 1980.

Keiter, Heinrich. *Handbuch der katholischen Presse Deutschlands, Österreich-Ungarns, der Schweiz, Luxemburgs und von Nord-Amerika*. 5th ed. Essen 1913.

Kertzer, David I. *Die Päpste gegen die Juden: Der Vatikan und die Entstehung des modernen Antisemitismus*. Berlin 2001.

Klueting, Harm. *Das Konfessionelle Zeitalter 1525–1648*. Stuttgart 1989.

Klug, Manfred. *Rückwendung zum Mittelalter? Geschichtsbilder und historische Argumentation im politischen Katholizismus des Vormärz*. Paderborn 1995.

Kocka, Jürgen. "Bildung und Bürgerlichkeit." In *Bürgertum im 19. Jahrhundert: Deutschland im europäischen Vergleich*. Ed. Margaret Kraul 3:45–73. Munich 1988.

Köhle-Hezinger. *Chrsitel. Evangelisch-Katholisch. Untersuchungen zu konfessionellem Vorurteil und Konflikt im 19. und 20. Jahrhundert vornehmlich am Beispiel Württembergs*. Tübingen 1976.

Kohn, Hans. *The Age of Nationalism: The First Era of Global History*. New York 1968.

Kösters, Christoph. "Katholische Kirche im nationalsozialistischen Deutschland. Aktuelle Forschungsergebnisse, Kontroversen und Fragen." In *Die katholische Schuld? Katholizismus im Dritten Reich*. Ed. Rainer Bendel, 21–42. Münster 2002.

Koszyk, Kurt. *Deutsche Presse im 19. Jahrhundert.* Geschichte der deutschen Presse. 2nd. ed. Vol. 2. Berlin 1986.

———. "Der jüdische Beitrag zum deutschen Presse- und Verlagswesen." In *Jüdische Unternehmer in Deutschland im 19. und 20. Jahrhundert*. Eds. Werner E. Mosse and Heinrich Pohl, 196–217. Stuttgart 1992.

Krämer-Badoni, Rudolf. *Judenmord, Frauenmord, Heilige Kirche*. Frankfurt 1992.

Krasnianski, Ben Tzion "The Untold Truth about the Passion." IsraelNationalNews, 18 March 2004. http://www.israelnationalnews.com/article.php3?id=3464.

Kraus, Elisabeth. *Die Familie Mosse: Deutsch-jüdisches Bürgertum im 19. und 20. Jahrhundert*. Munich 1999.

Kretschmann, Carsten and Henning Pahl, "Ein 'Zweites Konfessionelles Zeitalter'? Vom Nutzen und Nachteil einer neuen Epochensignatur." *Historische Zeitschrift* 276 (2003): 369–92.

Kröter, Thomas. "Political Correctness: Vom linken Wahn zur rechten Wirklichkeit." *Blätter für deutsche und internationale Politik* 40 (1995): 1367–74.

Lang, Josef. "Lernfeld der Judenfeindschaft: Urs Altermatt: 'Katholizismus und Antisemitismus.'" *Die Wochenzeitung,* 6 Jan. 2000.

———. "Ein trübes Kapitel Schweizergeschichte." *Israelitisches Wochenblatt* (Zürich), 3 March 2000.

———. "Kontroverse um Olaf Blaschkes und Urs Altermatts Antisemitismus-Thesen: Die Wörter übers Kreuz gelegt." *Israelitisches Wochenblatt* (Zürich), 3 Aug. 2000, 13.

Langer, Michael. *Zwischen Vorurteil und Aggression: Zum Judenbild in der deutschsprachigen katholischen Volksbildung des 19. Jahrhunderts*. Freiburg 1994.

Langewiesche, Dieter. "'Volksbildung' und 'Leserlenkung' in Deutschland von der wilhelminischen Ära bis zur nationalsozialistischen Diktatur." *Internationales Archiv für Sozialgeschichte der deutschen Literatur* 14 (1989): 108–25.

———. "Nation, Nationalismus, Nationalstaat: Forschungsstand und Forschungsperspektiven." *Neue Politische Literatur* 40 (1995): 190–236.

Langmuir, Gavin I. "Toward a Definition of Antisemitism." In *The Persisting Question: Sociological Perspectives and Social Contexts of Modern Antisemitism*. Ed. Helen Fein, 86–127. Berlin 1987.

Lässig, Simone. "Juden und Mäzenatentum in Deutschland: Religiöses Ethos, kompensierendes Minderheitsverhalten oder genuine Bürgerlichkeit?." *Zeitschrift für Geschichtswissenschaft* 46 (1998): 211–36.

———. *Jüdische Wege ins Bürgertum: Kulturelles Kapital und sozialer Aufstieg im 19. Jahrhundert*. Göttingen 2004.

Lehmann, Hartmut, ed. *Säkularisierung, Dechristianisierung, Rechristianisierung im neuzeitlichen Europa: Bilanz und Perspektiven der Forschung*. Göttingen 1997.

Lenk, Kurt. "Zum Strukturwandel politischer Ideologien im 19. und 20. Jahrhundert: Begriff und Phänomen des ideologischen Bewußtseins." In *Ideologien im Bezugsfeld von Geschichte und Gesellschaft*. Ed. A. Pelinka, 97–107. Innsbruck 1981.

Lenman, Robin. *Die Kunst, die Macht und das Geld: Zur Kulturgeschichte des kaiserlichen Deutschland 1871–1918*. Frankfurt 1994.

———. "Control of the Visual Image in Germany." In *Zensur und Kultur: Zwischen Weimarer Klassik und Weimarer Republik: Mit einem Ausblick bis heute*. Eds. John A. McCarthy and Werner von der Ohe, 111–22. Tübingen 1995.

Lepp, Claudia. *Protestantisch-liberaler Aufbruch in die Moderne: Der deutsche Protestantenverein in der Zeit der Reichsgründung und des Kulturkampfes*. Gütersloh 1996.

Lepsius, M. Rainer. "Parteiensystem und Sozialstruktur: Zum Problem der Demokratisierung der deutschen Gesellschaft." In *Demokratie in Deutschland: Soziologisch-historische Konstellationsanalysen,* 25–50. Göttingen 1993.

Leugers, Antonia. "Salonfähiger Antisemitismus?" *Newsletter zur Geschichte und Wirkung des Holocaust, Fritz Bauer Institut.* No. 26 (Autumn 2004). http://www.fritz-bauer-institut.de/rezensionen/nl26/ leugers.htm

———. "Review of Konrad Löw, *Die Schuld: Christen und Juden im Urteil der Nationalsozialisten und der Gegenwart (Gräfelfing 2002)*." *Gegen Vergessen: Für Demokratie* 41 (2004): 56–57.

Lichtblau, Albert. *Antisemitismus und soziale Spannung in Berlin und Wien 1867–1914*. Berlin 1994.

Lieber, Hans-Joachim. *Ideologie: Eine historisch-systematische Einführung*. Paderborn 1985.

Lill, Rudolf. "Die deutschen Katholiken und die Juden in der Zeit von 1850 bis zur Machtübernahme Hitlers." In *Kirche und Synagoge: Handbuch zur Geschichte von Christen und Juden*. Eds. Karl Heinrich Rengstorf and Siegfried von Kortzfleisch, 2:370–420. Stuttgart 1970.

———, ed. *Der Kulturkampf*. Paderborn 1997.

Lindemann, Albert S. *Esau's Tears: Modern Anti-Semitism and the Rise of the Jews*. 2d ed. Cambridge 2000.

Lipstadt, Deborah. *Denying the Holocaust: The Growing Assault on Truth and Memory*. New York 1993.

Löffler, Klemens. *Geschichte der katholischen Presse Deutschlands*. München-Gladbach 1924.

Löw, Konrad. "Kirche und Antisemitismus im Kaiserreich und im Dritten Reich," *Deutsche Tagespost,* 1 Oct. 1998.

———. *Die Schuld: Christen und Juden im Urteil der Nationalsozialisten und der Gegenwart*. Gräfelfing 2002.

Lowenstein, Steven M. *Umstrittene Integration, 1871–1918*. Vol. 3. Munich 2000.

Martin, Bernd. *Antisemitismus ohne Antisemiten. Studien zur Vorurteilsdynamik*. Frankfurt 2000.

Massing, Paul W. *Vorgeschichte des politischen Antisemitismus*. Frankfurt 1986.

Mattenklott, Gert. *Über Juden in Deutschland.* Frankfurt 1993.

Mattioli, Aram. "Das letzte Ghetto Alteuropas: Antisemitismus im Kirchenstaat bis 1870." In *Katholischer Antisemitismus im 19. Jahrhundert. Ursachen und Traditionen im internationalen Vergleich.* Eds. Olaf Blaschke and Aram Mattioli, 111–44. Zürich 2000.

———. "E salva l'Italia nel Duce. Die katholische Kirche im faschistischen Italien 1922–1938." In *Katholizismus in Geschichte und Gegenwart.* Ed. Richard Faber, 121–41. Würzburg 2005.

Maurer, Trude. *Die Entwicklung der jüdischen Minderheit in Deutschland (1780–1933): Neuere Forschungen und offene Fragen*. Tübingen 1992.

Mayer, Gottfried. *Österreich als "katholische Großmacht": Ein Traum zwischen Revolution und liberaler Ära*. Vienna 1989.

Mazura, Uwe. *Zentrumspartei und Judenfrage 1870/71–1933: Verfassungsstaat und Minderheitenschutz*. Veröffentlichungen der Kommission für Zeitgeschichte, Reihe B: Forschungen. Vol. 62. Mainz 1994.

McLeod, Hugh, ed. *European Religion in the Age of Great Cities 1830–1930*. London 1995.

Meier, Michael. "Hat Historiker Urs Altermatt abgekupfert?." *Tagesanzeiger,* 11 Mar. 2000.

Merton, Robert K. *The Sociology of Science: Theoretical and Empirical Investigations*. Chicago 1973.

Meyer, Michael A. "Heinrich Graetz and Heinrich von Treitschke: A Comparison of Their Historical Images of the Modern Jew." *Modern Judaism* 6 (1986): 1–11.

———. *Jüdische Identität in der Moderne*. Frankfurt 1992.

———. *Response to Modernity: A History of the Reform Movement in Judaism*. New York 1988.

———. "Recent Historiography on the Jewish Religion." *Leo Baeck Institute Yearbook* 35 (1990): 3–16.

Meyer zu Uptrup, Wolfram. Review of Berger Waldenegg and Georg Christoph. *Antisemitismus: "Eine gefährliche Vokabel"? Diagnose eines Wortes* (Wien 2003). H-Soz-u-Kult, H-Net Reviews, May 2004. http://www.h-net.org/reviews/ showrev.cgi?path=17501089995351

Michael, Reuven. "Graetz contra Treitschke." *Bulletin des Leo Baeck Instituts* 4 (1961): 301–22.

———. "The Unknown Heinrich Graetz: From His Diaries and Letters." *Leo Baeck Institute Year Book* 13 (1968): 34–50.

Millman, Richard. "Jewish Anticlericalism and the Rise of Modern French Antisemitism." *History* 77 (1992): 220–36.

Mollenhauer, Daniel. "Symbolkämpfe um die Nation: Katholiken und Laizisten in Frankreich (1871–1914)." In *Nation und Religion in Europa: Mehrkonfessionelle Gesellschaften im 19. und 20. Jahrhundert*. Eds. Heinz-Gerhard Haupt and Dieter Langewiesche, 202–30. Frankfurt 2004.

Mosse, George L. "Das deutsch-jüdische Bildungsbürgertum." In *Bildungsbürgertum im 19. Jahrhundert*. Vol. 2: *Bildungsgüter und Bildungswissen*. Ed. Reinhart Koselleck, 168–80. Stuttgart 1990.

Mosse, Werner E. *Jews in the German Economy: The German-Jewish Economic Élite 1820–1935*. Oxford 1987.

———. "Integration and Identity in Imperial Germany: Towards a Typology." *Leo Baeck Institute Year Book* 37 (1992): 83–93.

Motzkin, Gabriel and Jens Mattern eds. *Welt ohne Gott: Jüdisches Denken im Zeitalter der Säkularisierung: Festschrift für Stéphane Mosès*. Amsterdam 2000.

Moyn, Samuel. "German Jewry and the Question of Identity: Historiography and Theory." *Leo Baeck Institute Year Book* 41 (1996): 291–308.

Müller, Gerhard Ludwig, ed. *Erinnern und Versöhnen: Die Kirche und die Verfehlungen in ihrer Vergangenheit*. Freiburg 2000.

Müller-Dreier, Armin. *Konfession in Politik, Gesellschaft und Kultur des Kaiserreichs: Der Evangelische Bund 1886–1914*. Gütersloh 1998.

Nipperdey, Thomas. *Deutsche Geschichte 1866–1918*. Vol. 1: *Arbeitswelt und Bürgergeist*. Munich 1990.

Nolte, Ernst. *Nietzsche und der Nietzscheanismus,* 100–102. Frankfurt 1990.

Nonn, Christoph. "Ritualmordgerüchte als Form des populären Antisemitismus—eine katholische Spezialität?." In *Katholischer Antisemitismus im 19. Jahrhundert: Ursachen und Traditionen im internationalen Vergleich*. Eds. Olaf Blaschke and Aram Mattioli, 145–62. Zürich 2000.

———. *Eine Stadt sucht einen Mörder. Gerücht, Gewalt und Antisemitismus im Kaiserreich*. Göttingen 2002.

Novick, Peter. *The Holocaust in American Life*. Boston 1999.

Nowak, Kurt. *Kulturprotestantismus und Judentum in der Weimarer Republik*. Göttingen 1991.

Osinski, Jutta. *Katholizismus und deutsche Literatur im 19. Jahrhundert*. Paderborn 1993.

Owzar, Armin. Review of Urs Altermatt *Katholizismus und Antisemitismus: Mentalitäten, Kontinuitäten, Ambivalenze:. Zur Kulturgeschichte der Schweiz 1918–1945* (Frauenfeld 1999). 3 July 2000. http://hsozkult.geschichte.hu-berlin.de

———. *"Reden ist Silber, Schweigen ist Gold." Konfliktmanagement im Alltag des wilhelminischen Obrigkeitsstaates*. Konstanz 2006.

Oxaal, Ivar. "Die Juden im Wien des jungen Hitler: Historische und soziologische Aspekte." In *Eine zerstörte Kultur: Jüdisches Leben und Antisemitismus im Wien seit dem 19. Jahrhundert*. Ed. Gerhard Botz, et al, 29–60. Buchloe 1990.

Paucker, Arnold. "Die Abwehr des Antisemitismus in den Jahren 1893–1933." In *Antisemitismus: Von der Judenfeindschaft zum Holocaust*. Eds. Herbert A. Strauss and Norbert Kampe, 143–71. Bonn 1985.

———. "The Jewish Defense against Antisemitism in Germany, 1893–1933." In *Living with Antisemitism. Modern Jewish Responses*. Ed. Jehuda Reinharz, 104–32. Hanover, N.H. 1987.

Pauley, Bruce. *Eine Geschichte des österreichischen Antisemitismus: Von der Ausgrenzung zur Auslöschung,* 80. Vienna 1993. First published as *From Prejudice to Persecution: A History of Austrian Anti-Semitism*. Chapel Hill, N.C. 1992.

Peters, Paul. *Heinrich Heine "Dichterjude": Die Geschichte einer Schmähung*. Frankfurt 1990.

Phelps, H. "Dokumentation: Hitlers 'grundlegende' Rede über den Antisemitismus." *Vierteljahrshefte für Zeitgeschichte* 16 (1968): 390–400 (introduction); 400–20 (document).

Pickus, Keith. "Images of God and Country: Jewish National and Religious Identities in Wilhelmine Germany." *Aschkenas: Zeitschrift für Geschichte und Kultur der Juden* 8 (1998): 425–38.

Piper, Ernst. "Die jüdische Weltverschwörung." In *Antisemitismus: Vorurteile und Mythen*. Eds. Julius H. Schoeps and Johannes Schlör, 127–35. Munich 1995.

———, ed. *Gibt es wirklich eine Holocaust-Industrie? Zur Auseinandersetzung um Norman Finkelstein*. Zürich 2001.

Pollmann, Viktoria. "'Ungebetene Gäste im christlichen Haus': Die Kirche und die Juden im Polen des 19. und frühen 20. Jahrhunderts." In: *Katholischer Antisemitismus im 19. Jahrhundert. Ursachen und Traditionen im internationalen Vergleich*. Eds. Olaf Blaschke and Aram Mattioli, 259–86. Zürich 2000.

———. *Untermieter im christlichen Haus: Die Kirche und die 'jüdische Frage' in Polen anhand der Bistumspresse der Metropolie Krakau 1926–1939*. Wiesbaden 2001.

Prager, Denis and Joseph Telushkin. *Why the Jews? The Reason for Antisemitism*. New York 1983.

Prinz, Arthur. *Juden im deutschen Wirtschaftsleben: Soziale und wirtschaftliche Struktur im Wandel 1850–1914*. Ed. Avraham Barkai. Tübingen 1984.

Puhle, Hans-Jürgen. *Agrarische Interessenpolitik und preußischer Konservatismus im Wilhelminischen Reich 1893–1914*. 2d ed. Bonn 1975.

Pulzer, Peter. *Die Entstehung des politischen Antisemitismus in Deutschland und Österreich*. Gütersloh 1966.

Ragins, Sanford. *Jewish Responses to Antisemitism in Germany 1870–1914: A Study in the History of Ideas*. Cincinnati 1980.

Rahden, Till van. "Weder Milieu noch Konfession: Die situative Ethnizität der deutschen Juden im Kaiserreich in vergleichender Perspektive." In *Religion im Kaiserreich: Milieus, Mentalitäten, Krisen*. Eds. Olaf Blaschke and Frank-Michael Kuhlemann, 409–34. Gütersloh 1995.

———. "Ideologie und Gewalt: Neuerscheinungen über den Antisemitismus in der deutschen Geschichte des 19. und frühen 20. Jahrhunderts." *Neue politische Literatur* 41 (1996): 11–29.

———. *Juden und andere Breslauer: Die Beziehungen zwischen Juden, Protestanten und Katholiken in einer deutschen Großstadt von 1860 bis 1925*. Göttingen 2000.

Reichmann, Eva G. *Flucht in den Haß: Die Ursachen der deutschen Judenkatastrophe*. 6th ed. 99–107. Frankfurt 1969.

Reinhard, Wolfgang. “Gegenreformation als Modernisierung? Prolegomena zu einer Theorie des konfessionellen Zeitalters.” *Archiv für Reformationsgeschichte* 68 (1977): 226–52.

Requate, Jörg. *Journalismus als Beruf: Entstehung und Entwicklung des Journalistenberufs im 19. Jahrhundert: Deutschland im internationalen Vergleich*. Göttingen 1995.

Richarz, Monika, ed. *Jüdisches Leben in Deutschland.* 3 vols. Stuttgart 1976–1982.

———, ed. *Bürger auf Widerruf: Lebenszeugnisse deutscher Juden 1780–1945*. Munich 1989.

———. “Die soziale Stellung der jüdischen Händler auf dem Lande am Beispiel Südwestdeutschlands.” In *Jüdische Unternehmer in Deutschland im 19. und 20. Jahrhundert*. Eds. Werner E. Mosse and Heinrich Pohl, 271–83. Stuttgart 1992.

Rohrbacher, Stefan and Michael Schmidt. *Judenbilder: Kulturgeschichte antijüdischer Mythen und antisemitischer Vorurteile*. Hamburg 1991.

———. “Über das Fortwuchern von Stereotypvorstellungen in der Geschichtswissenschaft.” In *Shylock? Zinsverbot und Geldverleih in jüdischer und christlicher Tradition*. Eds. Johannes Heil and Bernd Wacker, 235–52. Munich 1997.

Rosenberg, Hans. *Große Depression und Bismarckzeit*. Berlin 1967.

Ross, Donald J. *The Failure of Bismarck's Kulturkampf: Catholicism and State Power in Imperial Germany, 1871–1887*. Washington 1998.

Rürup, Reinhard. “Die ‘Judenfrage’ der bürgerlichen Gesellschaft und die Entstehung des modernen Antisemitismus.” In *Emanzipation und Antisemitismus*. 2d ed. 93–119. 1975; Frankfurt 1987.

Rüsen, Jörn. *Historische Vernunft: Grundzüge einer Historik*. Vol. 1: *Die Grundlagen der Geschichtswissenschaft*. Göttingen 1983.

Sartre, Jean-Paul *Anti-Semite and Jew*. Translated by George J. Becker, 17, 53–54. New York 1948. First published as *Réflexion sur la question juive*. Paris 1954.

Scheil, Stefan. *Die Entwicklung des politischen Antisemitismus in Deutschland zwischen 1881 und 1912: Eine wahlgeschichtliche Untersuchung*. Berlin 1999.

Schilling, Heinz. “Die Konfessionalisierung im Reich. Religiöser und gesellschaftlicher Wandel in Deutschland zwischen 1555 und 1620.” *Historische Zeitschrift* 246 (1988): 1–45.

———. "Confessional Europe: Bureaucrats, La Bonne Police, Civilizations." In *Handbook of European History 1400–1600: Late Middle Ages, Renaissance and Reformation.* Eds. Thomas A. Brady, H. A. Oberman, and J. D. Tracy, 2:641–81. Leiden 1995.

———. "Konfessionelles Zeitalter, I–II." *Geschichte in Wissenschaft und Unterricht* 48 (1997): 350–70.

Schloßmacher, Norbert. "Antiultramontanismus im Wilhelminischen Deutschland: Ein Versuch." In *Deutscher Katholizismus im Umbruch zur Moderne.* Ed. Wilfried Loth, 164–98. Stuttgart 1991.

Schmidt, Heinrich Richard. *Konfessionalisierung im 16. Jahrhundert.* Munich 1992.

Schmolke, Michael. *Die schlechte Presse: Katholiken und Publizistik zwischen "Katholik" und "Publik" 1821–1968.* Münster 1971.

Schnabel, Franz. *Deutsche Geschichte im neunzehnten Jahrhundert.* Vol. 4: *Die religiösen Kräfte.* 270–71. 1937; Munich 1987.

Schoeps, Julius H. and Johannes Schlör. "Einleitung." In *Antisemitismus: Vorurteile und Mythen.* Eds. Julius H. Schoeps and Johannes Schlör, 10–12. Munich 1995.

——— and Johannes Schlör, eds. *Antisemitismus: Vorurteile und Mythen.* Munich 1995.

Schreiner, Klaus. "'Wann kommt der Retter Deutschlands?' Formen und Funktionen von politischem Messianismus in der Weimarer Republik." *Saeculum* 49 (1998): 107–59.

Schuller, Florian and Guiseppe Veltri, and Hubert Wolf, eds. *Katholizismus und Judentum. Gemeinsamkeiten und Verwerfungen vom 16. bis zum 20. Jahrhundert.* Regensburg 2005.

Sieg, Ulrich "'Der Wissenschaft und dem Leben tut dasselbe not: Ehrfurcht vor der Wahrheit': Hermann Cohens Gutachten im Marburger Antisemitismusprozeß." In *Philosophisches Denken—Politisches Wirken: Hermann-Cohen-Kolloquium Marburg 1992.* Eds. Reinhard Brandt and Franz Orlik, 222–48. Hildesheim 1993.

Smith, Helmut W. *German Nationalism and Religious Conflict. Culture, Ideology, Politics, 1870-1914.* Princeton 1995 Originally, *Nationalism and Religious Conflict in Germany, 1887–1914.* Ph.D. diss., Yale University, 1991.

———. "The Learned and the Popular Discourse of Anti-Semitism in the Catholic Milieu of the Kaiserreich." *Central European History* 27 (1994): 315–28.

———. "Religion and Conflict: Protestants, Catholics, and Anti-Semitism in the State of Baden in the Era of Wilhelm II." *Central European History* 27 (1994): 283–314.

———. *The Butcher's Tale: Murder and Anti-Semitism in a German Town.* New York 2002. In German: *Die Geschichte des Schlachters. Mord und Antisemitismus in einer deutschen Kleinstadt.* Göttingen 2002.

———. Review of *Konfessionen im Konflikt: Deutschland zwischen 1800 und 1970: ein zweites konfessionelles Zeitalter.* Ed. Olaf Blaschke (Göttingen 2002). German Historical Institute London, *Bulletin* 25 (2003): 101–106.

Sorkin, David. *The Transformation of German Jewry, 1780–1840.* New York 1987.

Spieler, Willy. Review of Urs Altermatt. *Katholizismus und Antisemitismus: Mentalitäten, Kontinuitäten, Ambivalenze:. Zur Kulturgeschichte der Schweiz 1918–1945* (Frauenfeld 1999). *Neue Wege* 94 (2000): 3.

Steinhoff, Anthony J. "Ein zweites konfessionelles Zeitalter?: Nachdenken über die Religion im langen 19. Jahrhundert." *Geschichte und Gesellschaft* 30 (2004): 549–70.

Sterling, Eleonore O. "Anti-Jewish Riots in Germany in 1819: A Displacement of Social Protest." *Historia Judaica* 12 (1950): 105–42.

———. *Er ist wie du: Aus der Frühgeschichte des Antisemitismus in Deutschland (1815–1850).* Munich 1956.

Stern, Fritz. "Die Last des Erfolgs: Gedanken zum deutschen Judentum." In *Demokratie und Diktatur.* Eds. Manfred Funke, a.o., 95–108. Bonn 1987.

Strauss, Herbert A. "The Jewish Press in Germany, 1918–1933 (1943)." In *The Jewish Press that Was: Accounts, Evaluations and Memories of Jewish Newspapers in Pre-Holocaust Europe.* 321–53. Tel Aviv 1980.

——— and Norbert Kampe. "Einleitung." In *Antisemitismus: Von der Judenfeindschaft zum Holocaust.* Eds. Herbert A. Strauss and Norbert Kampe, 9–28. Bonn 1985.

Suchy, Barbara. "The Verein zur Abwehr des Antisemitismus." Part 1: "From its Beginnings to the First World War." *Leo Baeck Institute Year Book* 28 (1983): 205–39.

———. "Die jüdische Presse im Kaiserreich und in der Weimarer Republik." In *Juden als Träger bürgerlicher Kultur in Deutschland.* Ed. Julius H. Schoeps. Stuttgart 1989.

Swartout, Lisa. "Culture Wars. Protestant, Catholic, and Jewish Students at German Universities, 1890–1914." In *Religion und Nation. Nation und*

Religion. Beiträge zu einer unbewältigten Geschichte. Eds. Michael Geyer and Hartmut Lehmann, 157–74. Göttingen 2004.

Tal, Uriel. *Christians and Jews in Germany: Religions, Politics and Ideology in the Second Reich, 1870–1914.* London 1974.

Thoma, Clemens. "Die katholische Weltkirche und der Rassenantisemitismus 1900–1939." In *Antisemitismus in der Schweiz 1848–1960.* Ed. Aram Mattioli, 445–64. Zürich 1998.

Tiedmann, Markus. *"In Auschwitz wurde niemand vergast": 60 rechtsradikale Lügen und wie man sie wiederlegt.* Mühlheim an der Ruhr 1996.

Todorow, Almut. *Das Feuilleton der 'Frankfurter Zeitung' in der Weimarer Republik: Zur Grundlegung einer rhetorischen Medienforschung.* Tübingen 1996.

Toury, Jacob. *Die politische Orientierung der Juden in Deutschland: Von Jena bis Weimar.* Tübingen 1966.

———. "'The Jewish Question': A Semantic Approach." *Leo Baeck Institute Year Book* 9 (1966): 85–106.

———. *Soziale und politische Geschichte der Juden in Deutschland 1847–1871: Zwischen Revolution, Reaktion und Emanzipation.* Düsseldorf 1977.

Verschaffel, Tom, et al. *Neostijlen in de negentiende eeuw.* Leuven 2002.

Vierhaus, Rudolf. "Bildung." In *Geschichtliche Grundbegriffe.* 1:508–51. Stuttgart 1980.

Volkov, Shulamit. *The Rise of Popular Antisemitism in Germany: The Urban Master Artisans, 1873–1896.* Princeton 1978.

———. "Antisemitismus als kulturelle Code." In *Jüdisches Leben und Antisemitismus im 19. und 20. Jahrhundert.* 13–36. Munich 1990. First published in *Leo Baeck Institute Year Book* 23 (1978): 24–45.

———. "Die Verbürgerlichung der Juden in Deutschland als Paradigma." In *Jüdisches Leben und Antisemitismus im 19. und 20. Jahrhundert.* 111–30. Munich 1990.

———. "Das geschriebene und das gesprochene Wort: Über Kontinuität und Diskontinuität im deutschen Antisemitismus." In *Jüdisches Leben und Antisemitismus im 19. und 20. Jahrhundert.* 54–75. Munich 1990. First published in *Vierteljahrshefte für Zeitgeschichte* 33 (1985): 221–43.

———. "Die Dynamik der Dissimilation: Deutsche Juden und die ostjüdischen Einwanderer." In *Jüdisches Leben und Antisemitismus im 19. und 20. Jahrhundert.* 166–80. Munich 1990.

———. "Die Erfindung einer Tradition: Zur Entstehung des modernen Judentums in Deutschland." *Historische Zeitschrift* 253 (1991): 603–28.

Volovici, Leon. "Discussion: A Broken Balance." *Vidal Sassoon International Center for the Study of Antisemitism Annual Report 1998* (1998): 15–17.

Wahl, Alfred. *Confession et comportement dans les campagnes d'Alsace et de Bade 1871–1939: Catholiques, Protestants et Juifs*. 2 vols. Strassbourg 1980.

Waldenegg, Berger and Georg Christoph. *Antisemitismus: "Eine gefährliche Vokabel"? Diagnose eines Wortes*. Wien 2003.

Walzer, Michael. "Liberalism and the Jews: Historical Affinities, Contemporary Necessities." *Studies in Contemporary Jewry* 11: *Values, Interests and Identity: Jews and Politics in a Changing World.* Ed. Peter Y. Medding (1995): 3–10.

Weber, Christoph. "Ultramontanismus als katholischer Fundamentalismus." In *Deutscher Katholizismus im Umbruch zur Moderne.* Ed. Wilfried Loth, 20–45. Stuttgart 1991.

Weber, Max. *Soziologie: Universalgeschichtliche Analysen, Politik*. Stuttgart 1973.

Wehler, Hans-Ulrich. *Deutsche Gesellschaftsgeschichte.* Vol. 3: *Von der "Deutschen Doppelrevolution" bis zum Beginn des Ersten Weltkrieges 1849–1914*. Munich 1995.

Weinzierl-Fischer, Erika. *Die österreichischen Konkordate von 1855 und 1933*. Vienna 1960.

Weiss, John. *Der Lange Weg zum Holocaust: Die Geschichte der Judenfeindschaft in Deutschland und Österreich*. Hamburg 1997.

Weiss, Otto. "Beim Lesen zweier Bücher über den katholischen Antisemitismus." *Traverse* 7 (2000).

West, Karl-Heinz. "'Der Stellvertreter'—Ein Stück und seine Wirkung." *Rottenburger Jahrbuch für Kirchengeschichte* 2 (1983): 203–47.

Wistrich, Robert S. Review of "Blaming the Victim." *Commentary* (Feb. 1998): 60–63.

Woerl, Leo. *Die Publicistik der Gegenwart: Eine Rundschau über die gesammte Presse der Welt.* 6 vols. Würzburg 1879–1881.

Wolf, Hubert. "'Pro perfidis Judaeis': Die 'Amici Israel' und ihr Antrag auf eine Reform der Karfreitagsfürbitte für die Juden (1928). Oder: Bemerkungen zum Thema katholische Kirche und Antisemitismus." *Historische Zeitschrift* 279 (2004), 611–58.

Wolffsohn, Michael. *Keine Angst vor Deutschland.* Erlangen 1990.

Wuthnow, Robert. "Antisemitism and Stereotyping." In *The Persisting Question: Sociological Perspectives and Social Contexts of Modern Antisemitism.* Ed. Helen Fein, 128–63. Berlin 1987.

Zalar, Jeffrey T. "The Process of Confessional Inculturation: Catholic Reading in the 'Long Nineteenth Century.'" In *Protestants, Catholics and Jews in Germany 1800–1914.* Ed. Helmut Walser Smith, 121–52. Oxford 2001.

Zimmermann, Moshe. *Die deutschen Juden 1914–1945* (Munich 1997).

Zucker, Stanley. *Ludwig Bamberger: German Liberal Politician and Social Critic* (Pittsburgh 1975).

Zumbini, Massimo Ferrari. *Die Wurzeln des Bösen: Gründerjahre des Antisemitismus: Von der Bismarckzeit zu Hitler* (Frankfurt 2003).

Index